D0121435

WINDSOR
V
WINDSOR

NIGEL BLUNDELL

BLAKE

Published by Blake Publishing Ltd,
3 Bramber Court, 2 Bramber Road, London, England W14 9PB

First published in Great Britain in 1995

ISBN 1 85782 115 7

All rights reserved. No part of this publication may be
reproduced, stored in a retrieval system, or in any form or
by any means, without the prior permission in writing of the
publisher, nor be otherwise circulated in any form of binding
or cover other than that in which it is published and without
a similar condition including this condition being imposed
on the subsequent purchaser.

British Library Cataloguing-in-Publication Data:
A catalogue record for this book is available from
the British Library.

Typeset by Datix International, Bungay, Suffolk

Printed in Finland by WSOY

1 3 5 7 9 10 8 6 4 2

Text copyright © Nigel Blundell 1995

Acknowledgement to Nicholas Constable for his sterling assistance, research and
journalistic expertise.

Contents

(Prologue): Shifting Sands

She is tall, slim and blonde, aristocratically elegant and still strikingly attractive, yet her face is downcast as she walks into the wind and rain on a bleak, sandy seashore. One of the saddest figures on earth, she leads a life of self-imposed exile.

It is all a far cry from her most golden day when, as a shy young bride with downcast eyes and shining blonde hair, she walked up the aisle to stand alongside her groom, twelve years her senior and heir to an ancient title. Their Westminster Abbey wedding, attended by the Queen, was the marriage of the year.

Just a few years later the fairytale was over. Among accusations of adultery, the marriage crumbled into a bitter struggle for custody of the children. The powerful husband, because of his position and his influence, won the day and the wife largely withdrew from public life. She was cast into the cold.

This is not the story of Diana, Princess of Wales . . .

but that of her mother Frances Shand Kydd who, after a marriage of misery, was finally forced to leave the family home, Park House on the Sandringham estate. Her daughter Diana was just six years of age when, sitting dejected at the foot of the stairs, she watched her mother drive off for the last time. It was a scene that has returned to haunt her ever since.

A car drove up to the royal train in the gloom of a winter's night and a blonde girl dashed into one of the elegant coaches. Aboard the train was Prince Charles. It was November 1980, just months before his marriage to Lady Diana Spencer. The location was a Wiltshire siding, just a short car drive from the home of Andrew and Camilla Parker Bowles.

A witness who saw the late-night comings and goings telephoned a newspaper, which ran a story stating that the blonde visitor had been Lady Diana. The report caused an unprecedented row and one of the great royal mysteries of modern times – but one which can now be resolved.

When the newspaper, the *Sunday Mirror*, hit the streets, Buckingham Palace reacted with fury. The Queen ordered: 'Protect Charles's image at all cost' and the Palace lie machine went into action with a categorical denial of the story. The unforeseen result of such an unequivocal denial was damaging speculation that, far from being Charles's future bride who had visited him that night, it was in fact her sister, Sarah, or Charles's lover, Camilla Parker Bowles.

Yet one witness, a policeman, swore that he saw Lady Diana Spencer, driving a small saloon car, arrive in the early evening and leave at 1 a.m. He also noted the car's number plate which, according to a later check, showed that it was in the name of Diana's mother, Mrs Shand Kydd, and registered in Oban, Scotland, where she lived. Diana, whose own car was out of action at the time, had been staying for a few days as a guest of the Parker Bowles family and, according to sources inside the house, had decided to pay a romantic visit to Charles.

The journalist responsible for the investigation, Peter Wilson, now a Scottish hotelier, later traced a second source for the story that had been so vehemently denied. This source, an officer of Scotland Yard's Special Branch told him: 'The story was true. The Palace went bananas because it broke just before they planned to announce the engagement of Charles to Diana. You nearly wrecked a royal romance.' And a decade and more later, they probably wished it had.

Yet one question remains. The original source for the newspaper story was within the Parker Bowles household. Is it likely that Diana, a shy, innocent virgin, would have let anyone else in that house into the secret of her illicit assignation? Perhaps only one person ... Charles's secret lover, Camilla Parker Bowles.

At that time, Camilla was conducting a passionate, illicit affair with Prince Charles – while at the same time tutoring Diana as a marriage candidate for him. It was not Camilla who fell into her lover's arms that night. But it was almost certainly Camilla who sent a timid and untested bride-to-be on her midnight journey to Charles's bed.

Upon the announcement of their engagement in February 1981, Prince Charles and Lady Diana faced the television cameras for an unprecedented interview. Eyes downcast, Diana said little, but charmed the millions of viewers. Charles was more loquacious – but hardly more eloquent. Asked about his feelings towards his bride-to-be and whether he was in love, the Prince answered: 'Yes ... whatever that may mean.' Diana was very soon to realise exactly what that would mean. As she now knows, Charles had left Camilla Parker Bowles's side only hours before the engagement announcement.

With only days to go before the marriage ceremony of the century, plump, rosy-cheeked Lady Diana Spencer sat nervously picking her nails and adjusting her dress as she watched her husband-to-be playing in a polo match. Feeling that the eyes of the world were on her, the twenty-year-old began shaking. She felt nausea. Then the tears began to flow and, without giving a second thought to her loss of public image, she fled to a royal car and wept freely.

It was not that she did not love Prince Charles. It was that, while she had for long been forced to call him 'Sir' in public, another woman seemed to be on far more intimate terms with him. She called him 'Fred'. He called her 'Gladys' or 'Girl Friday'. She knew this because she had recently opened what she had believed to be a wedding present to herself and Charles. It was, however, a gift purchased by him – a gift to Camilla of a gold bracelet with a 'G' and an 'F' intertwined.

Two days before his wedding on 29 July 1981, Charles and Camilla Parker Bowles made love.

On New Year's Eve 1989, Princess Diana lay on her bed at Sandringham and spoke on the phone to a close friend. She told him her life with Prince Charles was 'sheer torture'. The next day she escaped from her royal in-laws and walked alone along the empty, windswept sands of a Norfolk beach.

Some months afterwards, a nervous private secretary sat before Prince Charles and hesitantly pressed the 'Play' button on a tape recorder. They heard a man say: 'Oh Squidgy, I love you, love you, love you.'

And Diana reply: 'You are the nicest person in the whole wide world ... You're just the nicest person in the whole wide world.'

Later, again Diana: 'Playing with yourself?'

Him: 'No I'm not actually.'

And more. Diana: 'I don't want to get pregnant.'

Him: 'Darling, it's not going to happen.'

Prince Charles was incandescent with rage when he heard transcripts of the bugged phone conversation. 'It's that James Hewitt, isn't it?' he demanded.

'No sir, it's James Gilbey.'

It took hours before Charles's anger subsided. Then he began to smile ...

Princess Diana was told the news by a friend: an Australian magazine had published the transcript of a phone conversation between her husband and Camilla Parker Bowles. As she read it, she felt sick.

Charles: 'The trouble is I need you several times a week.'

Camilla: 'Mmm, so do I. I need you all the week. All the time.'

Charles: 'Oh, God. I'll just live inside your trousers or something. It would be much easier.'

Camilla: 'What are you going to turn into, a pair of knickers? Oh, you're going to come back as a pair of knickers!'

Charles laughing: 'Or, God forbid, a Tampax. Just my luck!'

And later, Camilla: 'I do love you and I'm so proud of you.'

Him: 'Oh, I'm so proud of YOU.'

Her: 'Don't be so silly. I've never achieved anything.'

Him: 'Yes you have.'

Her: 'No I haven't.'

Him: 'Your great achievement is to love me.'

Her: 'Oh, darling. Easier than falling off a chair.'

Him: 'You suffer all these indignities and tortures and calumnies.'

Her: 'Oh darling, don't be silly. I'd suffer anything for you. That's love; it's the strength of love. Night night.'

As she read on, Princess Diana's nausea subsided. Then she began to smile . . .

Only one man on the island knew that a royal visit was to take place that day but the word had somehow got around that something was up. A cluster of locals watched from the shore as the funnel appeared as a dot on the clearly defined horizon, then a bridge, then the whole of the royal yacht *Britannia*.

Soon after dropping anchor just beyond the reef, the *Britannia*'s launch was lowered and pointed its bow to shore. But the launch took a course towards the reef that would have ripped its bottom out on the coral — with possibly disastrous consequences for its VIP passenger, the Prince of Wales. The locals leapt into a boat and headed the visitors off.

'Where you tryin' to get to?' was the sing-song Caribbean inquiry shouted above the roar of the waves on the reef.

The royal party, they learned, were headed for a tiny islet within the reef but separated from the main island by a stretch of calm and crystal water. Obligingly, the locals transferred the visitors to their own boat, which swept them safely through a gap in the foaming coral and deposited them on the uninhabited strand of sand and scrub. Embarrassed by their inexpertise but grateful for their rescue, the dozen visitors paddled ashore.

Their Caribbean hosts, kindly, courteous and recognising their royal adventurer's wish for privacy, pushed out from the island and left them alone. The rest of his party also respected Charles's need of seclusion as they laid out a picnic on the sands. Which left the Prince and just one special guest alone to share each other's company. They swam together, laughed, held hands and lay together on the beach 4,000 miles from home and the zoom lenses of the paparazzi cameras.

For the *Britannia* had brought not just the heir to the throne to this little speck of paradise lost in the island maze of the Caribbean. It had also brought a girlfriend. Like the royal train more than a decade earlier, the royal yacht had become a secret lovenest.

After two hours, the islander's boat returned and plucked the couple and their retinue off the beach and returned them to the *Britannia*. As the royal yacht upped anchor and sailed on, the locals eagerly discussed the identities of their impromptu callers. 'No, it was not Diana,' the boatmen reported sadly. 'It was not the wife . . . it was the other woman.'

The islanders have long been speculating that it was Camilla Parker Bowles who briefly shared their romantic tropical haven. But it remains a closely guarded secret whether or not Prince Charles really did turn the proud yacht *Britannia* into a royal 'Love Boat'.

In January 1993 the editor of a well-known British magazine telephoned Buckingham Palace to warn about the strange photograph in her possession. It was a picture taken of a scantily-clad Lady Diana Spencer, apparently as a sixteen-year-old. It was a flattering photograph, showing her then-sensuous teenage curves, but it was so obviously a private snapshot that the editor realised that if it fell into the wrong hands its publication would be highly embarrassing to the Princess. She therefore immediately called the Palace to ask them to take possession of it.

When she got through, the editor briefly outlined her dilemma and asked to speak to a press officer specifically dealing with the Princess's affairs. Surprised that no one returned her call, she telephoned twice more. Wrongly thinking that the Palace still had Diana's best interests at heart, the editor was shocked when finally told: 'Just throw it in a skip.'

It took a long time for Princess Diana herself to realise fully that Buckingham Palace did not have her interests at heart. In 1994 it gradually dawned on her that the Royal Family and its devious diplomats had engineered her out of the mainstream of monarchy. She found herself isolated, marginalised, politically friendless and hopelessly forlorn.

All she had were the love and loyalty of her children, and she was determined to lose neither. Like a tigress, Diana turned to fight for her cubs . . .

The Princess of Wales asked her lawyers to draw up a sample petition for divorce — not on the 'amicable' grounds of two years' separation but on the more acrimonious grounds of adultery. She wanted to see what such a document would look like in black and white. She rather fancied that she would enjoy reading the legal jargon for an accusation that only she could make. It would be no more than a simple statement of the truth that few at that stage dared breathe . . .

(i) That the Respondent has committed adultery

and the Petitioner finds it intolerable to live with the Respondent.

(ii) That the Respondent has committed adultery on diverse occasions and locations, including the marital home of Highgrove House, for many years throughout the period of the marriage, with the Co-respondent Mrs Camilla Parker Bowles, of Middlewick House, Corsham, Wiltshire.

The more Diana thought about it, the more she knew that this was a battle she would win — even it cost her all rights to the throne.

She is tall, slim and blonde, aristocratically elegant and still strikingly attractive, yet her face is downcast as she walks into the wind and rain on a bleak, sandy seashore. One of the saddest figures on earth, she leads a life of self-imposed exile.

It is all a far cry from her most golden day when, as a shy young bride with downcast eyes and shining blonde hair, she walked up the aisle to stand alongside her groom, twelve years her senior and heir to an ancient title. Their Westminster Abbey wedding, attended by the Queen, was the marriage of the year.

Just a few years later the fairytale was over. Among accusations of adultery, the marriage crumbled into a

bitter struggle for custody of the children. The powerful husband, because of his position and his influence,
won the day and the wife largely withdrew from
public life. She was cast into the cold.

This is not the story of Frances Shand Kydd . . . but
of her daughter Diana, Princess of Wales.

1

Time Bomb

A chill December dawn broke over London. The early-morning traffic began to swirl down Parliament Hill and past the sombre granite flanks of Buckingham Palace. Westminster Corporation's garish green garbage trucks rumbled in and out removing the week's royal detritus. A reedy light began to glint on the gold flake atop the railings that guard the monarch from her gawking subjects. The bearskinned guards wheeled back and forth between their two sentry boxes watched by the earliest, most eager camera-clicking tourists. The Palace slowly awoke.

The royal standard fluttered at full mast above the massive edifice, which meant that Queen Elizabeth II was at home. Her consort, Prince Philip the Duke of Edinburgh, was in his own rooms down an adjoining corridor of the rambling building. Both had 'private engagements' to perform this day. The heir to the throne, Prince Charles the Prince of Wales, had already left his apartments in nearby St James's Palace. He was on his way to Newcastle upon Tyne to fulfil an all-day string of official engagements including a conference on Business in the Environment. His estranged wife, Princess Diana, was at home in London in the family apartments she had once shared with him at Kensington Palace. Their children, William and Harry, were in the safe custody of Ludgrove boarding school in leafy Berkshire.

As the British Royal Family awoke and went about their business this day, 9 December 1994, a time bomb ticked away – more insidiously damaging than any of the packages of Semtex that the Irish Republican Army had attempted to plant near royal personages over the years. This bomb had been primed exactly two years earlier – on 9 December 1992 – when the Prime Minister, John Major, had shattered the illusions of millions by announcing to a stunned House of Commons: 'With regret, the Prince and Princess of Wales have decided to separate. Their Royal Highnesses have no plans to divorce . . . The succession to the throne is unaffected. The children of the Prince and Princess retain their position in the line of succession and there is no reason why the Princess of Wales should not be crowned Queen in due course.'

Now, on the morning of the second anniversary of this announcement, the Prince of Wales in the far north of England and the Princess of Wales at home in London each noted the ominous date in their diaries. Two years' separation.

In the chambers of the Queen's solicitor, Sir Matthew Farrer, a bulging file was removed from the safe where only the most sensitive legal documents are stored. The file had been there ever since the separation announcement. It had gathered no dust, however, for it had been removed, added to and amended again and again over those two years. It was, to Sir Matthew, the most explosive set of documents in the land. If this time bomb were to be mishandled, it would prove devastating to the Royal Family. It could mortally damage the British monarchy. It could signal the surrender of power of the 1,000-year dynasty of the illustrious House of Windsor.

Sir Matthew, sixty-four-year-old senior partner of Farrer and Co., handled the information to which he was privy with kid gloves. He had been legal adviser to the Queen and her family since 1965. From their mansion offices with their Lutyens façade in historic Lincoln's Inn Fields, his trusted firm had dutifully and discreetly dealt with the Royal Family's most delicate briefings. Sir Matthew's office safe had been the repository of secrets that could have been splashed across every newspaper in the world; yet not a whisper of scandal had ever escaped from Lincoln's Inn. This time, however, it was different. This time there was no easy cover-up. This time he was dealing with a family at war. And the sum of evidence that the Prince of Wales had amassed against his estranged wife was dynamite. There was little hope of avoiding a scandal; scandal had already rent the royals. This was going to be a case of damage limitation.

A few hundred yards away from Lincoln's Inn, in a contrastingly modern office block next to a sandwich bar in bustling Southampton Row, off the Aldwych, another venerable lawyer also withdrew a stack of documents from his safe. Lord Victor Mishcon, a more flamboyant character than the privacy-seeking Sir Matthew Farrer, was the solicitor for the Princess of Wales. Lord Mishcon of Lambeth, a south London boy, son of Rabbi Arnold and Queenie Mishcon, was now a life peer and seventy-nine-year-old senior partner of the legal firm of Mishcon De Reya. Although officially retired, he had often attended his office over the past two years to help Princess Diana add ammunition to the traditionally ribbon-bound file containing her demands of her husband. Like the file at the offices of Farrer and Co., Lord Mishcon's secret brief contained claim and counter-claim in tortuously worded legal jargon. And like Prince Charles's file, it also held more explicitly worded evidence of explosive proportions.

Evidence of fornication, adultery, and other serious and damaging matters.

The battle plans had been laid in the war between the world's best-known couple. The long campaign of mistrust, unfaithfulness and eventually mutual hatred had at last culminated in the divorce of the century. The time bomb was primed and ready to explode.

The case of Windsor versus Windsor was about to begin.

Once upon a time, it was simple enough for a monarch to change, or at least to bend, the law to suit his or her own needs. Not so today. Remarkably, the embattled Prince and Princess of Wales have had to fill out precisely the same forms in precisely the same way as any other estranged couple. The fact that he is heir to the throne has no relevance in law. Nor indeed does the position of his wife — nor his mother, the Queen herself.

The principle task of a divorce court is to apportion responsibility for the secure upbringing of the children. In the case of Windsor versus Windsor, that was also the most acrimonious source of conflict on both sides.

To begin divorce proceedings in Britain, a Petitioner has to send two copies of his application to any one of the 170-plus county courts with a divorce jurisdiction. Alternatively, he or she can apply directly to the Divorce Registry at Somerset House, on London's Strand. In either case, standard forms have to be used.

One of these is a 'Statement of Arrangements for Children'. The Petitioner must also submit his marriage certificate and a 'Certificate of Conciliation' confirming that both parties have been offered the services of a conciliator whose job it is to iron out any disputed arrangements for support of and access to the children. In addition, there is this quaintly worded 'Prayer' for the divorce to be granted:

PRAYER OF THE PETITION. The Petitioner therefore prays: (1) That the said marriage be dissolved. (2) That the Petitioner may be granted the Residence of the children of the family namely William Arthur Philip Louis born on the 28th of June 1982 and Henry Charles Albert David born on the 15th of September 1984. (3) That the Respondent may be ordered to pay the costs of this suit.

These and other documents are deposited with the court and sent to the Respondent, who replies with his or her own comments. This is in the form of an 'Answer' – countering whatever allegations have been made by the Petitioner.

If, as is usually the case, the Respondent is not defending the divorce, there remain just three key matters to decide: residency of the children, the splitting of assets, and future maintenance. But when the assets belong to the heir to the throne, and residency of the children involves effective custody of the future King, the complex quagmire of claim and counter-claim can only be imagined.

Unfortunately, in the case of Windsor versus Windsor, the course of true loathing did not run even this smoothly. Princess Diana's demands were so stringent and Prince Charles's reaction so dismissive of them that an early, easy option was out of the question.

In 1994, realising at last that her husband, his family and their courtiers had engineered her out of the mainstream of monarchy and, far worse, were slowly gaining control of her children's futures, Diana's resolve hardened. Power, prestige and wealth were assets that the Princess was loath to lose. But the love and loyalty of her children were gifts that she would die for. The once diffident Di now turned to fight tooth and claw for her sons William and Harry.

Diana's 'teeth and claws' were her own rock-firm determination and her lawyers' tactical expertise. Foreseeing a battle royal over her role as mother of the heir to the throne, she instructed Lord Mishcon to fire a warning shot across the bows of Buckingham Palace. She had Mishcon De Reya draft a petition for divorce on the grounds of adultery – adultery by her husband with her hated rival, Camilla Parker Bowles.

The substantiation of this allegation would have been drafted by Diana and her lawyers in terms such as these:

(i) That the Respondent has committed adultery and the Petitioner finds it intolerable to live with the Respondent.

(ii) That the Respondent has committed adultery on diverse occasions and locations, including the marital home of Highgrove House, for many years throughout the period of the marriage, with the Co-respondent Mrs Camilla Parker Bowles, of Middlewick House, Corsham, Wiltshire.

Lawyers talk. Far more chat goes on outside the courtrooms of the country than within them. Mishcon De Reya would have been in regular contact with Farrer and Co. from the start. And threats of an adultery suit would have brought an immediate response in kind.

Although the details of these negotiations between the two legal firms a few hundred metres apart in central London will never be known, it is certain that any threat by the Princess's side to petition on the grounds of adultery would have incensed the Palace. Farrer and Co. would have retaliated with the threat of a petition by Prince Charles on the same grounds: adultery. But Sir Matthew Farrer is likely to have recommended that this be backed up with an additional allegation: unreasonable conduct. This latter petition could have read:

(i) That the Respondent has behaved in such a way that the Petitioner cannot reasonably be expected to live with the Respondent.

(ii) That the Respondent (the Princess of Wales) has throughout the period of the marriage behaved publicly in a manner likely to bring disrepute upon the Petitioner (the Prince of Wales) and embarrass his family, including Her Majesty the Queen, in the eyes of their friends, their servants and their subjects. Furthermore, the Respondent has received the attentions of male admirers in a manner likely to cause humiliation to the Petitioner. Furthermore, the Respondent has encouraged a book to be written and newspaper articles to be published maligning the Petitioner and likely to subject him to public disrepute and contempt.

All of this was clever swordsmanship by some of the mightiest legal warriors in the land. They had parried blows with their adversaries along these battle lines in many similar skirmishes over the years. Yet the battle that lay ahead awed even them. And it positively petrified the Palace. For the first time in her life, Princess Diana had her hated husband, his haughty mother, his furious father and all their courtiers ('oilers', as she called them) running scared. And she loved it . . .

2

Scheming and Schism

The notion of divorce is not new to the British Royal Family. It has been around ever since the early sixteenth century when King Henry VIII felt the need to rid himself of a hated wife. When he found that she could not give him a male heir, he sought to divorce her in order to marry his mistress, Anne Boleyn. Turned down by the Pope, Henry broke with Rome and created the Church of England – then sacked the monasteries, only to squander their wealth. When the old lecher died, grotesquely obese and riddled with syphilis, England was bankrupt.

Monarchs of England, Wales and Scotland have since been at pains to avoid such extreme solutions to their domestic difficulties. And that is where advisers like Sir Matthew Farrer have played their part.

Since taking over from his father Sir Leslie as keeper of the Queen's secrets, Sir Matthew has dealt with an extraordinary array of crises. He handled the divorce of Princess Margaret and Lord Snowdon, an unprecedented event at the time. In recent years he negotiated the settlement arrangements in the divorce of Princess Anne and Mark Phillips, the separation of the Duke and Duchess of York, and the constitutional implications of the separation of the Prince and Princess of Wales. He even tackled the thorny problem of the Queen's finances when she came in for a storm of criticism for not paying taxes.

The role of Farrer and Co. as 'firemen' to scandal-hit royalty predates any of these events, however. The legal firm (founded 1761) had been commissioned to solve the problems of the royal 'Firm' for almost a century. Sir Leslie Farrer was solicitor to George VI and had to tackle the House of Windsor's previous near-disaster: the abdication of King Edward VIII so that he could marry his mistress, Wallis Simpson. That was the moment that the British Royal Family learned to fear one word more than any other in the English language.

Divorce!

As Prince of Wales, Edward could not resist the lure of dominant women. He enjoyed a string of mistresses, most of them the wives of his friends. (One such mistress was Alice Keppel, whose great-granddaughter was to play a central part in a later royal scandal. Her name: Camilla Parker Bowles.) In 1931 Edward was introduced to Wallis Simpson and was immediately besotted by her and by the severe, matronly treatment she meted out. The problem was not that Edward had found a new mistress to dominate him. It was that the heir to the throne had fallen in love with a divorcee — twice wed and still married to her second husband, Ernest Simpson.

Edward frolicked around Europe's smarter resorts with Wallis, creating an international scandal reported in every country of the world but Britain. The Royal Family became a laughing stock but the Prince refused to give up his beloved dominatrix. Finally, told by the British government that they could never sanction their future King and head of the Church of England marrying a divorcee, Edward meekly signed his abdication papers on 10 December 1936. The next day he told his country: 'It is impossible to carry the heavy burden of responsibility and to discharge my duties as King as I would wish to do without the help and support of the woman I love.' Accepting the title Duke of Windsor, Edward went into immediate exile, married his Wallis and never returned to his own shores.

The abdication crisis almost put paid to the House of Windsor. In disarray, Edward's shy, stuttering brother was crowned George VI and, against all the odds, proved an exemplary monarch. With his wife Elizabeth, he carried Britain through World War II on a wave of patriotic support, and on his death in 1952 his daughter, Elizabeth Alexandra Mary, was handed an untarnished crown. Even then, the new, young

Queen Elizabeth II and George's widow, now Queen Elizabeth the Queen Mother, refused to forgive the Duke of Windsor or Wallis. Both mother and daughter blamed the errant Edward and his divorcee wife for forcing George VI to take the throne, unprepared and seemingly unsuited to the job – the toll of which, they believed, was his early death.

The Queen deigned to visit the Duke of Windsor at his Paris home only once in his life, in May 1972. Eight days later he was dead of throat cancer. Wallis, paralysed by arteriosclerosis, died in April 1986 and was allowed to be buried alongside her husband at Frogmore, on the royal estate at Windsor. The inscription on her coffin read: 'Wallis, Duchess of Windsor 1896–1986'. Even in death she was denied the three letters that her husband had fought for and she had craved throughout their lives: HRH – 'Her Royal Highness'.

The Royal Family do not forgive easily. They never forget. And because of the Duke and Duchess of Windsor, they had added reason to hate that word: 'divorce'.

Which was again proved true when the Queen's sister, Princess Margaret, fell for a married man. Group Captain Peter Townsend was sixteen years older than the impressionable, glowingly beautiful teenager. The romance went largely unnoticed until 1952 when Margaret, then aged twenty-two, and Townsend, by now divorced and having been appointed Equerry to the

Queen, broke the news of their planned engagement to other members of the Royal Family.

Shocked, the Queen, Prince Philip and the Queen Mother sought the advice of political, religious and constitutional advisers. The reaction of Queen Elizabeth's most senior adviser, Tommy Lascelles, was direct and to the point. An old friend of Townsend, Lascelles turned on his fellow courtier and told him: 'You must be either mad or bad.' He then warned the Queen that it mattered not a jot that Townsend was an innocent party in his divorce. The Queen was head of the Church of England and, under canon number 107 of the year 1603, she could give her consent to such a marriage only if the Prime Minister and his Cabinet agreed.

Winston Churchill was Prime Minister and was sympathetic to Townsend, who had been a heroic Spitfire pilot during World War II. 'What a delightful match,' he commented. Then he began to have second thoughts. Here were the makings of another royal scandal only sixteen years after the abdication crisis of Edward VIII had shaken the monarchy. Churchill had been heavily attacked at the time for taking the side of Edward and Mrs Simpson. Now, as Prime Minister, he worried lest a trauma of 1936 proportions should again rock the Royal Family. As he dithered, his wife Clemmie warned him: 'Winston, if you are going to begin the abdication all over again, I am going to leave.' Churchill sighed resignedly.

Over the next three years, Church, State, Parliament, courtiers and eventually the Queen herself all rejected the pleas of the forlorn Princess Margaret. After one last night together, she and Townsend parted for ever, having drafted one of the most moving official statements ever released by the Palace. Issued on 31 October 1955, it read:

> I would like it to be known that I have decided not to marry Group Captain Peter Townsend. I have been aware that subject to renouncing my rights of succession it might have been possible for me to contract a civil marriage. But mindful of the Church's teaching that a Christian marriage is indissoluble and conscious of my duty to the Commonwealth, I have resolved to put these considerations before any others. I have reached the decision entirely alone, and in doing so have been strengthened by the unfailing support and devotion of Group Captain Peter Townsend. I am grateful for the concern of all those who have constantly prayed for my happiness.

Peter Townsend disappeared from the scene, settling in Paris, where he quietly married a French woman and raised three children. Princess Margaret, on the other hand, threw herself into a round of partying, seeking forgetfulness with an array of high-living and sometimes eccentric acquaintances. In 1959 she fell for photographer Antony Armstrong Jones, and the Princess and the commoner (by now having been given the gratuitous title 'Lord Snowdon') were wed at Westminster Abbey in May 1960.

Despite two children and a free-and-easy lifestyle, the marriage was not to endure. Margaret's assignations with society gardener Roddy Llewellyn were published in the press and a humiliated Lord Snowdon telephoned the Queen with an anguished plea: he wanted out.

Now the Queen had to come to terms with the previously unthinkable. That dreaded word 'divorce' within the Royal Family itself.

Edward VIII's marriage to divorcee Wallis Simpson had been one thing; Margaret's bid to marry divorcee Peter Townsend was another; but this was to be a divorce by a sister of the Queen, the sister of the head of the Church of England. It was to be the first divorce by an immediate member of the Royal Family since the head-chopping days of Henry VIII.

The Queen sought Prime Minister Harold Wilson's help in successfully keeping the Cabinet in line. Then Matthew Farrer was summoned to the Palace to negotiate a legal separation and a financial settlement. Snowdon gratefully signed on the dotted line. His eventual divorce in 1978 left him free to remarry that year. Margaret remained alone – with the memories of two passionate romances that had both ended with the word 'divorce' ringing in her ears.

Ironically, the divorce of Princess Margaret and Lord Snowdon actually helped another royal romance to a fruitful conclusion. While the 'Princess Margaret Affair' had been giving the monarch and her advisers sleepless nights, another delicate family romance had been maturing for nine months or so until it, too, had to be brought to the Queen's attention. Her cousin, thirty-six-year-old Prince Michael of Kent, had fallen in love with a divorcee. In any other family, the fact that a young man's bride-to-be was a divorcee would not have presented a problem. For the Queen, head of the Church of England, it was a double blow – for Marie-Christine, Baroness von Reibnitz and lately Mrs Tom Troubridge was not only a divorcee but a Roman Catholic!

At any other stage of history, Prince Michael's request to his aunt for permission to wed would have prompted a heartbreaking refusal of royal sanction. This time, however, the fates were on the side of the young lovers, because their plea to marry had come at the time that the Queen was treating the trauma of own sister's divorce with uncharacteristic leniency. Having let Margaret off the hook, she could hardly object to a liaison between Prince Michael, one of her favourite relatives, and the divorced Mrs Troubridge.

The Queen consulted the Prime Minister, at that time James Callaghan, and her Privy Council of advisers, who have the power to approve or reject all royal marriages. They rubber-stamped the arrangements but they and the Queen attached three conditions to their acceptance, otherwise permission for the marriage would be instantly withdrawn. They stipulated that Michael must forfeit his right of accession to the throne, that the couple must guarantee that any children be raised as Anglicans and not Roman Catholics and, thirdly, that they must marry abroad. Despite appeals by the couple to the Archbishop of Canterbury, Dr Donald Coggan, he failed to give the marriage his blessing. Not only could the Prince not marry his divorced bride in any Church of England establishment, it was impossible under the Act of Settlement for any member of the Royal Family to be married in a register office or in any form of civil ceremony in Great Britain.

The wedding of Prince Michael of Kent and Marie-Christine went ahead in an incredibly modest civil ceremony in Vienna town hall. The haughty divorcee felt utterly humiliated — as was the case throughout much of her marriage as the Queen and the rest of the Royal Family (who labelled her 'Princess Pushy') continued to snub her.

Princess Michael of Kent may have got her way and her man, but her ambitious visions of a life of grandeur within the Royal Family had been blighted by that one word: 'divorce'.

It is not known whether Sir Matthew Farrer was involved in the negotiations behind the Queen's conditional approval of Prince Michael of Kent's wedding, but it is likely that he was. He certainly played a major role in the divorce of the Queen's only daughter, Princess Anne, later made Princess Royal.

Anne had married commoner Captain Mark Phillips at Westminster Abbey in November 1973. They lived the relatively unregal lives of country gentlefolk at Gatcombe Park, Gloucestershire, a mansion and farm which the Queen bought for them as a belated £5 million wedding present. There fiery, passionate Anne and awkward, retiring Mark raised two children before their totally disparate characters and lifestyles drew them apart. Anne was revealed to have written love letters to a Royal Navy officer, Commander Tim Laurence, while Mark was romantically linked with several lady friends before being named in a paternity suit as the father of a six-year-old girl born to a New Zealand art teacher. A royal sex scandal and messy divorce was on the cards.

Enter Sir Matthew Farrer. His guiding hand was there from the start to nip yet another royal crisis in the bud. In August 1989 Buckingham Palace un-dramatically announced that Princess Anne and her husband were to separate. It was said that there were no plans for divorce. It was, of course, a stalling tactic. Princess Anne waited a full two and a half years before instituting divorce proceedings. When she even-tually did, it was all very 'gentlemanly'. Indeed the announcement was delayed so that it would not clash with the 1992 general election. By then, Sir Matthew had sorted out the 'business'. It was agreed that Anne would continue living at Gatcombe with the children, while Mark, with access granted and a healthy settlement, would move down the road to Aston Farm.

On 13 April 1992 an historic but typically terse statement from Buckingham Palace signalled the end of the eighteen-year marriage: '. . . Her Royal Highness is starting the necessary legal proceedings . . .' The Princess's petition was presented to the Divorce Registry the very same day. Just ten days later, the first of the Queen's children to dissolve a marriage was granted a four-minute 'quickie' divorce in dingy Court Three of Somerset House. Thanks to Anne's common sense and Sir Matthew Farrer's diplomacy, she was able to pick up the pieces of her life, continue her royal duties, marry her new love, Commander Laurence – and remain friends with her new neighbour, her ex-husband!

Such an amicable conclusion to a marriage was unique in royal annals (and, sadly, set a precedent now looking increasingly unlikely to be followed). How Sir Matthew pulled off this coup of diplomacy is a secret few shall ever know. That wise old counsellor to the Royal Family would never speak of such matters. His profile is not so much low as invisible. He flits like a shadow between his homes in London and Sussex, which he shares with his German wife Johanna Creszentia Maria Dorothea Bennhold. He travels anonymously by bus between his London house and his firm's offices. A car is summoned for his invitations to Buckingham Palace but no one recognises him as the limousine sweeps through the gates. No photograph of him is known to exist in the public domain. He is the real-life 'Invisible Man' and that is the way he likes it.

Sir Matthew, knighted in one of the Queen's New Year Honours lists, is Establishment to the core, a loyal monarchist who fears that the actions of the younger royals have permanently damaged the fabric of the House of Windsor. He hates royal separations and would do anything to avoid a situation that could land the Royal Family with another divorce scandal. Yet, as an acquaintance said: 'He knows his role is to represent, not to admonish.' Which is why he must have bitten his stiff upper lip many a time while dealing with the House of Windsor's most squalid marital crisis: that between the Duke and Duchess of York.

Prince Andrew and flame-haired Sarah Ferguson had wed amid high pomp and high hopes at Westminster Abbey in July 1986. The marriage hit the rocks only five years (and two daughters) later. Sir Matthew was so upset by the tawdry nature of the pair's separation that he escaped to China for three weeks midway through the most delicate part of the negotiations – much to the Duchess's loudly expressed indignation. 'Fergie' had been tutored by her 'financial adviser' and lover, the toe-sucking Texan Johnny Bryan, to ask for the earth in her interim settlement. After Sir Matthew Farrer's intervention, she fared less well than she or her boyfriend had expected. She retired hurt to a rented house in suburban Berkshire, pending a divorce.

Sir Matthew was now able to concentrate on the most crucial royal problem he had handled in his entire career. He even delayed his retirement because of it. The problem that threatened to tear the House of Windsor apart and sink it for ever in the eyes of the public, the press and half of Parliament was the schism between the Prince and Princess of Wales ... The divorce of the heir to the throne ... The case of Windsor versus Windsor.

At one stage it had looked as if the introduction to 'the firm' of the Princess of Wales and the Duchess of York had heralded a reincarnation of the Royal Family. Never had there been two women quite like them. Throughout the 1980s they appeared to be more than mere sisters-in-law. They were close friends, allies against the stuffy Palace old guard, in tune with the youth of Britain, the future of a glamorous new monarchy.

Even the Archbishop of Canterbury described blushing Diana Spencer as a fairytale princess when she wed Charles at St Paul's Cathedral in July 1981. When, five years to the month later, shy Di was followed up the aisle by worldly redhead Sarah, the nation applauded this second 'breath of fresh air' in royal affairs. The fact that Sarah's Westminster Abbey wedding was to dashing Falklands War hero Prince Andrew only added to Britons' pride.

The press dubbed Di and Fergie the 'Merry Wives of Windsor' as they skittered across the national stage, putting a sparkle into every event on the royal calendar. With or (usually) without their respective husbands, they livened up London society. At the other extreme, they supported one another in the stuffy outposts of the Royal Family: Sandringham and Balmoral. And when the magic went out of their marriages, they continued to support each other as they found themselves again 'outsiders'. There was even a strong suggestion that the pair had made a naïve pact that, if all went wrong, the two would announce the breakdown of their marriages in unison.

It never happened, of course. As separation became inevitable for both wives, they grew not closer but further apart. As their marriages to Charles and Andrew collapsed, so Diana and Sarah's friendship collapsed along with them. The Princess of Wales felt that her former friend's extravagant and sometimes lascivious antics were letting the side down. The Duchess of York felt equally let down — by Diana herself, whom she accused of egging her on towards independence then dumping her like a too-hot potato.

Now that the Merry Wives of Windsor had become

the Warring Wives of Windsor, the bubbly Fergie characteristically bounced back and forged her own life, independent of the Palace. Diana, however, could find no solace to overcome the stigma of being party to the biggest crisis ever to threaten Britain's royal house. Ignored by the Queen, spurned by the royal household, humiliated by her husband, caricatured by the press, the brightest hope for the future of the British Royal Family stood alone. Alone and out for revenge – in the divorce of the century.

So was this to be the culmination of 1,000 years of royal history? In a single decade, a vision of great promise had blossomed, withered and died. The most publicised marriage of the century was ending in mistrust, unfaithfulness and eventually mutual hatred. In accusations of fornication and adultery. In crisis, in scandal, and inevitably in defeat.

From such golden beginnings, how on earth had Charles and Diana made such a fearful hash of it . . .?

3

Charles: Born to be King

Charles Philip Arthur George Windsor was born at Buckingham Palace on a clear, crisp day on 14 November 1948. Weighing in at 7 pounds 6 ounces, Charles was the forty-fourth heir to the throne and the first male in direct succession for more than eighty years. Accession to the throne would make him King Charles III.

Prince Charles came into the world at a time when Britain was struggling to recover from World War II and ration books were still in use. They were austere years and there was to be no wet-nursing, no mollycoddling and no private tutors for this heir of the new Elizabethan Age.

From his earliest years, his contact with his parents was restrictively formal and limited. The child spent all his time with his nannies, being taken to see his mother for only half an hour in the morning and being in the company of both parents for only an hour and a half in the evening. Since neither his mother nor father was given to displays of affection, even these brief interludes provided fewer bonds of affection than he forged with his principal nanny, Mabel Anderson, who was devoted to him and who assumed the role of 'surrogate mother'.

There was even less chance of parental care when Charles came of school age. The Prince was the first royal to be sent to day school: Hill House in London. Then, like his father Prince Philip, he went on to attend boarding schools: Cheam and Gordonstoun.

It was during his time at Cheam that Charles showed the beginnings of his talent for art. While there, he did hundreds of drawings and paintings. He kept his parents amused with the little pictures he sent home every term. He was a perfect pupil and, whether his parents knew it or not, a perfect son, gentle and loving, writing assiduously to them every week he was away. But the Prince also had a mischievous streak which revealed itself in the many pranks he indulged in as a pupil at Cheam. This was to be the start of the joker trait that was to stay with him throughout his life.

At fourteen, his parents sent him to Gordonstoun, the tough Scottish boarding school his father had attended as a teenager. Gordonstoun was founded by Dr Kurt Hahn, a Jew who set up the school when he was hounded out of Germany by Hitler in 1933. The sons of royalty mixed with the sons of ordinary folk, all of whom in Charles's time paid an average £519 a year. Life was spartan at the school, where a pupil's day started at 7 a.m. with a brisk run around the grounds, come hail or shine, followed by a cold bath before breakfast. The day's solid studies were interrupted only by afternoons on the playing fields or on adventure courses. The only time a pupil got for himself was an hour after supper when he was allowed to listen to the radio or watch certain television programmes.

When he joined the school, Charles at first floundered then began to retreat into a shell. He grew to regard Gordonstoun as 'a prison sentence'. He hated the mindlessly strict regime, the harshness and crudeness of his fellow pupils – but most of all he feared the bullying. This is the constant theme of letters he wrote to friends far away, almost every one a tragically lonely cry for comfort.

'I hate coming back here and leaving everyone at home,' he wrote during his third term. 'Papa rushed me so much on Monday when I had to go that I hardly had time to say goodbye to Mabel properly. He kept hurrying me up all the time ... I hardly get any sleep because I snore and get hit on the head the whole time. It's absolute hell ... I don't like it much here.'

More than a year later he was still writing: 'It's such hell here, especially at night. I don't get any sleep practically at all nowadays ... The people in my dormitory are foul. Goodness they are horrid. I don't know how anyone could be so foul . . . Last night was hell, literal hell . . . I still wish I could come home. It's such a HOLE this place!'

And again: 'People in this house are unbelievable. They have hardly any manners worth mentioning and have the foulest natures of any people I know. I don't know why people are like that . . . The language people use is horrid. I think it is because they are too lazy to use anything else.'

The obvious disgust that Charles felt towards his young contemporaries must have revealed itself to them. The royal whose life had been so sheltered was mercilessly taunted, and the more he displayed what they must have viewed as his prissy nature, the more they bullied him.

Although Charles poured out his heart in letters to young friends, he never complained to his masters. He took his punishment and retreated still further into his shell. His only outgoing displays were in his writing and his drawing, in both of which he found solace from his 'foul-natured' fellow pupils. Although the Prince was only a middle-stream pupil, he proved himself artistic and musical. He also revealed a telling need for escapism . . .

During this time the Goons, the famous radio comedy team, were introducing a new zany brand of British humour. Charles was instantly addicted and mastered all of their weird accents. He even insisted to friends that should he mimic the character 'Seagoon', then the person he spoke to had to answer back as 'Bluebottle'. His powers of mimicry stood him in good stead when in later years he trod the boards at Cambridge.

His love of the Goons lasted and he struck up friendships with all four members: Spike Milligan, Harry Secombe, Peter Sellers and Michael Bentine. He became, in effect, the fifth Goon and spent hours volleying jokes back and forth with them. Even when he was away they exchanged cabled gags.

Meanwhile, back at Gordonstoun, Prince Charles was involved in what was considered at the time to be a huge scandal. Considering the scandals that were to dog the young royals in years to come, it is revealing of this age of innocence that all the hapless fourteen-year-old was guilty of was being caught drinking cherry brandy while on a school trip. The press went wild. Charles described the episode years later in a radio interview, still with much of the naïveté of a teenager:

At the time I thought it was the end of the earth. I was all set to pack my bags and leave for Siberia. What really happened was this. I was on a cruise from Gordonstoun in the school yacht and we went to Stornaway. I was recognised by the press and I suddenly thought 'I can't bear this any more' and decided to go off somewhere else. The only other place I could find was the bar. Having never been in a bar before, the first thing I thought I ought to do was to have a drink. I was terrified and asked for the first drink that came into my head. It just happened to be cherry brandy. I had drunk it before when it was cold and I was out shooting. I had hardly taken a sip when the whole world exploded around my ears. It caused a terrific uproar.

The result was that Charles was hauled in front of the headmaster, who dismissed the pupil's explanation. He was demoted. What hurt Charles more, however, was the punishment exacted on his private detective, Donald Green, who was dismissed from royal duty. Charles said many years later: 'I have never been able to forgive them [the Metropolitan Police] for doing that because he defended me in the most marvellous way and he was the most wonderful, loyal man. I thought it was atrocious.' In Charles's own words, the Prince was also 'severely punished by my parents — and I think that's why they packed me off to Australia and Geelong Grammar School'.

Perversely, Charles's need of solitude was to put him on the front pages time and time again in the coming years. But the boy Prince did not have long to wait until his next press appearance. A copybook full of his school essays was stolen and sold to a national newspaper. It was dubbed the 'Exercise Book Affair'. An investigation carried out by the school failed to reveal the culprit who had sold the Prince's golden words, which included an essay on his mother and father. Again the teenager was in his parents' bad books.

Not long after, the seventeen-year-old Prince, just like many noble miscreants before him, was on his way to Australia. There, at Timbertop, the bush annexe of Geelong Grammar School, he was able for three escapist months to live a life out of the public eye. His tough Aussie contemporaries seemed to take to him immediately. He raised a laugh among fellow pupils when he wore a classic City of London suit, a bowler hat and carried an umbrella for his debut at the school. He accepted his affectionate nickname 'the Pommie Bastard', but privately, he found Timbertop every bit as tough and sometimes as Philistine as Gordonstoun.

Back home in England, he went straight to Trinity College, Cambridge, entering the ancient university among controversy that his qualifying grades were too low for such a prestigious seat of learning. Nevertheless, the student Prince worked hard and threw himself into acting, starring in several amateur revues. He left Trinity with an unimpressive 'class two, division two' degree. He also left with a highly tuned sense of humour and wit, finely honed by such comedy greats as Peter Cook, Dudley Moore and David Frost, former students whom he later befriended. Prince Charles also studied at the University College of Wales, Aberystwyth. He diligently learned Welsh and made an historic speech in the language – typically including a reference to his comic hero, Welshman Harry Secombe.

The title Prince of Wales does not come automatically and its bestowal is at the discretion of the sovereign. Charles, who had been created Prince of Wales at the age of ten, was not formally invested with the title until eleven years later. He became the twenty-first English Prince of Wales since 1282 when Edward I, having killed the Welsh Prince Llewellyn ap Gruffudd, gave the title to his own son. Taking his oath of allegiance to the Queen at Caernarfon Castle on 1 July 1969, Charles pledged: 'Faith and truth I will bear unto you to live and die against all manner of folks.' Charles was true to his word. Of all twenty-one English princes of Wales, he is considered to be the best ever. Until his investiture, his ancestors had taken little interest in the place. But Charles is a firm believer in the Prince of Wales's motto 'I Serve' and has always done his bit to promote Wales in his travels.

Prince Charles followed in his father's footsteps and joined the Royal Navy. There the real adventurer started to surface, with Lieutenant Charles Windsor giving full rein to his daredevil streak, often with potentially dangerous results. Action man at heart, he went on to excel as a deep-sea diver, sailor, helicopter pilot and parachutist. Some felt his antics were down-right reckless, exposing the heir to the throne to unnecessary risk. However, throughout his life in the services he was an advertising man's dream: his image proved to be a real recruit-puller.

There was a less sure-footed side to the Prince, however, as the immature prankster in him reared its head again. While at Cranwell RAF College in 1971, he noticed that fellow student officers all wore the same, expensive, hand-sewn shoes. The Prince announced on the Tannoy system that all of the shoes were faulty and the manufacturers were withdrawing them to replace them with brand-new ones. More than half the cadets complied with the request that they hand their shoes over to a porter bribed by Charles. It wasn't until three days later that the Prince owned up to the shoeless students. Charles's naval career is dotted with similar, schoolboy stunts, and the Prince used to spend a fortune in joke shops buying exploding cigars, stinkbombs, imitation doggie-dirt and the like. So exasperated were his fellow officers at these childish japes that Charles was frequently 'debagged', exposing the royal rump.

Quite what such activities said for the mentality of this fully-grown Senior Serviceman was difficult to discern at the time. But it did forewarn of a need for escapism, if not a deep-seated desire to take less than seriously his role as heir to the throne – and later his role as a father and indeed as a husband.

Of all the influences on the Prince throughout his life, none was stronger than that of his uncle, Earl Mountbatten of Burma. Charles was so attached to his beloved Uncle Dickie that he dubbed him 'Honorary Grandfather'. He enjoyed his company so much that, like his parents before him, he would one day choose to spend the first night of his honeymoon at Mountbatten's family home, Broadlands, in Hampshire.

Lord Louis Mountbatten may have been a hero to Charles and a cornerstone within the Royal Family but he was no pillar of society. His proximity to the royals once prompted MI5 to classify him as a security risk. Such was Uncle Dickie's greed for constitutional power that he strove throughout his life to have the title of the House of Windsor changed to incorporate his own family name of Mountbatten. (It is now known to be the wish of Prince Charles, backed by his father, to rename the royal house 'Mountbatten' rather than 'Windsor' whenever he assumes the crown.)

The duplicitous Lord Louis was known to have been consulted by press magnate Cecil King in his attempted political coup against the Labour government of Harold Wilson in 1966. More scandalously, it had long been apparent that Lord Louis was a practising homosexual, both he and his wife Edwina shocking their close circle with a string of affairs. The Royal Family has always turned a blind eye to homosexual practices among its members – but it has often been marvelled at that Prince Charles was allowed to become so close to his adoring Uncle Dickie. Few fathers would have been as trusting and as understanding as Prince Philip when his son spent so long in the company of a surrogate father figure with such sexual predilections.

It was with heart-stopping horror that Charles heard the news that his uncle had been killed by a terrorist bomb while holidaying at his Irish home, Classiebawn Castle, in August 1979. Charles was utterly devastated and wept openly. He could barely contain himself when he read the lesson at the earl's funeral.

Following Mountbatten's death at the age of seventy-nine, the thirty-one-year-old Prince turned to another man he had known since childhood: the gentle, softly-spoken philosopher, Laurens van der Post, who was to become his greatest spiritual mentor. Sir Laurens's basic principle of life is that man must live in harmony with himself, animals and the land. That is something that Charles has striven to achieve in his solitary pastimes. The result is that, like van der Post, he has come to be regarded as rather eccentric.

The major influences in his life have not always been male, of course. Prince Charles may not be the most handsome man in the world but he has never had any trouble attracting beautiful women. Doubtless that has something to do with his position. What he has never been able to do, however, is to keep them. And that is despite his reputation as a particularly well-endowed lover!

In his youthful years, the gossip columnists were kept busy with speculation about Charles's principal loves and predictions as to his future bride. The Prince gave them a run for their money. He dated a string of women, jokingly referred to as 'Charlie's Angels' after the American television series.

Charles's most constant confidantes have shared his interest in horses, hunting and outdoor pursuits. Apparently, they must also be good listeners. These friendships, which have endured to the present day, include women whose influence on the Prince has been considerable. Among them are Sarah Lindsay, widow of skiing victim Major Hugh Lindsay, Patti Palmer-Tomkinson, who was severely injured in the same accident, Lady 'Kanga' Tryon and of course Mrs Camilla Parker Bowles, formerly Camilla Shand.

Charles first met Camilla in 1972 when they were both twenty-three. He was shy and awkward; she was the blonde, vivacious daughter of a wealthy wine merchant, master of foxhounds and deputy lord lieutenant of East Sussex. She is also the great-granddaughter of Mrs George Keppel, a mistress of Edward VII. Prince Charles was utterly smitten with Camilla, despite the fact that she was being wooed by Charles's polo friend, cavalry officer Andrew Parker Bowles. For eight months she dated Charles before he went to sea with the Royal Navy. Early in 1973 they said their farewells in his Palace rooms. Weeks later she announced her engagement to army officer Andrew. But, as we now know, this was to be far from the end of the astonishing influence that Camilla was to have on the life of Britain's heir to the throne . . .

Over the following years, Charles was linked to a string of society belles and European royals, none of whom he felt inclined to make the future Queen.

In June 1977 the revelation that all of Britain had been awaiting hit the newsstands. In big, bold type, the headline read: 'Charles to Marry Astrid – Official'. The Astrid referred to was Princess Marie-Astrid of Luxembourg. It was not to be, however. The press had been the victim of a political ploy to root out a suspected mole who was a member of the Queen's Privy Council. The false story had been planted.

Charles's reaction at the time was one of incredulity; he had never even met his so-called bride-to-be. In an unprecedented move, he issued a statement: 'There is no truth at all in the report that there is to be a formal announcement of an engagement to Princess Marie-Astrid of Luxembourg.' The next day, when newspapers refused to let go of such sensational speculation, he issued another statement through the Queen's press secretary, this one even more emphatic: 'They are not getting engaged this Monday, next Monday, the Monday after, or any other Monday, Tuesday, Wednesday or Thursday. They do not know each other and people who do not know each other do not get engaged.'

There were plenty of real escorts, however, for the newspapers to report on. Among them were Princess Caroline of Monaco, Maltese Governor General's daughter Sybilla Dorman and Sabrina Guinness of the wealthy brewing family. Charles again made headlines when he invited the latter to a ball at the Earl of Pembroke's house, along with her twin sister Miranda, then left the two of them like Cinderellas at the end of the night's dancing.

Charles is the ultimate chauvinist and his many dates were expected to behave in an old-fashioned, subservient role. One who fell foul of his pig-headed attitude was Davina Sheffield, a beautiful twenty-five-year old blonde whom Charles met in 1976 at a dinner party in Fulham. Davina was invited to Balmoral to be put through the 'test' — one that was designed to see if the woman was suitable for a continuing relationship. Poor Davina failed to grasp the message that she was expected to stay at home with the ladies of the household while the Prince and the other men went stalking through the Scottish heather. She insisted on tagging along and the hard-hearted Prince ran her into the ground by trekking through the toughest terrain he could find. She left the next morning for London. When revelations of her past romance with another man hit the headlines, she was never seen with Charles again. She did not fit the bill as the acquiescent bride.

Another woman who failed to fit Charles's ideal was Lady Jane Wellesley, daughter of the eighth Duke of Wellington. A BBC researcher and representative of the National Union of Journalists, he found her a touch too radical and outspoken for his taste.

Anna Wallace, daughter of a Scottish landowner,

was the only woman apart from Lady Diana Spencer to whom Charles ever proposed marriage. He was thirty-two and no nearer finding a wife than when he made his first conquest (of an exotic young lady named Lucia Santa Cruz) thirteen years earlier. However, Anna was more spirited than most of his escorts and would not accept his cool, unromantic, passionless approach to the art of love. This was epitomised by the occasion on which he infuriated her by inviting her to a Windsor Castle ball marking the Queen Mother's eightieth birthday, then ignoring the poor girl all evening. Nicknamed 'Whiplash Wallace' as a testament to her hot temper, Anna certainly cracked the whip that night when she stormed out at midnight – and out of his life.

Yet another seemingly serious contender for his hand shattered his male ego when she spoke frankly about her feelings for him to the press. Lady Sarah Spencer was on a skiing trip with the Prince in 1978 when she was asked where their relationship was going. She replied: 'Charles is a fabulous person but I am not in love with him. He is a romantic who falls in love easily. I would not marry a man I did not love, whether it was a dustman or the King of England. If he asked me I would turn him down.'

By now the ageing Prince was getting quite worried about his failure to find a future Queen. Then, quite by chance, he met up with Sarah Spencer's younger sister Diana.

4

Diana: Born to be Queen?

Diana, then aged sixteen, was introduced to Charles at her home, Althorp, in Northamptonshire, which her father had inherited, along with the title Earl Spencer, upon the death of her grandfather two years before. Diana was away from school for half term when Charles arrived for a pheasant shoot. It was by no means a question of a member of royalty dropping by at the ordinary home of an ordinary girl. The Spencer family, by virtue of its aristocratic name and links, had always mingled closely and freely with the royals. Earl Spencer had been an equerry to George VI, and Diana had been born at Park House, rented from the Royal Family on the Sandringham estate in Norfolk. It was inevitable that the Spencers and the Windsors would become friends. That is how Diana's older sister Sarah first came to meet Charles – and become his girlfriend.

That weekend pheasant shoot heralded another sport much loved by the upper classes: bagging a marriage partner to better oneself even further! No one would dare to suggest that Diana made the decision to steal Charles away from Sarah but steal him she did, by winning smiles, flirting and an unconscious determination to be noticed. Charles remarked later that he was absolutely enthralled by the gawky teenager. 'She was a jolly, amusing and attractive sixteen-year-old,' he said. Diana told friends her heart was lost on that very first introduction but she never dreamed that the Prince who impressed her with his man-of-the-world air and royal control would one day be her husband.

It was sad that neither ever sat down to evaluate what one partner could give the other. Charles was the product of a typical royal upbringing and schooling. He was well read, serious to the point of being stuffy, a maker of polite conversation, but totally detached from the everyday lives of everyday people. He hunted, rode, preferred intense debate to socialising with large groups of friends. No one could ever forget that here was a man groomed one day to be King.

Diana was twelve and a half years his junior – born on 1 July 1961 to Viscount Althorp, then thirty-seven, and the Viscountess, who was also twelve years her husband's junior. The Viscount had been hoping for a boy and had not even considered a girl's name. However, he hid his disappointment at the birth of a third daughter, named her Diana Frances and described her, at 7 pounds 12 ounces, as a 'perfect physical specimen'.

Physically perfect was what she certainly grew up to be. But mental scars remained from those early days when she came to realise that her very birth had been an anti-climax for parents who had longed for a male heir to carry on the Spencer dynasty. The sense of disappointment was heightened by the fact that just eighteen months previously Diana's mother Frances had given birth to a sickly, deformed baby boy named John who had died only ten hours after entering this world.

'I was supposed to be a boy,' Diana would forlornly tell her pals.

Diana was christened in a modest ceremony at Sandringham Church. When three years later the longed-for son arrived, he was christened with full pomp at Westminster Abbey, with the Queen as godmother. Diana, however, was never jealous of her baby brother Charles. The two youngest children shared a deep bond as they grew up together at Park House amid an increasingly acrimonious atmosphere caused by their parents perpetually warring with one another. Worse, as was revealed many years later, good old 'Johnnie' Spencer not only hurled abuse at his wife but occasionally more than that.

Some of Diana's first memories are those of her parents arguing as she and her two sisters, Lady Sarah and Lady Jane, her elders by six and four years, covered their ears with their hands. As she grew older, she helped comfort baby brother Charles as he cried himself to sleep. Moody Diana learned to suffer in silence as, with her parents permanently at loggerheads, she was fought over and eventually passed from one to another, with nannies providing the only sense of permanence for the impressionable child.

Diana received plenty of expensive presents and attended lots of lavish children's parties. But all she really wanted was the loving attention of her mother and father. Somehow she came to blame herself for the desperate unhappiness of the entire family. She became sullen, introverted and rebellious. Early photographs of her seldom catch her smiling.

Then, when she was just six years old, the nightmare worsened. She sat dejected at the foot of the main staircase of Park House as her mother drove off for the last time. It was a scene of sorrow that has often returned to haunt her over the years.

One of the very first personal conversations she had with Prince Charles when their friendship flourished was about the divorce of her parents. He realised that it had had a profound effect on such a sensitive, sheltered girl. For Diana, divorce was a particularly heart-breaking word. Close friends believe that the bond Diana has with her own children has come about through a determination to shower as much love and security upon them as possible after her own unhappy childhood. The vitriolic rows of those years are recalled vividly by Diana. So one private vow she made to herself was that her children would never hear harsh words between their parents, no matter how intolerable the relationship became.

After the break-up of the Spencer marriage, Diana grew closer to her father, who was given custody of the children after a long and bitter court battle in which the Viscountess was too much of a lady even to breathe the phrase 'domestic violence'. Instead she suffered the ignominy of being labelled an adulteress because of her affair with a married man. The Spencer divorce went through in 1969 and within months Frances quietly wed her lover, Peter Shand Kydd, heir to a wallpaper fortune.

As Diana grew older, the feeling of guilt that she had harboured – 'I was supposed to be a boy' – gradually diminished. Yet she was still a moody child. She would often visit the grave of lost baby John in Sandringham churchyard. 'In Loving Memory' read the inscription on his gravestone. Had he lived, would her parents have tried for another child? Would Diana have ever been conceived?

The young country girl's morbid curiosity was also strangely reflected through her menagerie of pets. A horse rider from the age of three, Diana also had a cat called Marmalade, rabbits, hamsters and guinea pigs, which often ended up skeetering across the stone floors of ten-bedroomed Park House. When any of these creatures died, their young proprietor would arrange elaborate funerals, laying them to rest under crosses and headstones in shady corners of the rambling grounds.

Diana loved Park House and was loath to leave it when in 1975 her grandfather, the seventh Earl Spencer, died and the family moved from her Norfolk idyll to the stately (and gloomy) home of Althorp, Northamptonshire. Its echoing corridors, its dark corners, its many musty rooms all made the young teenager nervous. The move also meant that she saw even less of her father, who had become the eighth Earl Spencer. Looked after by a succession of nannies, then by governesses, the younger Spencers did not even dine with their father. It was a throwback to a distant, aristocratic age — and to a lifestyle that was hardly helpful to the emotional make-up of a young girl wounded by rejection and torn apart by deeply buried guilt.

So the little girl retaliated. Even while still at Park House, Diana was known as a menace by nannies who came and went with predictable regularity. One of them, Mary Clarke, recalled that during her interview for the job in 1970 Viscount Spencer put these problems of domestic staffing down to her 'high spirits'. In fact, she later discovered that the errant nine-year-old had locked one nanny in the lavatory and thrown another's clothes on to the roof!

Mary Clarke lasted two years with the Spencers. Many years later she described the young Diana thus: 'I can see her now, this child with fair hair down to her shoulders, rosy cheeks and downcast eyes, always talking about love. She so needed to be loved. She once told me: "I shall only get married when I am sure I am in love so that we will never be divorced." Even then, all she wanted was simply to get married happily. It's so sad.'

Moving from homely Park House to grand Althorp only made matters worse. For now one of the family's occasional weekend visitors ('that friend of Daddy's') became the new mistress of the house. Just a year after moving to Althorp, Earl Spencer married again. His new wife was the Countess of Dartmouth, better known as Raine, daughter of romantic novelist Barbara Cartland.

Diana became a daughter torn. She worshipped her father but found it hard to accept her stepmother. She divided her time between Althorp and her mother's home in Scotland. But although Diana found it hard to love Raine, she was eternally gratefully for the care the Earl's wife bestowed on him after he had a massive stroke when Diana was eighteen. It was that devoted care that enabled the proudest father in the world to walk down the aisle to see his daughter married to the Prince of Wales.

Diana was growing up into a pretty, though unremarkable, teenager. Her friends found her dreamy, her elders found her moody, and her schoolteachers at West Heath private boarding school in Kent found her sullenness less than attractive.

She had certainly turned out to be 'a perfect physical specimen', as her father had blandly described her at birth. But unlike Prince Charles, she turned out to be anything but an academic. She passed no exams at school, where her reports could do no better than say she was kind to animals and younger children (although she did win a prize at West Heath for being enthusiastic and 'nice').

How Diana must have hated having her father and her new stepmother read out such reports. Lady Raine Spencer – or 'Acid Raine' as she was dubbed by her stepchildren because of her fearsome tongue – was not the warm, understanding stepmother that Diana and her brothers and sisters needed. 'Raine was not meant to be a stepmother; she doesn't have the right temperament' was how Lord Spencer's aunt, Lady Margaret Douglas-Home, described her. 'Haughty', 'arrogant' and 'more regal than the Royal Family' are other descriptions her critics have provided.

When she married the eighth Lord Spencer ('my dearest Johnnie') she didn't pay close attention to the children. For instance, the children were not allowed to use the front door at Althorp; they could enter only by the tradesmen's entrance. She would address them as 'Lady Sarah' and 'Lady Diana' – seldom, if ever, by their Christian names alone. As one friend of the family said: 'She made insufficient effort to recognise the importance of the children. They were three little girls and a boy crying out for love and affection, and all she gave them was formality.'

The Spencer children deeply resented the way their

haughty stepmother 'took over' their father, and subsequently of the way she assumed control of the Althorp estate. To raise funds, valuable paintings and silver, most of which had been in the Spencer family for centuries, were sold. This supposed depletion of what they regarded as their rightful inheritance infuriated the children. One heirloom was sold to local dealers for £40,000 and was resold in New York for £270,000.

At the same time, Raine was the saviour of Earl Spencer when in 1978, just two years after their marriage, he suffered his massive stroke and hovered close to death. Raine banned everyone, including the children, from his hospital bedside and spent up to seventy-two hours at a time with him, talking about times past and future — literally bullying him back to life. The Earl later said: 'The doctors had me on the death list eight times. Raine was my miracle. It is entirely due to her — her love for me, her determination not to let me go — that I'm still around.'

Diana's father was still around but Diana was not. Seeking independence, she moved to London and stayed with friends. She took several jobs, including cleaning, and she learned how to type and how to ski at a finishing school in Switzerland. Basically she was being groomed for nothing other than to marry well.

No one can guess what would have happened to Diana if Charles had not become a serious part of her life. What is certain is that she knew that, because of the personal traumas her own parents' divorce had caused her, whomever she married, it would be for ever.

It was a year after Charles and Diana's first meeting that their paths were to cross again. She was finding her independence in a London flat she shared with three friends. He occasionally asked her along to make up the numbers at private gatherings. Diana thought no further than getting closer to the Prince to discover the real man behind his detached, regal image. She certainly never envisaged becoming his wife, but she always kept up her hopes that she would become more than just 'Sarah's little sister' to him.

At that time Sarah was having her own emotional problems: she was suffering from the eating disorder anorexia nervosa. Prince Charles was highly supportive towards Sarah – in stark contrast to the way he was to react to his own wife's similar illness a decade later. Sarah's weight plummeted from eight stone to four and a half stone at the time she was seeing the Prince, but she overcame her anorexia quietly without drama or headlines. (Sarah went on to marry Neil McCorquodale, a Lincolnshire farmer and former Coldstream Guards officer, after a whirlwind romance in 1980.)

Charles was now watching with sharpening interest as Diana blossomed from an awkward girl into an attractive young woman. By the time the Queen invited Diana and Sarah to Balmoral for a house party in 1979, the love match was taking shape. The invitation, Charles was to admit later, was a put-up job. He was no longer escorting Sarah. They had remained good friends, but inviting the two girls to the royal home was the only ruse he could think of to begin his courtship of Diana.

Royal courtships must be slow by ordinary standards, for it was not until early 1980 that Diana received another invitation, this time to join the Royal Family at Sandringham. A couple of months later Charles invited Diana to watch him play polo. Two weeks after that, she joined him on the royal yacht at Cowes. As one wag remarked: 'The Di was now cast.'

The romance progressed unnoticed by the press until the summer of 1980. Lady Diana had decided to join her now-married sister Jane, along with her husband Robert Fellowes, assistant private secretary to the Queen, and their new baby at a holiday cottage at Balmoral. A sharp-eyed reporter peered through his binoculars and at last identified the pretty young woman he had seen at other functions yet had never managed to put a name to.

A month later she was again spotted with Charles, at a race meeting in the Midlands. This time, however, they had a chaperone: the Prince's old flame Camilla Parker Bowles. Diana thought it odd that Charles paid Camilla so much heed. Inexperienced as she was, shy Di soon learned that she was expected to fit in with everything Charles and Camilla suggested ... or be ditched. Extraordinarily, what young Diana failed to realise was that Camilla Parker Bowles had vetted her and was now grooming her to be a suitable bride for her own ex-boyfriend!

Royal watchers were now on the scent of the romance of the century. Fleet Street was ecstatic and spent the next six months following Diana everywhere she went. Diana, although growing deeply in love with the earnest Prince, was unprepared for this intensity of press interest. Her past was dug into, no one believing that there was such a thing as a virgin in these modern times. Her academic achievements (or lack of them) were commented upon. Diana was hounded wherever she went.

One incident particularly endeared her to the press, at the same time as filling many a newspaper page. She was pictured holding a small child at the London kindergarten where she worked – unwittingly wearing a cotton skirt that was virtually transparent when photographed against the sun! Everyone marvelled at the fine pair of legs belonging to Charles's likely wife-to-be.

The press laid siege to the £50,000 London bachelor-girl apartment bought for Diana by her father as an eighteenth birthday present. Her flatmates, Anne Bolton, Carolyn Pride and Virginia Pitman, were all but bribed to discover exactly what Di got up to behind the doors of the Colherne Court flat in London's upmarket Knightsbridge. In fact, the three girls were the first to know how serious Diana's relationship with Charles was. But even they were unprepared for what greeted them one night when they got home. Diana had fled the bachelor girls' nest just before her engagement was officially announced. All that remained of her was a note saying: 'Please call me, I'm going to need you.'

5

The 'Fairytale' Marriage

The announcement of the engagement between Prince Charles and Lady Diana Spencer was made on 24 February 1981, with Diana sporting a beautiful £28,000 diamond and sapphire engagement ring. It was to be the biggest, fairytale, royal wedding the world had ever seen and, for the romance-loving British, it was to be an occasion of pomp and pageantry that would lift the spirits of the nation and unite everyone in a heart-stirring day long to be remembered. It was natural that at times it all seemed too much for the bride-to-be.

The announcement was a merciful release for Diana, but the intensity of press coverage did not let up. There were pictures of Diana as a child, pictures of Diana as a teenager, and even pictures showing what her wedding dress *might* look like. At least she now had the powerful protection of the Royal Family and a private apartment at Buckingham Palace to shield her.

A month after her engagement the Privy Council gave permission for the marriage; only then, because of protocol, could Diana be photographed with the Queen. Five gruelling months of pre-wedding royal tuition followed to prepare her as wife of the future King of England. Diana's first public engagement with Charles was attending a recital in London. She caused a stir by wearing a low-cut, black taffeta evening dress and got her first real taste of being the world's most photographed woman. There followed three state banquets, Trooping the Colour, the service of the Order of the Garter and a host of exhausting walkabouts to allow the public to get to know their future Princess.

It was the belief of everyone who saw the couple that they were made for one another, and that the marriage itself was to be made in heaven. This trusting view by the monarchy's loyal subjects could not have been more wrong . . .

It was upon Diana's official acceptance into the Royal Family that Prince Charles gave his first comments about his feelings for her. He was asked if he was in love. The Prince replied: 'Yes, whatever that may mean.' His bride-to-be was soon to discover just how prophetic those words were . . .

As Earl Spencer perceptively said at the time: 'I'm happy for my girl because she has got the man she adores. For myself, in my heart I wish she wasn't marrying the Prince of Wales. I shall see so much less of her. Sometimes I feel very worried, as if I'll never see her again.' In fact, the Earl had told friends that he had always wanted Diana to marry 'an ordinary chap' so that they could live close to him at Althorp.

It is a tragedy for Diana that she did not.

With only days to go before the marriage ceremony of the century, Lady Diana, still a plump, rosy-cheeked girl who blushed when she met the gaze of a stranger, was having to suffer the eyes of the whole world upon her as she waited to take her place in history. On one occasion, she sat nervously adjusting her dress, picking her nails and desperately trying to cope with cameras trained at her as she watched her soon-to-be husband ride in a polo match. Despite an all-out effort to swallow the nausea she felt and to choke back the tears, the twenty-year-old newest recruit to the Royal Family could cope with the ordeal no longer. The tears began to flow and, without giving a second thought to the loss of public image, she fled to the safety of a Range-Rover where she could weep freely.

It was all put down to the stress of the monumental change that was to happen in Diana's life. But close friends knew differently. Deep down, Diana was wondering if she had not made some terrible mistake. It wasn't that she didn't love Charles. Or that she was just having cold feet about coping as part of Britain's monarchy. Diana was in turmoil over her husband-to-be's relationship with another woman, a relationship which was to batter and bruise Diana and Charles's marriage and eventually tear it asunder.

None among an adoring public knew this, of course. They knew nothing of Charles's insistence that Diana call him 'Sir' during the early days of their courtship, while his female confidante and long-term married woman friend, Camilla Parker Bowles, called him by his nickname of 'Fred'. Charles, in turn, nicknamed Camilla 'Gladys'. Only those well inside the Buckingham Palace circle were aware of the many telephone calls Charles made to Camilla on his private line, sometimes overheard by a distraught Diana. And only the closest of friends were told by a weeping Diana of how she had unwrapped a gift that arrived at the Palace to discover that it wasn't a wedding present to them but a gold chain bracelet bearing the initials 'G' and 'F' intertwined which Charles was to give to Camilla. The initials stood either for 'Gladys' and 'Fred' or for 'Girl Friday', which was another pet name Charles had for Camilla.

So when Diana fled crying from the polo field that day, all that the onlookers saw was a frightened girl finding the glare of publicity before her marriage just too, too much. But eleven years later Diana was to break down in tears in full public focus again, amid amazing private and royal turmoil. Diana has felt like running away again many, many times over.

The wedding of Charles and Diana on 29 July 1981 was the grandest in memory. Upwards of 750 million television viewers worldwide watched her walk down the aisle of St Paul's Cathedral wearing a dress created specially for a Princess by designers David and Elizabeth Emanuel. Despite rehearsals, Diana still managed to get Prince Charles's four names in the wrong order when she repeated her marriage vows. But all it did was to endear the Royal Family's newest Princess to the nation even more.

Diana was looking forward to a dream of a honeymoon. It began at Broadlands, the old home of Charles's beloved Uncle Dickie, to be followed by a cruise around the Mediterranean. On the first morning of the honeymoon, however, Charles showed that he had not lost his bachelor habits – by leaving his marital bed to go fishing in the River Test. Neither was the cruise the romantic, private interlude she had envisaged. The newly-weds barely had a moment to themselves. What should have been intimate dinners were similar to official functions as officers on the royal yacht *Britannia* waited on them. Far from cuddling up to his new bride and planning their happy future, Charles read his heavyweight, thought-provoking tomes and discussed mysticism and the meaning of life. It heralded a marriage of loneliness and frustration for Charles's young bride. It was a portent of the difficulty he has in bonding mentally and emotionally with another human being.

Yet on the surface, everything went well at the start of the 'radiant reign' of the new Princess of Wales. Her very first official engagement with Prince Charles had the Queen and royal advisers breathing a great sigh of relief. The couple went to Wales and, despite heavy rain that made the feather on Diana's beige hat go limp, their walkabout among the people of Carmarthen was an astounding success. The love she had for Charles positively glowed through. Her eyes sparkled. Her demure smile won people over wherever she went. Her way with children touched hearts. Slowly her confidence grew, together with the fashion style that brought praise throughout the world. They were heady days, but they were soon to become wistful memories as, with bitter challenges in her private life, 'Shy Di' became 'Sad Di'.

Some say it was the twelve-year age gap between her and Charles that made them grow apart. Upon marriage, she was a very young twenty-year-old, while he had the attitudes of a man much older than his thirty-two years. She was the Pop Princess, he the Philosopher Prince. Tales were told of how Diana would dance her way through Kensington Palace listening to rock bands on her personal stereo, or exasperate her serious-minded, money-conscious husband with her love of shopping. 'On occasions, Charles was concerned that the earnestness and serious-mindedness built into him were not as strong in his beautiful young wife,' said one acquaintance. 'But he would have had the same doubts about any woman he might have married. No woman ever born could have lived up to expectations as unrealistic as his.'

In an interview four years earlier, Charles had unwittingly given a few, telling clues as to what he expected from married life when he said: 'I think an awful lot of people have got the wrong idea of what love is all about. It is rather more than just falling madly in love. It's basically a very strong friendship. I think you are very lucky if you find the right person attractive in the physical sense and the mental sense. If I am deciding whom I want to live with for fifty years, well that's the last decision on which I'd want my head to be ruled by my heart.'

One royal observer accurately described Charles as 'judging marriage as an additional burden in an already busy life'. And his words were to ring true a few months after Diana gave birth to Prince William on 21 June 1982, when there arose the first of many clashes of private and public obligations.

Diana, suffering from depression and a feeling of being trapped, begged not to attend the annual Remembrance Day Service at London's Royal Albert Hall. She wanted to be at home with her new baby and she wanted her husband to stay with her. There was a violent row, overheard by royal staff. Charles was stunned at the sudden change in his wife. It was her duty to attend the official function, he said. And duty always came first. She *had* to understand that.

There were anxious moments at the service when an obviously ruffled Prince Charles arrived without Diana. He whispered the official reason for her absence, pleading sickness on his wife's behalf. Five minutes later Diana turned up, confirming that Charles had left Kensington Palace not knowing exactly what she had decided to do. In fact, it was only the gentle cajoling of Palace advisers that put Diana in her rightful place: at her husband's side on a royal engagement.

But deep down, the little girl who was blessed enough to be born into the aristocracy was already beginning to regret that she had tried so hard to win the hand of a man whose character and family would force her into a cold-blooded, albeit very blue-blooded, existence.

Her husband became jealous of the public adoration for Diana, which had once made him proud. He felt clumsy and ignored when he and his wife fulfilled official duties together. Once, a crowd even let their disappointment show when they were expecting Diana to make an appearance first but instead saw Charles step out of the car. There was an audible groan, followed by a jubilant cheer as they then set eyes on their beloved Princess. For photographers there was no comparison between pictures of Charles in his staid suits or of Diana looking stunning whatever she wore, wherever she went.

Their first overseas tour, to Australia and New Zealand, in April 1983, was a triumph. More than a million people turned out to see them during the visit. And Charles could not help but be aware that the welcome was so warm because of his young, beautiful wife. Diana had decided to take her new-born son with her, a gesture that touched public hearts even more.

Eventually, Charles turned his resentment into anger aimed at his young wife. She felt inadequate, present at discussions he knew she would find too deep to share. He criticised her choice of friends, the way she spent her spare time and the way she looked. All the time, he kept in regular contact with Camilla Parker Bowles, the married woman he felt understood him in a way his wife never could. And all the time, Diana was sliding further and further down into a despair she felt she would never shake off.

A year later, the couple gave an interview to television broadcaster Sir Alastair Burnet. It was extraordinary, in that Diana came across as totally articulate and utterly in control, while it was Prince Charles who looked uncomfortable. There was reason for discomfort, for the couple had just suffered vitriolic revelations in the press. One bitter ex-valet had branded Diana a spoilt child who had got rid of many of Charles's loyal and trusted staff (indeed in the four years after their marriage, forty staff members were to leave) and who had stopped her husband from enjoying his favourite pursuits of hunting and shooting. Reports said Charles was being 'pussy-whipped' by a petulant wife.

In a bid to correct much of what was being said in those early days, Diana and Charles invited Fleet Street editors to an informal lunch to discuss the situation. It was a wasted effort. The editors simply enjoyed their lunch and the chat, but gave no orders that coverage of the royal couple's marriage should be modified. The Prince and Princess made another mistake, too, in their attempt to tell the world that all was well in their private lives. They invited television cameras to their Highgrove home in Gloucestershire to record scenes of domesticity and the quiet calm of a royal couple away from the public eye. Instead, viewers were irked at the glimpse into a privileged existence that allowed the Princess to spend time deciding which costly designer clothes she would add to her wardrobe. Instead of the public being endeared to a future King of England finding quietude among his herb gardens, they smirked at his confession of talking to his plants. That rare insight into the sensitive Prince's mind earned him the nickname the 'Loony Prince'.

The pervading influence of his aged guru, Sir Laurens van der Post, became apparent at this time. Following the line of his spiritual and intellectual mentor, Charles stunned doctors when he addressed the British Medical Association in 1984 and suggested that they did not have the monopoly on healing. He attacked conventional medicine, with its dependence on drugs, and advocated that more 'alternative' holistic medicine should be employed.

Until then, the Prince had had a good relationship with the press, their stories approvingly reporting a young man at first sowing his wild oats then settling down to family life. Bit by bit, however, his popularity waned. At times he became but a shadow in the glare of the spotlight on his beautiful wife. His love of painting, his quaint architectural vision, his devotion to the 'natural', his need for self-contemplation, all lost him his earlier 'action-man' image.

A little brother for Wills, Prince Harry arrived on 15 September 1984. The Princess was a model mum but, in contrast to her new-found *joie de vivre*, her husband became noticeably stiff and formal in her presence. Trying to reach a compromise in marriage between a wife who revelled in parties and girlish chatter and a husband who worried about unsightly modern architecture and the royal obligations he was born into became impossible.

In public they mastered the art of putting on a united front. In private, things began to go badly awry. Diana felt a stranger in her own home. Her husband was cold and detached. He didn't appear to show great interest in his sons.

Worst of all, an eating disorder, little understood at the time, was taking a dangerous grip on her life. Diana had begun to suffer from the slimming disease, bulimia nervosa, shortly after becoming engaged to Charles. Since then, the disorder of gorging and then making herself vomit had become a regular part of her life. Her self-esteem was at rock-bottom. Her weight went up and down. Often Diana looked painfully thin – yet she laughed off questions about her figure.

'I eat like a horse,' she told people, fooling them and herself. She sought medical and psychiatric help on occasions when she really felt she couldn't cope. She even made cries for help by cutting herself with a knife and hurling herself hysterically against a glass cabinet. Way back when Diana was three months pregnant with William, she was so insecure in her royal marriage that, after falling down a few stairs, she claimed she had been driven to the verge of suicide. It has even been alleged that some time later, in sheer desperation, she took too many pills.

Charles treated all the incidents as irritating dramas he hoped would never be known outside the tight Palace circle; he feared the embarrassment they would cause. He turned more and more to Camilla Parker Bowles, the 'safe' girlfriend whose friendship with him had the blessing of her husband.

Despite shining on every public appearance, Diana's smile hid feelings of despair that her life was a total sham, a mess, centred on a meaningless marriage. By 1986, Charles and Diana were desperately unhappy and were inexorably drifting further and further apart. It was not just the problems they were trying to solve in their marriage, but the further pressure put on it by a public forever looking for signs of those problems.

One particular incident made Diana realise that she would never be able to look to her husband for support. They were at the Expo World Fair in Vancouver when Diana, whose dramatic weight loss had caused comment among her hosts, grabbed Charles's arms, muttered a few words and then collapsed in a heap. She had fainted because of her erratic eating habits – as well as the strain of trying to live a normal existence with such an abnormal and inattentive husband. Far from receiving sympathy for her public faint, Diana instead received harsh words from her husband for not waiting until she was in private before making an exhibition of herself. At the end of that particular day's touring, Diana locked herself away in her room and sobbed.

It was becoming increasingly difficult for Diana to hide her frustration and feelings of isolation. She started to confide in close friends about her unhappiness, despairing that her marriage had become one By Royal Appointment rather than one of passion. A telling remark came as Diana visited a hospital. She saw a romantic novel by a patient's bed and commented: 'I enjoyed that one, too, but my husband doesn't approve of the books I read.' That one comment hinted at the incompatibility between the couple and the kind of terse conversations that obviously took place between them behind the closed doors of their private apartments.

Later in the year, Diana's absence was noticeable when Charles attended a Mountbatten party, that of Timothy Knatchbull to celebrate his twenty-first birthday. The Princess, having had a run of arguments with Charles over his not showing enough interest in his family and herself, threw a sulk. She turned down the joint invitation to the party in a fit of pique. The official reason was that Diana needed time with her children.

In August that year, Charles and Diana went on holiday to Majorca but the Prince flew home earlier than his wife. Despite the 'official smiles' the couple put on for the cameras during a tour of the Persian Gulf a few months later, the strain between them was obvious.

The next year, 1987, began badly, doing little to improve the image of the Royal Family. The new Duchess of York, formerly Sarah Ferguson, and her husband Prince Andrew joined Charles and Diana on a ski trip to Klosters. Di was allowing herself to be influenced by her fiery, redheaded friend, and it caused many a royal eyebrow to be raised. On this skiing trip, as the four lined up for press photographs, the two young women playfully pushed each other on the slopes, laughing as they lost their balance. Charles was not amused at this unruly, unregal behaviour. 'That's enough,' he scolded them testily. There were reports from the same trip that Diana was forever teasing her husband and leaving him in their chalet alone while she went looking for nightlife. Eventually she left Klosters to return to London alone.

In April, the press pounced with glee on the news that Charles was spending four days trekking through the Kalahari Desert with Sir Laurens van der Post. It was claimed the Prince was searching for the 'meaning of life'. When he returned, newsmen poured further scorn when Charles went on to moan about his battery-powered razor failing during his magical mystery tour! Soon after arriving back in London he took off again, this time on a painting trip to Italy. Speculation over Charles and Diana's marriage problems grew stronger. In October, Charles travelled to Balmoral to see his sons. He stayed just one night, without even catching up with the wife he hadn't seen for a month. Much was made of the fact when the couple eventually spent a night under the same roof together. Even then, Diana was off twenty-four hours later. The next month, she was absent from another private, family occasion: the marriage of his old friend Amanda Knatchbull, granddaughter of his beloved Uncle Dickie, Earl Mountbatten.

Diana spent all night dancing with Philip Dunne at the wedding of the Marquess of Worcester. An incensed Charles stormed over to her in the early hours to say it was time to leave. Diana refused and once again a very public display of personal differences had Charles going home on his own.

The situation got to the stage that, at one point, the couple had spent only one day together in six weeks. Even when they visited flood victims in Wales, the Prince and Princess made their way there separately. She arrived from Highgrove, he flew in from Aberdeen. They paid their condolences to the victims then left separately, too.

Amid fierce speculation that the royal marriage really was on the rocks, Princess Diana and her Prince put on a brave front during their visit to Berlin in November 1987. The Princess was mobbed by the crowds and the couple wore determined smiles throughout. By this time, Charles was throwing himself into various 'causes' to take his mind off his marital problems. But his sudden desire to become a high-profile Prince did not fool the public.

A tragic event was to sour the image of the young royals just a few months later, in March 1988. Diana and Charles were on another Klosters ski trip, staying with close friends Patti and Charles Palmer-Tomkinson. Also in the skiing party were the Duchess of York and mutual friend Major Hugh Lindsay. On this particular occasion, not long after the obligatory photo call for the world's press, the Duchess and Princess decided not to continue their skiing fun. Instead, they stayed behind to relax indoors. That decision could have saved their lives.

Within hours, they learned that Major Lindsay was dead and Patti Palmer-Tomkinson was critically injured. A giant avalanche had swept over them as the ski party tore down a slope of deep virgin snow that was off the normal piste. Major Lindsay was killed outright. Mrs Palmer-Tomkinson was revived by mouth-to-mouth resuscitation. Her legs were horrifically crushed. The rest of the group, including alpine guide Bruno Sprecher and a Swiss policeman, had literally missed death by inches. They could only watch in horror as their friends were swept away.

It was a very humble and bowed group who returned immediately to London. Their tragedy was obviously treated with sympathy. Yet there was also public concern that the privileged royals had put themselves and their hapless companions at risk.

The tragedy was, however, a turning point in Diana's life. She had surprised herself at the practical way in which she had coped when faced with such a crisis. It was she who had organised the skiing party's return home, the packing of the dead man's belongings and the sensitive breaking of the news to Hugh's pregnant wife, Sarah, back home in London. Diana found a sudden maturity. She had been amazed at the way Charles had let her take control of the situation ... and now, for the first time since meeting the Prince, she began to feel in control of her own life.

Diana returned from Klosters a far more confident woman. Yes, the obsessive slimmer's disease still regularly reared its ugly head and there were times when she shut herself away and wept, but she had discovered a new determination. She had also begun to despise the way her husband made her feel inadequate.

The Princess no longer felt embarrassed when well-meaning but unknowing members of the public asked her about having more children. Diana brushed aside their enquiries with a joke. She knew there was little likelihood of her becoming pregnant again. She and

Charles had separate sleeping quarters. She could barely stand being in his presence.

It was at the end of that year that Diana chose to make her first major speech. It was on behalf of the children's charity Barnardo's and she spoke with feeling about children's needs within the family. Diana revelled in her new-found confidence and independence. She realised she was capable of a lot more than simply being a pretty patron of a charity or the perfect clothes-horse for the British fashion industry.

As 1989 dawned, Diana seemed to make a New Year's resolution to throw herself more and more into work. As patron of the Welsh National Opera, one of her major overseas visits was to watch them perform at New York's Brooklyn Academy of Music. Guests paid £500 each for the privilege of attending an after-concert party at which the Princess was present. She carried out an increasing number of official engagements for Turning Point, a group for those with drink, drug and mental problems, of which she had become patron in 1987.

In a very telling move, the Princess also became patron of the marriage guidance group, Relate, and made it clear she wanted to be more than just a figurehead. During her official visits to Relate offices, Diana would listen intently as the counsellors described their work and how they encouraged partners to open up about the problems in relationships. On one particular Relate visit, Diana witnessed counsellors acting out different roles, pretending to be partners coming to them for advice. The Princess's attentiveness throughout was not overlooked, and she was not slow in asking pertinent questions about marriage guidance.

6

The Sham Marriage

Gossip about the royal couple's marriage began to grow, almost imperceptibly. The beautiful Princess took to driving around London late at night on her own. She was also seen out and about enjoying herself at cinemas, pop concerts and restaurants. Most disturbingly, other men began to feature in her life. In society circles, such male escorts are called 'walkers' — attractive men who escort wives on outings when the husband is absent. In the view of a distressed Charles, however, they had absolutely no right to be photographed alongside his wife. Diana also took exception to the press interest shown in her socialising. She snapped: 'Just because I go out without my husband, doesn't mean that my marriage is on the rocks.'

City banker Philip Dunne was a regular member of house parties invited to stay at Windsor for Royal Ascot, and he joined Diana and Charles on a skiing trip to Klosters. Diana once spent a weekend at the country home of Philip's parents while Charles was out of the country, and she was guest of honour in 1989 when Philip married Domenica Fraser, daughter of the former Rolls-Royce chairman Sir Ian Fraser. Charles had declined his invitation in favour of a day's hunting.

Tongues began to wag when the Princess was photographed with Household Cavalry officer David Waterhouse at a David Bowie concert at Wembley. The couple whispered and giggled together in front of 72,000 witnesses. The couple were also often spotted leaving the homes of friends together.

The seriousness of the friendship was only realised towards the end of 1987 when Diana was spotted giggling and acting playfully in a quiet Kensington mews in the early hours of the morning. She had just emerged from the home of her close friend, stores heiress Kate Menzies, whom the Princess had often visited to escape the rigours and formalities of life at Kensington Palace. Diana would hop into her car and quietly nip around the corner to nearby Queensgate Mews where friend Kate had a small maisonette. The immediate neighbours had often marvelled at the comings and goings there and at the many Sloane Ranger girls and dashingly handsome young men who made up this exclusive circle. Neighbours were more than once tempted to complain about the late-night movements of motor cars in the narrow mews, but the knowledge that the Princess of Wales was a friend and guest prevented them. Her solo visits were well known to them.

It was only when a particularly assiduous photographer followed her one night that her nocturnal escape route was revealed to a wider public. He waited outside and when Diana left Kate Menzies's home in the early hours he photographed her laughing and larking and acting altogether like a coquettish young girl alongside a particularly handsome young man — David Waterhouse.

Diana spotted the photographer and immediately became distraught. Such pictures could not possibly be published. In tears, she begged the photographer not to use the pictures and to hand them over to her. It was the desperate act of a desperately unhappy woman. Some agreement was reached. The pictures did not appear but reports about the incident did. It was no wonder that the Queen summoned Charles and Diana to Buckingham Palace to order them to put right what was fast becoming a right royal farce of a marriage.

Other close men friends of the Princess included Nicholas Haslam, former equerry to Charles, Mervyn Chaplin, who runs an audio installation business, and Rory Scott, a young man for whom Diana had sometimes done some ironing back in her single days.

Most of her male friends appreciated the privileged position they held but one of them made abundantly clear his closeness to the Princess. Sandy-haired army officer James Hewitt became obsessed with Diana after he was chosen to teach Prince William to ride. His charm encouraged Diana to return to riding too. It was no mean feat; she had become terrified of horses after falling off one when she was a child. The friendship was to continue while he served with the Life Guards in Germany and during his periods of leave at his family's riding school near Exeter, Devon. While he was in the Middle East during the 1991 Gulf War, Diana wrote regularly to the tank captain. Shortly after his return, Hewitt ended his relationship of five years with girlfriend Emma Stewardson, who claimed that James had become totally smitten with Diana. Hewitt, by then a major, was made redundant from the army in 1993.

There was another 'old flame' of long standing whom no one knew about, however: society car dealer James Gilbey. A member of the famous gin family, Gilbey first met Diana when she was living with her three best chums in their London bachelor-girl apartment, Diana and the dashing 6 foot 3 inch Gilbey struck up a deep friendship which lasted throughout her marriage. They regularly dined together at San Lorenzo, Diana's favourite restaurant, in Beauchamp Place, near to Kensington Palace. Gilbey was on the exclusive list of close friends allowed easy access to the Princess at Kensington Palace and Highgrove.

James was the shoulder for Diana to cry on. He

listened silently as she talked about her obsessive eating problems, her loneliness, the times she had threatened to kill herself just to get a spark of reaction from her husband. James had heard it all before but now he felt a growing unease. He sensed a more sinister mood in his old friend yet he knew that there was little he could do. Whom could he warn that the Princess of Wales might one day really attempt suicide?

As one of Diana's few and trusted *real* friends, James knew that the last thing he should do was to tell anyone about what the Princess had revealed to him. However, he was later to be asked to speak out about the Princess's health and emotional troubles and would thereby become part of a group whose aim would be to raise Diana in the favour of the British public at the same time as alienating it from Charles.

Diana's closeness to James Gilbey was first discovered when she was tailed by two journalists one evening in the autumn of 1989. The Princess drove to James's apartment in fashionable Lennox Gardens, Knightsbridge, accompanied by her private detective Sergeant David Sharp. On arrival, she jumped out of the car at 8.20 p.m. – and dismissed the policeman. She was in the apartment for a little over five hours. The reporters saw no one else arrive or leave.

Sergeant Sharp, obviously acting on instructions, returned to collect his charge at 11 p.m. but it was gone 1 a.m. when Diana made her exit. On leaving, she furtively looked up and down the street to make sure the coast was clear. Her face was hidden by a hat pulled firmly over her eyes. She was taken home by Sergeant Sharp, who had hung around for over two hours.

The reporters later questioned James Gilbey, who was at that time still the soul of discretion. He told them that the Princess had visited his home to make up a foursome at bridge. He was unable to comment when the newsmen pointed out that he had had no other visitors that night!

Prince Charles was well aware of the friendships that his wife was forging. What angered him and deeply offended his pride was that the public saw only one side of the picture. He was always portrayed in the press as the cold, unfeeling husband; she was always the mix of Madonna and Mother Teresa. It infuriated him, but there was no way that he could change the impression given to the world.

Yet Prince Charles's sometimes theatrical displays of angst disguised a great measure of hypocrisy. For while his wife was disporting herself with men friends, he was secretly continuing his relationship with his own 'old flame'.

As we shall learn more fully in a later chapter, the sad truth about the mismatched Prince of Wales is that, although he has known many close female confidantes, he has had only one real love in his life,

Camilla Parker Bowles. She was equally firm in her regard for him, right up to his marriage to Diana. Indeed, he told his friends that from the moment of that fairytale wedding on 29 July 1981 he did his utmost to make his marriage work. He certainly saw Camilla (and Kanga and others) during the early years of his marriage, but never once, he vows, did he imperil it.

It was five long years before he threw in the towel as a husband, five years during which Diana grew apart from him just as obviously as he from her. Only then did Charles and Camilla start meeting again for secret trysts – and by then, Diana too was finding friends outside the marital homes. Diana knew about Camilla, just as Charles knew about his wife's men friends. The difference was in their respective reactions to what each saw as the other's infidelities. The Princess, an impetuous, hot-blooded woman, was incandescent with rage and hungry for revenge. The Prince's attitude was somewhat less emotional – his main concern was that his future Queen was flaunting her friendships in far too public a manner.

This is not to pretend that Charles did not suffer. There must have been many times when he wished for a reconciliation, if only for the sake of their children, but only he and his wife know whether he ever attempted one. Meanwhile, the hypocritical pretence went on . . .

In public, the Princess of Wales was battling to

adhere to what the Queen describes as 'the necessary training some of the younger members of the family find hard to cope with'. In private, Diana was on the verge of a nervous breakdown. She often absented herself from Royal Family gatherings. She found excuses to break free, if only for a few hours, from a marriage that made her feel trapped.

Servants were more than once disturbed to observe Diana's manner when the couple were alone together. Said one: 'She could barely bring herself to look at him when he was talking to her. It was as if she just wanted to scream.' Another commented: 'There were rows, terrible rows. Anyone who has met the Princess in public would find it hard to believe how she could behave in private. You could feel the tension when you entered the room. Once, she walked along rows and rows of books, punching each one as she went, shouting "No, no, no" as Charles tried to talk to her.'

Even dinner guests at Kensington Palace noted at the time just how difficult the Princess found it to be pleasant to her husband. One visitor noted how her knuckles were clenched and white whenever he passed an observation about her. 'I didn't then know whether it was nerves or fear or frustration at being talked down to,' said the visitor. 'I know now, however. It was hatred.'

By now, the Princess and her husband were leading totally different lives, coming together only through necessity. Diana spent as little time as possible at

Highgrove; Charles rarely stayed overnight in London. Whenever Princes Harry and Wills enjoyed a day out, it was always with their mother. Diana no longer had any qualms about going out on her own. She took to driving around London unescorted just for the sheer feeling of freedom it gave her.

The Princess also began paying more attention to her physical and mental health. She started having acupuncture sessions to help her relax. Then there were the visits to a chiropractor to iron out the nagging pains that had come with incessant standing and sitting for long periods at a time. Diana underwent reflexology, the theory of which is that certain parts of the feet are connected to vital organs in the body. She took up swimming regularly, something she had abandoned when she started to suffer depression.

In an attempt to straighten out her mind, Diana called upon an astrologer and an interpreter of dreams. She became obsessed with how astrology could determine one's fate. It was ironic that Diana should turn to things mystic, something for which she had always scorned her husband, to try to work through her failing marriage and desperate turmoil. She believed spirits were looking after her and guiding her. Diana no longer simply dressed to suit an occasion or win fashion acclaim. The colours she wore were carefully picked to help her inner karma.

It was an almost robotic Princess who switched on the smiles for public appearances. But she switched off in private, becoming disturbingly child-like and unsociable. Only her own children and the support of a secret circle of friends allowed Diana to keep her grip on reality.

At the same time, Prince Charles was seeking his own spiritual solutions. Long past were the days when the Prince was criticised for putting the heir's life in danger by virtue of his many macho pursuits. Now 'Macho Man' had become 'Mystic Man'. His fascination for spiritual matters became an obsession. He even appointed his own spiritual advisers for medical treatments. As well as his devotion to bringing harmony between humans and the planet, Charles had stepped back in time, calling on Mother Nature for her healing powers.

The Prince, like his mother, is a great believer in alternative medicine, so much so that he is a patron of a homoeopathic medicine group in London. Charles regularly and secretly attends meetings, and he called on the group's doctors to help him with one particular problem, which also highlighted once again the deep rift between himself and his wife.

The Princess was in London in June 1990 when news reached her that Charles had taken a tumble playing polo at Cirencester and had broken his arm in two places. (Once again, the couple were spending their leisure time apart.) On hearing of Charles's accident, Diana was put in a quandary over what she should do. For the sake of public appearances, she knew she should rush to his side but, quite frankly, she couldn't face it. She chose instead to keep a date with her lady-in-waiting, Anne Beckwith-Smith, who was holding a leaving party.

Later in the evening, the Princess had arranged to attend Puccini's *La Bohème* at Covent Garden with old friend Carolyn Bartholomew. It was only when warned that it wouldn't look good if she failed to visit Charles that night that she reluctantly drove down to Cirencester Hospital. Charles's injury was such that he later underwent a second operation and was out of action for several months. Diana's workload increased dramatically. Diana fulfilled not only her own scheduled duties but Charles's too, to avoid disappointing those who had long been on his itinerary of visits and engagements.

Diana also dutifully turned up to see her disgruntled husband at the Queen's Medical Centre in Nottingham, where he underwent his second operation. During her visits, Diana befriended the parents of a young man who was in a coma after a motorcycle accident. The Princess held his hand and helped bring him round. When the news leaked out, Diana's secret dedication, coupled with her gruelling round of extra royal engagements, made her shine like a saint in the eyes of her adoring public.

Tellingly, as soon as Charles was discharged from hospital, Diana once again went about her own independent life. The Prince flew off to France to recuperate, accompanied by his physiotherapist, Sarah Key.

He then went to Balmoral to rest, where he was nursed by old flame Camilla Parker Bowles while Diana remained in London. Further restful days at Highgrove were also accompanied by Camilla. Royal lapdogs insisted the Waleses' separation simply reflected the Prince's need for time alone after his serious injury, and that he wanted to spend some weeks with the Queen Mother in Scotland, but they had no answer to the simple fact that a man who had suffered tremendous pain did not have his wife with him. It was the most natural thing for any married couple to be together when one most needed the other. Charles wasn't around either when William returned for his first weekend home after starting boarding school. It was Diana, as always, who was there for her children.

For the couple who had by now perfected living a lie, Charles's solitary recuperation was a welcome break for them both. Diana knew he was regularly in contact with Camilla Parker Bowles and that he was visited by her, but she was now past caring. Had they been an ordinary couple, she and Charles would have gone their own ways a long time before. However, there were the children. There was also, above all else, the fact that Diana was married to the man who could one day be King. Even though the chances of Charles ever making the throne were becoming more and more remote, Diana was nevertheless firmly ensconced as part of the higher echelon of the Royal Family. The charade she and Charles played out for the public seemed vital, but in private, life was a nightmare for them both.

The agony that the Princess of Wales was going through at this time has been well reported. But what is little known is the very private agony of the Prince. For while the world saw only a disgruntled, sour and seemingly selfish royal hiding himself from his wife and the world, the truth is that Charles was hiding a secret that, if made known at the time, might have altered the public's critical perception of him.

After the fall from his polo pony, it was reported that the Prince might one day have to give up his beloved sport because of injuries caused to his arm. A senior medical source has revealed, however, that a far more serious ailment was caused by the accident, and was destined to plague him ever after. The polo fall exacerbated an old back injury, the consequence of which was, the Prince learned, that he would be in pain – not constantly but often enough to affect his sense of wellbeing – for the rest of his life.

At this stage of his marriage, his ailment was sheer agony for him. He has always tried to hide it but, to those who know him closely, it has often shown. Charles has begged his homoeopathic specialist friends to provide treatment for sufferers like himself. 'Charles is often in agony with his back,' said one specialist. 'Standing is sometimes excruciating for him. He has made it clear to us that this is the most hindering health worry he has.'

What became doubly worrying was that Charles's back complaint may well have affected his outlook on life. The physical pain, along with the mental anguish over his failed marriage and concerns over his suitability to become King, may have turned him into the inward-looking and self-centred figure he has become. The Prince of Wales has built a wall around himself, stubbornly ignoring advisers, believing himself to be on a far greater level of awareness. How ironic that these failings are exactly the same as those for which the Princess of Wales has also been criticised.

7

Blind Hatred

Gushing tributes poured forth as the royal couple approached their tenth wedding anniversary. Princess Diana, in particular, was the focus of umpteen books, newspaper reviews, magazine articles, colour supplements and television programmes. Universally, praise rained down upon her for her victory in struggling out of her chrysalis to emerge a beautiful, regal butterfly — confident, grown up and mistress of a marriage 'made in heaven'.

The Prince and Princess of Wales were by this time the proud parents of two sturdy sons, Prince Harry, aged seven, and Prince William, nine. But whereas Charles seldom seemed demonstrative towards his boys, Diana was portrayed as the perfect, genuine mother, showing no restraint when it came to exhibiting the joy her children gave her. At a more worthy level, she was the patron of nearly forty charities and organisations. She was seen as the royal who, against adversity, composed herself at all times in a manner which was exemplary. She was held up as one of the hardest-working royals, fulfilling her duties without demur and always with a smile. Diana had become a stunning ambassador for Britain. Her face had been seen on more magazine covers than anyone else in the world. And when it came to style, everyone agreed that no one did it better. Unlike the devil-may-care Duchess of York, Diana's fashion flair was rarely criticised, but almost invariably copied and cooed over. She was, with her English-rose looks, willowy figure and impeccable demeanour, the Perfect Princess.

Yet, for most of her married life since she had walked down the aisle of St Paul's Cathedral on 29 July 1981, the Princess of Wales had been oppressed by suffering and sickness — although most of her crying had been behind closed doors. Diana's brave face was the one she put on for her doting public and loyal supporters. She spoke gentle words to the little children she crouched down to meet during official engagements and to the elderly and the sick whose hands she shook on visits. The real feelings of Lady Diana Spencer turned Princess of Wales were kept for the private turmoil she suffered as wife of a distant, totally unsuitable husband with whom she had nothing in common.

Very few knew the real Diana or the real Charles, and those two fiercely protective cliques were too aware of the unique positions they held in the royal lives to reveal the awful truth. Yet the cracks in the wall of silence built around their joint misery were beginning to show. Rumours about the intensity and enormity of their marital problems, and in particular Diana's deep depression, began to circulate.

There was yet more even than these chilling revelations to threaten the Royal Family. For the core of the looming crisis was the Princess of Wales's mental health. The terrifying truth was that Diana, wife of Britain's heir to the throne, the woman who would one day take over from the Queen as the nation's female figurehead, was alleged to have become so disturbed by living a royal lie that she had actually considered taking her own life . . .

The startling effects of Princess Diana's bulimia nervosa were fairly clear for all to see. Not everyone knew of the clinical condition that was causing her such obvious distress, but those around her became increasingly concerned for her wellbeing. Even workers at the Waleses' office at St James's Palace had noticed what one of them could only describe as 'irrational behaviour'. Staff there, as well as at Kensington Palace and Highgrove, generally found that dealing with Charles, crusty and formal though he could sometimes be, was preferable to answering to the Princess's whims. One worker who left their employ revealed that Diana's voice on the end of the phone made some of the hearts there sink. Charles, it was said, might demand instant action in a polite but determined manner; Diana, on the other hand, might be chatty and charming at one moment then carping and critical the next.

Friends (though it must be said, principally friends of Charles) have spoken of their belief that Diana sometimes lacked touch with reality. She was rarely other than enchanting when in public, but in private her moods and sulks were becoming an embarrassment. She burst into tears in front of visitors. She stormed out of rooms full of people. She became hysterical in moments of upset, anger or frustration.

All this is perfectly symptomatic of bulimia. The Consumers Association issued a *Drug and Therapeutic Bulletin* on the disorder, which warned that sufferers:

> . . . indulge in episodes of massive overeating associated with a sense of loss of control. Between episodes of eating most sufferers fast or induce vomiting. Binges tend to be secret, sometimes preplanned and are often followed by strong mood swings expressed as guilt, depression, self-hate and even suicidal behaviour. Unlike anorexia nervosa, bulimia survives by disguise. It is a sophisticated illness in that sufferers do not admit they have a problem. They always appear to be happy and spend their lives trying to help others. Yet there is rage beneath the sunny smile, anger which sufferers are afraid to express.

They may, according to the bulletin, dislike their

own bodies and feel guilty about caring for themselves. That disgust is translated into violent purging by vomiting or laxatives. Sufferers, it is said, 'have a sense of failure, low self-esteem and loss of control'.

Few knew of Princess Diana's traumas throughout the first decade of her marriage. However, 'loss of control' was clear for all her household to see. Her sickness would transcend mere 'female hysterics'. Charles knew these mood swings to his cost and did his best to make himself scarce whenever the glint in his wife's eyes forewarned him of trouble, but there was one occasion at Highgrove in the summer of 1990 when he could not escape in time.

Thoroughly embarrassed by his wife's voluble pursuit of some domestic row that no one can now recall, Charles tried to draw her away from the ears of the staff into a private room. Diana at first allowed herself to be led gently by the arm – then suddenly became animated. She began to rage at her husband and, according to one witness, was incoherent with anger at something he said to her in reply. She wrested herself away from him, arms flailing. Charles ineffectually raised an arm as Diana swung towards him. He blocked the blow but Diana appeared to hurt her wrist in the process. The fact that the incident was witnessed was excruciatingly embarrassing to Charles but seemed not to affect Diana one jot. She simply stormed upstairs.

Aides talked only in hushed whispers about such

examples of Diana's hysterics. They were concerned at the regularity of their occurrence at a time when a public-relations exercise was being orchestrated to show their master and mistress in the best possible light.

Wholly unaware of the bubbling cauldron of domestic disharmony inside Highgrove at this time, a visitor turned up one day for a very special commission 'By Royal Appointment'. Accepted as a photographer who took 'nice' pictures of the royals, he was invited to Highgrove for a session of at-home portraits. He arrived on a sunny day in 1990 to undertake the assignment any of the regular rat pack of royal paparazzi would have killed for. However, as soon as he set foot inside the door of the Prince and Princess of Wales's country mansion, an aide felt obliged to pull him aside and caution him that there was disharmony in this English idyll. The photographer had arrived at a bad time. The photo session could not be cancelled but the cameraman was told that he was likely to hear some raised voices. In an extraordinary briefing, the aide was obliged to warn, effectively, that if the photographer heard the warring royals rowing, then he was to 'just ignore it'!

The glossy magazine photographs that emanated from this 'perfect' at-home session were all smiles, sweetness and light, but the fearsome rows that had been going on behind the scenes only got worse. Charles became increasingly frustrated at his inability to handle his wife's behaviour. Diana began to cut herself off in private life, not just from her husband but from most of the Royal Family. It became a war of nerves as the Waleses organised separate schedules to ensure that they seldom met even on official duty. The Princess, drained and traumatised by more than a decade of bulimia nervosa – and blaming her husband for most of her misfortunes – was at the end of her tether.

During these times Diana sought solace from within her tiny circle of loyal friends, and it was to them she turned when her marriage hit the greatest crisis of all. But it was more than mere platonic comfort she was receiving. The Princess of Wales, it appeared, had been so in need of emotional support that she did not discourage the advances of admirers – and of one young man in particular. Indeed, Diana had been repaying her husband for his interest in other women – and repaying him in kind.

In truth, she had done no more than her husband had done. Like Charles, she had found the most comfort *outside* her marriage. Like Charles with his Camilla, she had found one special confidant to share the loneliness of her elevated station. Long after her husband had abandoned intimate love talk, that special person provided the warm words and support she so desperately craved. And only that special someone knew the real extent of her emotional turmoil. It was a disclosure of feelings Diana had never dared share with anyone else.

The two came to rely on each other, meeting surreptitiously and sharing intimate secrets. Here at last was someone to whom she felt an equal. He did not sneer at her sometimes extraordinary naïveté, but found it endearing, just as Charles had once done. Here, too, was a man who brought out the 'daddy's girl' in Diana, gently chiding her when she showed self-doubt but firmly encouraging her when she felt able to fight back at the world.

The result of Diana finding a new and stronger relationship outside her marriage was beneficial to her state of emotional health. She became more confident and better equipped to deal with the rigours of royal life. With her new-found feelings of self-worth, Diana was able to take on more duties. She at last felt a fully 'trained' member of The Firm. She also felt strong enough to fight back when news of her secret friendship leaked out. And leak out it did, in the most extraordinary circumstances . . .

The Princess of Wales was warned of the existence of a tape recording of her and her friend from teenage days: James Gilbey. Worse still, the tape clearly illustrated that their relationship had gone far beyond the bounds of friendship. The tape was of the two of them sharing not only small-talk but love-talk. It was circulated in Fleet Street and two newspapers acquired copies and put them 'on ice'. Several journalists on other newspapers, however, were aware of the contents. It was a frightening new development that threatened to throw the entire royal machine into turmoil.

The reaction of Princess Diana when she was first tipped off about the existence of the tape is hard to imagine. She would instantly have known of its veracity — and of the effect its publication would have on her 'Fairytale Princess' image. The senior royals have always been aware that sensitive stories about them are kept 'on ice' in newspaper offices (Andrew Knight, chairman of News International, announced as much in relation to *Sunday Times* revelations about the Princess in 1992). Diana could have panicked. Instead she moved surely but swiftly. She accused royal aides of monitoring her phones and she ordered a debugging of her private apartments. Then she set about organising a 'damage-limitation exercise' . . .

Diana promptly consulted close friends about what action she should take to counter the crisis. Cold-shouldered by royal advisers, she felt that drastic and unprecedented measures were warranted. But most of all she needed a shoulder to lean on. Naturally, that was James Gilbey's. He gathered round her five others, who constituted the Princess's 'war cabinet'. They were her brother Charles Althorp and friends Carolyn Bartholomew, Rory Scott, Angela Serota and Adam Russell. None had to be sworn to secrecy; they were all so close, and they all knew the burden the Princess was bearing. Yet they could barely believe the bizarre plan of campaign.

Diana was so determined to reveal her desperation over her marriage to Charles that she was willing to sacrifice her public esteem by exposing her own mental and health problems to tarnish her husband. Diana's 'own story' would be told to the world. And the chosen mouthpiece was the former Fleet Street royal-watcher, author Andrew Morton.

Said a friend: 'Diana was determined to settle what she sees as old scores with an awful lot of people. She had been pushed into the incredible position of wanting intimate facts made public. Most of us thought it was an astonishingly brave thing to do. But there was this tremendous feeling of unease — or of fear, if we were honest.'

Diana felt she really had nothing to lose. Her marriage could not suffer any more than it had done already. Her relationship with the inner royal circle was already strained. She also believed that, with Charles being increasingly seen as no more than a mild but ineffectual eccentric, some of the pressure had been taken off just what the nation expected of *her*. She felt it was doubtful her husband would ever become King of England. She realised she would never be Queen. Her dreams and those of her bedazzled public would never come true.

So she allowed the reports of her private traumas to filter out, fuelled by her ever 'helpful' friends. When the stories began to circulate about her slimming sickness and her suicide attempts — including the occasion when she was said to have taken an overdose of painkillers before sounding the alarm – it all came as a relief both to the Princess and to those who had spent the years since her marriage desperately trying to shield her from any hint of scandal.

The Queen viewed it all with horror. She had already seen the marriages of her only daughter, Princess Anne, and her middle son, Prince Andrew, fall apart, both in the most spectacularly headline-making fashion. Now she felt that the latest revelations were potentially the most damaging of all.

If Princess Diana felt she had passed through the saddest, most challenging time in her life, she was wrong. Shortly before the shock revelations were unleashed on the world, Diana was on a skiing trip when Earl Spencer died in hospital. Returning to Britain as soon as was humanly possible, she was nevertheless wracked with guilt that she had not been with the father she worshipped in his final hours. She felt alone in her grief. Charles, as usual, was unable to provide the emotional crutch she so desperately needed.

The shock revelations of Diana's personal problems came out that summer in a book entitled *Diana, Her True Story* by Andrew Morton. The book, seen by many as Diana firing the first broadside at the Royal Family and her husband, sparked an all-out war. Friends of Charles hit back, claiming Diana had continually gone out of her way to stage public appearances that ensured herself good publicity. They alleged that she deliberately organised engagements on the same day as Charles was due to make personally important speeches or visits, knowing she would steal his thunder. In short, it was suggested, far from being the sweet-natured wife, Diana was really a vixen.

Another book serialised in newspapers the same year was even more sensational. The author, Lady Colin Campbell, was quite a story in her own right, being a beautiful, titled socialite who had been brought up for a short period when she has very young as a boy. Many of her allegations, including references to Diana's private life, were considered so outrageous at the time that the Princess was able to laugh them off. But one claim stung Diana deeply. It was that one of her former bodyguards might have been killed off by the security services because he got too close to her. Sergeant Barry Mannakee was transferred from his royal post to the Diplomatic Protection Squad amid suggestions of over-familiarity with the Princess. Eight months later, the thirty-nine-year-old father of two was killed when the motorcycle on which he was riding as pillion passenger was hit by a car in London. Lady Colin Campbell claimed that MI5 agents may have had a hand in his death.

Quite apart from Diana, there was another woman for whom all this adverse publicity was exceptionally embarrassing. Diana's older sister Jane was torn between supporting the emotionally weakened Princess and sticking with the Royal Family's stiff-upper-lip party line. Jane, wife of the Queen's private secretary Sir Robert Fellowes, could not condone the unofficial publicity campaign Diana had started for herself, yet at the same time she also felt desperately sad for her sister. The two women found themselves in a very strained situation.

Matters were brought to a head when Diana accused Sir Robert Fellowes of permitting the bugging of her private phone calls at both Kensington Palace and Highgrove. The Princess said certain conversations with close friends had filtered back to her. She claimed it was all a Palace ploy to provide proof that she had masterminded the leaking of revelations in Andrew Morton's book. Courtiers dismissed her allegations as paranoia.

How cruelly wrong they were. The truth about the bugging was bound one day to emerge. Charles's friends would take comfort from the tape recording of Diana and her admirer. It did, after all, redress the balance of public opinion in his favour. The Prince had long been cast solely in the role of marriage wrecker. The existence of the tape was to change all that — and make many people believe that Diana must share the blame.

Throughout all the private traumas, the Princess of Wales had always managed to keep her emotions under control when she ventured out in public. It was no easy task. The eyes of the whole world were upon her. It took Diana back to those weeks before her marriage to Charles, and to that day when she fled weeping from the polo field. In amazing, unprecedented scenes, the Princess of Wales again found herself sobbing in full public view.

Desperately trying to carry out her official duties as normally as possible in the midst of all the dramatic newspaper coverage, Diana visited a hospice on 11 June 1992 to cheer up the terminally ill patients. A crowd of hundreds welcomed her as if greeting a saint. 'We love you,' they told her. It was all too much for Diana. Despite biting her bottom lip and trying to carry on with the visit, she was overcome. The Princess of Wales broke down and had to flee. Some of the most startling royal pictures ever seen hit the front pages the next day – Diana, her face creased with sadness, weeping pitifully.

Were those tears for the patients? For her marriage? For her family? For herself? Or were they the most honest, humble reaction to the words of Bill Davidson, chairman of the Queenscourt Cancer Hospice at Southport, Merseyside, who had just told her: 'By your example, you have won the admiration and devotion of caring people worldwide. God bless you and may you always remain, Ma'am, just you.'

8

Exhibit 'A' – The 'Dianagate' Tape

The conversation that became known as 'Dianagate' took place on New Year's Eve 1989. A tape recording was made of a telephone call personally dialled by the Princess of Wales from her rooms at Sandringham, where she and her family were spending the holiday. The call was to a male friend, who received it on a mobile phone in his car.

It is evident from the conversation that the couple were at pains to disguise their identities from eavesdroppers. The Princess never addressed the man by his name. Likewise, he never addressed Diana by name, instead referring to her as 'Darling' and by the nicknames 'Squidge' and 'Squidgy'. Yet the clues they inadvertently dropped into their conversation provided clear evidence as to the identities of the pair – and the nature of their relationship.

The deeply personal and obscure detail contained in the exchange left no room for doubt that the female voice on the tape is that of Princess Diana. But what confirmed the identity of her male friend?

The man on the tape was said to be thirty-three years old at the time the recording was made, a Libran (born between 23 September and 22 October). He lived within 'knocking distance' of Diana's Kensington Palace home. He enjoyed hunting and shooting, like his father, he had a car telephone, wore brown suede Gucci shoes and on the night of the call was dressed in denim jeans (a new pair which he said he'd bought the day before), green socks, white and pink striped shirt topped with a dark, apple-green V-neck pullover. He referred to a friend, City businessman Mark Davis, as being a fellow guest at a recent tea party hosted by Simon Prior-Palmer and his wife Julia, adding that Davis hunted with the Belvoir and Quorn Hunts.

Only one man, James Gilbey, could fit – or have been privy to – all those facts. Gilbey, a Libran born on 4 October 1956, lived at the time in Lennox Gardens, not far from Kensington Palace. The handsome bachelor had been Diana's friend for fifteen years. He had been quoted as saying: 'Diana is a private person who likes to keep her meetings with friends covered up. I am lucky to count her as a very good friend. We go back a long way. I knew her well before she got married.'

Diana used Gilbey as a shoulder to cry on. But at times, he needed her shoulder to cry on as much as she needed his. After leaving Ampleforth, the leading Roman Catholic public school, James had headed for London to indulge his passion for cars at the upmarket end of the motor trade. His jobs included a brief spell with BMW prior to joining Tom Dodd-Noble to set up the Holbein Motor Company, with franchises for Saab and Subaru. In 1991 the company fell victim to economic recession and crashed, owing £500,000. Gilbey went on to work as a specialist marketing and sponsorship consultant for Lotus, driving a limited-edition Lotus Carlton. Former business associate Dodd-Noble said of him: 'He is a very good bloke. He's extremely nice to girls. He's understanding and a good listener. A problem can be talked over with James.'

Problems were presumably being talked over at length in October 1989 when they were caught out on their secret tryst at his Knightsbridge flat. Gilbey subsequently admitted: 'I suppose it wasn't that wise for Diana and myself to meet in those sort of circumstances. No doubt tongues will be wagging and there will be gossiping.'

His words were prophetic. Just a few weeks later, on New Year's Eve 1989, they were caught out again, in the now-infamous 'Dianagate' tape recording. But this time it was Gilbey and the Princess who were gossiping, and it was *their* tongues that wagged too freely . . .

The 'Dianagate' tape exposes the Princess of Wales

at her most vain and vindictive. But it also reveals compassion, humanity and humour. Diana is childishly coquettish at times, but she also reveals a sad frailty and vulnerability. Here is a woman crying out for the affection she fails to get from within her marriage and from within the Royal Family.

Diana speaks of a visit she had made that day to nearby Park House, the home on the Sandringham estate where she was born and spent her early years. Park House is now a convalescent home for the severely disabled, and the compassionate Princess had considered entering quietly through a back door. Instead, she summoned up her courage and walked straight in through the front door. She then spent one and a half hours with the inmates, being photographed as they surrounded and hugged her. It must have been a moving occasion.

Another example of Diana's sensitive nature is revealed when she speaks of an encounter with the Bishop of Norwich, the Right Reverend Peter Knott, who was a guest of the Queen at Sandringham that Christmas. The Princess seems to have given the poor man something of a hard time. Diana told him she had lived before and that friends who had died still looked after her. The cleric was apparently horrified, while the Princess herself delighted in the way she had shocked him.

The Princess talks also of her puzzlement at the constant watch the Queen Mother keeps on her.

Diana wonders wistfully why it is that, whenever she looks up, she catches 'his grandmother' staring at her with a strange look – a mixture of interest and pity.

At one stage, the taped conversation centres on a female friend, whose restaurant is closed over the New Year holiday. Mara Berni, a long-standing friend of Diana, is co-owner of James and Diana's favourite meeting place, San Lorenzo, which was indeed closed during that period.

Diana talks of going swimming near Sandringham with the Duchess of York the following day. The two were pictured swimming together at a hotel during the course of that week.

She refers to a man called Ken taking her to London. Diana's Royal and Diplomatic Protection Squad bodyguard is Ken Wharfe, who took the wheel of her car on many occasions.

On the tape, there is a reference to Diana having avoided the urge to 'binge' and is asked about her weight – long before details of her desperate struggle against the disorder bulimia nervosa became public knowledge. Diana speaks of buying clothes for James Hewitt, the cavalry officer and Gulf War hero who had become an extremely close friend and was pictured alongside her at polo matches.

There is a reference to Nigel Havers, the dashing, forty-one-year-old movie star of whom Diana once said prior to a royal premiere of one of his films: 'I don't care what it's about as long as Nigel Havers is there.' In the tape, Diana gloatingly reveals that the Duchess of York had called her that day to say that she has had lunch with Havers and that there had been only one topic of conversation – Princess Diana!

Diana also mentions Charlotte Hambro, who had just become Countess Peel, second wife of landowner Earl Peel. Charlotte, from the wealthy Hambro merchant banking family, is a long-standing friend of Diana, whose daughter was a bridesmaid at her wedding to Charles. There is also a reference to Lady Lucy Manners, a thirty-year-old former school chum of Diana. She became Fergie's lady-in-waiting, until she left the post in March 1992. She is a former girlfriend of Lord Linley.

Also among the *dramatis personae* in the world's most sensational phone call are Diana's own children, William and Harry. She raises the volume of her television set to drown out her phone conversation as they wander in and out of the room. Which may be just as well, given conversational snippets such as these . . .

Early in their conversation, the Princess speaks of the difficulty she has in trying to grin and bear the 'confines' of her marriage. She explodes: *'Bloody hell! What I've done for this f . . . ing family!'*

On the debate she had conducted with the Bishop of Norwich about the afterlife: *'Bloody bishop . . . I said I know this sounds crazy but I've lived before.'*

On her visit to her former home, Park House: *'Bugger that, I went round to the front door and walked straight in.'*

And on the utterly consuming subject of a pink top she has been wearing . . .

Him: *'Do you know the one I mean?'*

Her: *'I know.'*

Him: *'Very good – shit hot, actually.'*

Her laughing: *'Shit hot.'*

Him: *'Shit hot.'*

Her: *'Umm.'*

Much of the conversation is made up of similar inconsequential gossip about parties, meetings, friends and acquaintances, including a long discussion about astrology and the latest predictions of Diana's stargazer.

At times sounding disturbed, the Princess also reveals that TV host and charity fundraiser Sir Jimmy Savile has been in touch with her, showing concern about her wellbeing. Diana gloats that the star has referred to 'the Redhead' (the Duchess of York) as a 'lame duck' while calling Diana his 'number-one girl'. At this, James Gilbey interrupts – insisting that she is *his* 'number-one girl'.

The most explosive parts of the conversation come when Diana and Gilbey talk about each other. Gilbey is obviously ardently in love with the Princess and says so repeatedly, as in this excerpt . . .

Him: *'Oh Squidgy, I love you, love, love, love you, love you.'*

Her: *'You're the nicest person in the whole wide world.'*

Him: *'Squidgy, kiss me [sound of kissing by both]. Oh it's wonderful, isn't it, this sort of feeling? Don't you like it?'*

Her: *'I love it. I love it.'*

And her again, passionately: *'Love it. Never had it before. Never had it before.'*

Elsewhere in the tape the conversation becomes more intimate. Two sections of the tape were not made public at the time; most newspapers were not aware of them. However, these most damning segments were later published in an Australian magazine — and in hours had been faxed around the world.

In the first excerpt, the pair joke about solo sex — or *'Playing with yourself'* as Diana refers to it — and they dissolve into giggles on the subject . . .

Her: *'Playing with yourself?'*

Him: *'What? No I'm not actually.'*

Her: *'I said it's just like, just like . . .'*

Him: *'Playing with yourself.'*

Her: *'Yes.'*

Him: *'Not quite as nice. Not quite as nice. No, I haven't played with myself. Not for a full forty-eight hours. Not for a full forty-eight hours.'*

The second excerpt is even more disturbing. In it, the Princess voices her fears of becoming pregnant and Gilbey reassures her . . .

Her: *'I don't want to get pregnant.'*

Him: *'Darling it's not going to happen.'*

Her: *Sigh.*

Him: *'All right?'*

Her: *'Yeah.'*

Him: *'Don't worry about that. It's not going to happen, darling. You won't get pregnant.'*

Her: *'I watched "EastEnders"* [*the TV soap*] *today and one of the main characters had a baby they thought was by* [*indistinct*] *another man. Ha-ha.'*

Even Diana, who failed her school biology exams, cannot believe that anyone can become pregnant by 'playing with themselves'! But she still proves herself sadly lacking in knowledge of human sexual relations. The Princess of Wales is a patron of AIDS charities; she has all but made them her mission in life. Yet at one stage in the tape, she refers to a famous friend whom she suspects is bisexual – and reveals that she does not know the difference between that and heterosexual!

This astonishing naïveté surprises even Gilbey, who has to give her a lesson in the English language . . .

Her: *'He's sort of heterosexual.'*

Him: *'That's not heterosexual, darling. Oh Squidge, do you know what heterosexual is?'*

Her: *'No.'*

Him: *'You and me. That's heterosexual.'*

The existence of the 'Dianagate' tape was revealed in a uniquely wipe-out front page of the *Sunday Express* on 23 August 1992. It quoted from the forthcoming book *Fall of the House of Windsor* by Nigel Blundell and Susan Blackhall. The story caused immediate derision among royal 'experts' and 'authorised biographers', who labelled the tape a fake – or an inconsequential piece of chit-chat between platonic friends. However, when the transcript,* as published in *Fall of the House of Windsor*, was more closely studied, its authenticity became obvious. Moreover, the conversation proved that the couple were utterly familiar, totally at ease, on the most intimate terms with one another. The inescapable conclusion of the 'Dianagate' tape was that here was a couple having an affair over the telephone.

Princess Diana's emotions upon the public revelation of the tape's existence were, naturally enough, anger and embarrassment. Charles's reaction, however, was more detached. Like Diana, he had long known of the existence of such tapes – and had clinically appraised the benefits that they afforded him . . .

The notion of 'divorce', however distant, had already been considered. The tape, Charles judged, should ensure his wife's compliance in a settlement that the heir, his old friends, his most trusted advisers and his solicitors would soon be formulating. It would be a settlement in the overriding interests of a stable monarchy – but, as it happened, one that also happened to be most suitable to the heir to the throne himself!

---

* A full transcript, following computer enhancement in a sound studio and laboratory, is printed in Appendix 1 to this book, p. 387.

9

Dirty Tricks

Authors of coffee-table tomes on royalty, 'authorised' royal biographers and stuffy television pundits were quick to pick up another healthy cheque by expressing their knowledgeable verdicts on the 'Dianagate' tape. Almost to a man and woman, they pooh-poohed them. The tape was a forgery. Or a practical joke. Scribblers who had earned a packet by repeating the syrupy myth of Charles and Diana's rock-solid marriage found it difficult to change their tune. But change it they sordidly did. At first the tape recording was fake. Then it was just 'chit-chat' – the royals, it had to be explained to commoners, always spoke in this manner, with lots of 'love you, love you' and 'darlings' galore. Finally the 'experts' had to admit what the 'gutter press' of Fleet Street had been saying all along: that the tape was genuine and that the fairytale marriage of the century was a disgraceful sham. Their tardy admission was no surprise to the few experts who had actually heard the conversation. Nor, as we now know, to Charles and Diana themselves . . .

The experts who first heard the tape were immediately convinced of its authenticity. For it was not only the depth of feeling of Diana and her ardent admirer that had been captured; the sheer minutiae of detail and the clarity of recording were shattering. They posed the inescapable question: Who made it and why?

Was the Diana love tape simply the result of a radio ham scanning the airwaves and stumbling, by pure chance, across her intimate conversation, as was first claimed?

Was the conversation monitored by a member of household staff – perhaps a 'kiss and tell' merchant anxious to elicit easy money out of the tabloid press?

Or was this the work of a 'dirty tricks' department, possibly operating on behalf of Britain's secret service or even at the behest of the Palace itself?

Ironically, the Prince and the Princess were both anxious to know how investigations into the recording were progressing – Diana because she was keen to have proof that her phones and her apartments had been bugged on the orders of the Palace; Charles because he was anxious that no one be able to flaw the 'evidence' thus garnered against his wife in any future divorce negotiations.

At the time the recording was made, questions were already being asked about Princess Diana's role in her uneasy marriage to Charles, though it was long before any public furore or suggestion that their differences were irreconcilable. If Diana's telephones were being *officially* tapped, the orders to bug the future Queen could only have come from the very highest level. It seemed beyond belief. The notion of a royal aide carrying out such a sophisticated operation seemed even less credible.

The more easily accepted option was the story being examined by executives of *The Sun*, the newspaper that was first offered the tape. This was that an amateur radio ham had used a simple scanner, available at High Street stores, to capture the conversation midway between James Gilbey's car and the nearest transmitter/receiver in the mobile phone network. This lucky enthusiast, it was said, had recognised that he was indeed listening to the voice of Diana – and had had the perspicacity to make a recording and offer it to the newspaper.

The author of this book was the first person to investigate all theories. Every expert whose advice has been sought has found highly implausible the suggestion that a scanner was used randomly to pluck Princess Diana's conversation from the airwaves. British and American voice experts, security-service contacts, police and FBI all veer towards the more controversial theory – and the one that helps Diana's divorce submissions the best – that the call was professionally monitored at her end of the line.

The story of the 'Dianagate' tape — how it was uncovered, how it was passed on, how it was analysed and, after a thousand twists, turns and blind alleys, how it was finally proved to be what it is — is a saga at the very crux of Diana's divorce allegations and Charles's defence of them . . .

The first person seriously to delve into the innocent-looking little cassette was an American. Tom Owen is one of the United States' most experienced voice analysts. He was chief engineer at the Archive of Recorded Sound at the Lincoln Center and systems planning officer for the Performing Arts Research Center. Not only is he a certified voice-print examiner, he is in charge of vetting other experts on the Board of Certification of Voiceprint Licensing. Owen said the tape had been edited heavily and considerable time and trouble had been taken to 'clean it up'. An extremely powerful Digital Adaptor Filter had been utilised to eliminate background interference. It is an instrument that costs about $15,000 in the US and rather more in the UK. It is, to quote Owen, 'restricted equipment used by high-tech security organisations, such as MI5'.

Tom Owen went even further in his dismissal of the 'amateur' theory, thereby raising entirely unexpected question marks over the way the call had been recorded. He said the recording, so obviously of a mobile phone conversation, showed no signs whatever of the use of a mobile phone! There were no so-called 'drop-outs' (when sound is lost for microseconds) which are the trademarks of such mobile phone tapes. There were no signs of the phone's handset even being held – the movement of a telephone receiver in a person's hand can normally be detected by Mr Owen's amazingly sophisticated equipment. There is not even the sound of a passing car (Owen's analysis would detect even the wind in the trees), which reinforces his view that the tape was cleaned with a Digital Adaptor Filter.

Mr Owen said: 'I find no evidence of carrier noise, crosstalk or interference normally associated with mobile communications.' The whole scenario of the scanner is, in the verdict of Mr Owen, a 'not very palpable story'.

An FBI expert on the taping of mobile phones also gave his verdict on the possibility of such a conversation being recorded with a scanner. The FBI man had been involved in more than one 'sting' in conjunction with British law-enforcement agencies and was therefore well aware of UK telecommunications systems. He had found that when working in Britain it was 'impossible to pick up crosstalk for any length of time . . . the conversations were always interrupted'.

The FBI man said that in Britain mobile phone calls were 'bounced around' the frequencies to a far greater degree than in the US. This is simply because the communications companies' aerials are far closer together and they constantly 'fish out' the best frequencies and change them in a microsecond without the user knowing. A scanner cannot follow such changes. Indeed, said the FBI expert, when working in Britain he was forced to use not one but two scanners to have even a chance of keeping tabs on a conversation.

One of the most respected British experts on voice authentication is Derek Faraday, for more than forty years vice-president of the Association of Professional Recording Studios. Mr Faraday, who spent World War II serving in His Majesty's Radio Security Service, has regularly appeared as an expert witness in cases involving magnetic tape recording in both civil and criminal courts, and before disciplinary tribunals and courts martial. He has been retained as consultant by the regional police authorities, by the investigative branch of Her Majesty's Customs and Excise, and by industrial security organisations. He is officially recognised by the Law Society as an expert witness – and would undoubtedly make one if ever needed in a case such as Windsor versus Windsor. What then is his verdict on the 'Dianagate' tape?

According to Derek Faraday, the chances of such a recording being made in impromptu fashion were 'infinitesimal'. Observing Tom Owen's tests in the United States, the English expert concurred with his American counterpart's findings. Mr Faraday pointed to the lack of background noise on the 'Dianagate' tape. He said: 'A mobile phone conversation has an immediate "trademark" obvious to an expert. Whenever a person stops talking, if only for a second, the receiver tries to pick up any other sound and amplify it during the gap in the conversation. The background would thereby rise and fall. But in the "Dianagate" tape, the background noise is level.'

Mr Faraday stated: 'The most plausible theory is an in-house recording because the voices, particularly the Princess's, are so clear, and because there are no radio noises on the tape.' He added: 'This is a very professional recording which has none of the trademarks of a radio link. It was obviously made by someone who was ready and waiting, with all the apparatus set up for a recording, and probably taken off a hard-wire line. This is the one conclusion that fits all the known parameters – except for the theory of the random scanner.'

Checks with Britain's two mobile phone services at the time, Vodaphone and Cellnet, confirmed that few scanners can pick up both sides of a conversation for very long. And even if they did, the quality would not be up to the level of the Diana-Gilbey call. There would 'inevitably have been some electronic background or associated radio noises. Using a scanner, an even higher level of background noise, on both voices, would have been clearly detectable on the tape.' It is not – and the only explanation for this is the use of the top-range Digital Adaptor Filter.

An expert who had been involved in selling such equipment in the United Kingdom confirmed that the purchase of such a piece of equipment by an ordinary member of the public would immediately set alarm bells ringing. Security clearance is required before the sale of such devices is allowed ... because the customers for such DAFs are sometimes the Special Branch but more usually the military or MI5 and MI6.

Electronic experts Audiotel International were allowed to analyse the frequency of speech and data signals on the tapes. Their report: 'The balance of probability suggests something irregular about the recording which may indicate a rebroadcasting of the conversation some time after the actual conversation took place.'

Mr David Benn, the head of London surveillance experts Lorraine Electrics, said that a standard domestic telephone could be bugged by a transmitter inside the phone itself: a tiny device costing about £450. The two-way conversation could then be transmitted to a £3,000 automatic radio receiver up to 1,500 metres away. The remote receiver tape records the calls without requiring constant manning. But according to Mr Benn, the equipment more likely to have been used would have been a more sophisticated £700-plus transmitter fitted on the land line between a building and the exchange. 'This does the same job but is easier to fit and remove,' he said. 'It is electronically invisible.'

Mr Benn added: 'This is all basic stuff. And the Royal Family have all the security expertise of the government agencies at their fingertips.'

Most sophisticated of all, however, is a £10,000-plus computerised scanner that is seldom seen outside Special Branch, MI5 and GCHQ. This piece of hardware is so 'clever' that once it has locked on to a particular number, it can begin recording again whenever that number is in use.

Contacts in the British security services were naturally reluctant to discuss the analysis of the tape. However, an MI5 source who was a specialist in this field told the author that a 'security and protection unit' within one of the official security services would be the most likely users of the equipment required for such an operation.

So what of these various theories – all extraordinary to say the least? Was the recording of Diana's phone conversation really a million-to-one chance? Was it beamed to amateur scanner-users having previously been recorded by professionals? And if it was the work of professionals, who were they – and why were they bugging the Princess of Wales's line?

The answer might, of course, be the Royal and Diplomatic Protection Squad, which regularly makes official security checks on the various royal households. But the organisation more likely to be interested in the relationships between senior royals and 'outsiders' would be a section of the Special Branch.

It would not be surprising to learn that the Special

Branch makes regular checks on the activities of the Royal and Diplomatic Protection Squad, so would know of any covert phone-tapping operation in which they were engaged. Their inside knowledge of the Royal Family's private activities is enhanced by the fact that they operate a hush-hush liaison group which links the operations of the Metropolitan Police and St James's Palace. The liaison group spends much time monitoring official royal movements — foreign tours and so forth — but its security checks run a great deal deeper. The Special Branch also has ready access to the experts of the Met's little-known and extremely well-equipped 'tape laboratory'.

There is also a straightforward link with the most secretive security arm of all, MI5. Although Scotland Yard strongly denied that Royal Protection Squad officers had ever been asked to supply details of secret assignations to MI5, it can be revealed that MI5 officers regularly inspect a detailed log kept by the royals' bodyguards at their headquarters at Buckingham Palace. The log is filled in daily by every officer and even covers the private moments when royals ask protection officers to stay at a discreet distance. Every week copies of that log go straight to MI5.

In fact, in all areas the Special Branch is in constant communication with MI5 and its external security arm, MI6. There is a kind of Eton-and-Guards 'mafia' of senior officers who have worked in military intelligence. Only a senior courtier or Prince Charles himself

Top: Born to be king: Prince Charles out riding at the age of 12 in the spring of 1961.

Above: Born to be queen? An ungainly Lady Diana, aged seven, in the summer of 1968.

Above: Lady Diana arrives home after staying at Sandringham in November 1980.

Opposite: Bride and mistress: Diana and Camilla Parker Bowles at the races in 1980.

Kindergarten Kid: Diana silhouetted against the sunlight in March 1981.

Top: Shy Di: Uneasy with the cameras as she poses with her fiance in 1981.

Below: The newly-weds: Crowd-pleasers on the balcony of Buckingham Palace in 1982.

Fairytale marriage: The action-man husband and the model wife at a polo match.

Above: The strain shows: The 'marriage made in heaven' is beginning to crumble.

Sham marriage: Smiles for the camera but, in private, vitriolic rows.

would have been able to recruit the services of one of these experts to 'screen' in secrecy the telephone traffic at Sandringham.

Princess Diana had no doubts about who was to blame for the bugging: Charles himself. What she didn't know was how it was carried out.

The Princess had become paranoid about her need of secrecy from the prying eyes of the Palace machine. In 1991 the suspicious Princess had her apartments 'swept' for bugging devices but found none. She also had a shredder installed to destroy private mail. In June 1992, however, she was confronted by a senior member of the Queen's Household over damning evidence of a phone call that 'might damage the reputation of the Royal Family'. Diana hotly denied any knowledge of such a call – but it fuelled her paranoia for secrecy. When a few weeks later a phone conversation she had had with her old pal Carolyn Bartholomew was fed back to her, an angry Diana retaliated. She complained to the Queen's private secretary Sir Robert Fellowes that her private calls were being monitored on the orders of the Palace. And she effectively told Fellowes: 'If I discover that my calls are bugged, then I'm off!'

Prince Charles too was wary of bugs. That same month, June 1992, he also had his apartment 'swept' for listening devices. According to the *Sunday Times*, the Prince's private secretary, Commander Richard Ayling, employed an independent security firm, Ian

Johnson Associates, to search Kensington Palace. The decision to hire a private firm rather than use the police or MI5 was ominous in that it meant that even the Prince of Wales felt he could not trust the state's security officers.

So Charles relied on his friends and Diana on hers. Their bodyguards and official security advisers were left out in the cold. This was not entirely true in the case of the Princess, however. She still relied utterly on the confidence of her trusted and slavishly loyal detective from the Royal and Diplomatic Protection Squad, Inspector Ken Wharfe. It was he who had danced with the Princess on the Caribbean island of Necker; it was he who had won the fathers' race at Prince William's sports day; and it was he was was referred to as 'Ken' on the 'Dianagate' tape. Ken Wharfe was known in the force as 'Mr Flamboyant' but to Diana he was a firm friend who could be trusted with running errands, making deliveries and carrying messages without the knowledge of Palace officials.

Diana also used the home addresses of her oldest pals from her single days as 'dead letter boxes' to collect mail that she did not wish to go through Palace sorting offices. Her third precaution to top cloak her movements was to use mobile phones rather than go through Palace switchboards. On this occasion, however, she had dropped her guard because, although James Gilbey may have been conversing on a mobile phone, Diana herself was almost certainly talking into a handset on a fixed line in Sandringham House.

The conspiracy theorists — Diana included — had had a long battle to prove their case. Indeed, in claiming from the very start that she had been bugged on her Sandringham line, the Princess of Wales was working on no more than a hunch, or on womanly instinct, or perhaps on a realistic assessment of her husband's nature. But she was almost certainly right . . .

Until this point in our story, we have, for simplicity's sake, talked only about a 'Dianagate' *tape*. We should, however, be referring to *tapes* — because there were indeed at least *two*. Best known is the recording made in Abingdon by Cyril Reenan. But there was another recording, made by another radio enthusiast just seven miles away in Cowley, a suburb of Oxford. This recording was made by a twenty-four-year-old secretary, Miss Jane Norgrove, in the terraced home she shared with her parents and used as an office. The recordings are of the same conversation (or conversations, edited together) and although they have considerable overlapping stretches, the starting and finishing points are different.

Both Mr Reenan and Miss Norgrove coincidentally sold their tapes to reporters and both eventually ended up at the offices of *The Sun* newspaper, whose executives accepted at face value that they were identical and had been recorded at the same time and on the same day. But, as we shall reveal, they most certainly had not. Let's examine the evidence for this crucial point – the evidence of a massive and officially engineered conspiracy scandal which influenced the divorce strategies of both Charles and Diana.

Mr Reenan, sixty-nine, who became an amateur radio enthusiast after retiring from his bank manager's job in 1981, was in the sitting room of his home when his £1,000 scanner, tuned to a random search of the airwaves, began to pick up the voices of Gilbey and the Princess on the evening of 4 January 1990. He immediately recognised Diana's voice as, fascinated, he walked across the room to switch on the very basic, hand-held tape recorder that sat on a shelf with its microphone dangling down to a point about six inches from the scanner loudspeaker. The time was approximately 9.30 p.m.

After a few minutes, Cyril roused his wife Muriel who was dozing in another chair. As the couple listened in growing disbelief to the sometimes banal, sometimes sexually charged conversation, they never doubted for a moment that they were hearing it 'live'. Afterwards, however, several aspects of the recording gave them cause for doubt.

1. The scanner remained firmly locked on to the conversation for fifteen minutes without interruption. When reception was suddenly lost, Mr Reenan managed to twiddle the dial and retrieve it for a further

five minutes. 'That is quite unusual,' said Mr Reenan. 'Normally the scanner will not stay locked on to a single conversation for anything like that time.'

2. Mr Reenan could hear both parties speaking at the same volume and with similar clarity. 'This also is very unusual,' said Mr Reenan. 'Virtually always there is one voice of poorer quality than the other.'

3. The recording, as Mr Reenan affirmed, began at about 9.30 p.m. on the night of 4 January. Yet the conversation is obviously taking place at an earlier hour of the evening on New Year's Eve, 31 December 1990 – a full *four days* earlier.

In his tape, Mr Reenan could clearly hear Diana telling her male suitor that she planned to go swimming with Fergie the following day. Mr Reenan only realised the strangeness of his recording when he saw a front page of *The Sun* in a newsagent's shop on the morning of 5 January. It contained a picture of Diana and Fergie, both with wet hair, emerging from a Kings Lynn, Norfolk, hotel's private swimming pool the previous day. That day was 4 January – *four days* after New Year's Eve.

4. And yes, as far as she can recall, Miss Norgrove did indeed make her recording up the road in Oxford a full *four days* earlier. (Her only cause for doubt is by virtue of the fact that, having made the tape recording, she tucked it away in a drawer for a year before her curiosity got the better of her and she retrieved it to

play again. A local reporter heard of it and contacted *The Sun*.)

Mr Reenan's evidence for there having been a conspiracy was wholly ignored at first. But after the author tested and confirmed his theories for *Fall of the House of Windsor*, experts began to back the claim.

Mr Reenan himself acknowledges that he could have been used in a plot to discredit the royals. He said: 'I have always been adamant that I heard that conversation on the fourth of January. I have no doubts about it. The Princess was talking of going swimming the next day and, sure enough, four days later there were pictures in *The Sun* of her at a swimming pool. That is why I phoned them on the spur of the moment. When their reporter arrived, I agreed to give them the tape for safe keeping and so that Princess Diana could be warned about such easily-overheard conversations. I got some money for my trouble but was assured the tape would never be published.'

He added: 'Looking back on it, there were certain strange things about that tape. Normally when you hear phone calls on the scanner between land-line phones and mobile phones, one caller is much clearer than the other. On this occasion both came through at the same level. Bearing in mind the man was supposed to be on a mobile phone, one would expect to hear wind, noise and general rustling as the phone rubbed against his clothes. There was none of that.

'I cannot rule out the possibility that I was meant to hear what I did by some sinister, behind-the-scenes element. But I never wanted to be part of this conspiracy. I don't find it very amusing when people suggest I work for MI5, GCHQ or whoever.'

Yet that, it seems, was exactly what had happened to the hapless Cyril Reenan. It took some time, however, for many to admit it . . .

Months after *The Sun* ran its first 'Dianagate' reports, its sister paper, the *News of the World*, reported that they now believed that the Squidgy tape was not recorded by amateurs. They quoted the results of a secret investigation by the Cellnet network that the recording was taken from a listening device on the actual phone line out of Sandringham. After detailed technical analysis, they concluded that a spy tap was planted inside Diana's private quarters or attached to a telegraph junction box. Concerned Cellnet executive William Omstrom said: 'We have dismissed this as an example of our network being eavesdropped.'

Another newspaper in the same stable, the worthy *Sunday Times*, in January 1993 came down firmly on the side of the conspiracy theorists. They commissioned one of Britain's top communications consultants, John Nelson, to carry out his own investigations. He concluded that electronic noises had been added to the 'Dianagate' tape in an 'attempt to disguise a local tap by making it appear that it was recorded over cellular radio'.

The *Today* newspaper (another *Sun* stablemate) came to a similar conclusion that year. Their verdict was that the same recording had been played over the airwaves repeatedly, so that scanning enthusiasts would pick it up and pass it on. The newspaper said that two separate sources involved in royal security hinted that private investigators may have been recruited by the royals themselves. Special Branch, MI5 and the government's electronic spy centre at GCHQ, Gloucestershire, all had the expertise to carry out such an operation.

At about this time, MI5 officers were spurred to initiate an investigation at both British Telecom headquarters and at GCHQ. Many thought that MI5 interrogating GCHQ workers about the royal bugging was the height of cynical irony.

There was a further 'wild card' theory that utterly confused the hunt for the snoopers. In March 1993 James Rushbridger, a former officer of Britain's foreign security organisation MI6, stated that US intelligence agents regularly tapped royal calls on behalf of GCHQ. Mr Rushbridger said that two top-secret listening stations, operated by America's National Security Agency – at Morwentsow, Cornwall, and at Menwith Hill, Yorkshire – illegally tap large numbers of private conversations. 'By getting the Americans to do it,' said Mr Rushbridger, 'the British Government is able to say truthfully but misleadingly that GCHQ does not bug domestic phone calls. The reason the government is resisting an official investigation into the tapping of royal conversations is that it would be forced to admit this.'

Rushbridger went on to claim that special operatives at GCHQ monitor all royal communications, including phone calls, faxes and telex messages. 'There are six officers on duty at any time,' he said, 'whose sole activity is to monitor the royals in order to keep a discreet eye on their private lives. It is mainly to secure their safety — especially if they are enjoying secret trysts in lonely lanes or country houses.'

Who gets the benefits of this information? Here we turn full circle . . . For whether it is the Americans or GCHQ or Special Branch that carries out the bugging, it is of course good old MI5 who receive the end results.

That being the case, Diana felt vindicated and morally fortified for the battle ahead.

10

Furore!

Doubts may remain over the origins of the 'Dianagate' tape but there can be no question that the eavesdroppers responsible knew full well the explosive consequences of their actions. Within hours of a transcript being published in the British newspapers, the scandal was rocketing on to front pages and news bulletins around the world.

For the first time in those turbulent summer months of 1992, the spotlight tilted from Charles's behaviour towards his wife to Diana's private intimacies. Suddenly, the public perceived that the future Queen of England had indulged in a close — most would say unacceptably close — relationship with another man.

The man himself, James Gilbey, went into hiding and largely vanished from the scene for the ensuing months. His efforts at secrecy, however, had their farcical moments as the British press attempted to hunt him down. In a car chase with a persistent photographer from *The Sun* on 27 August 1992, their two vehicles collided, almost writing off Gilbey's white Montego saloon. The fugitive from the press did not hang around to exchange insurance details, however; he abandoned his crumpled car and 'legged it' down a country lane.

In September Gilbey was spotted sunning himself on the Italian Riviera with Diana's brother Lord Charles and wife Victoria. With them in sneak paparazzi photographs was Gilbey's new blonde girlfriend, the attractively topless Lady Alethea Savile. By December, however, she and Gilbey had broken off their engagement, and the latter successfully faded from the public arena. (Lady Alethea was not so fortunate; two years later, still heartbroken over the split, she was found dead in her London apartment from a pills overdose.)

Unlike Gilbey, Diana faced the breaking storm more stoically than most expected. She reacted with brief panic, though her initial horror soon turned to resignation. She had heard rumours of the tape's existence for some time but hoped and believed it would never come to light. Now she suspected a clique of pro-Charles Palace courtiers had engineered its appearance in the media as part of an orchestrated smear campaign against her as the opening shots in a divorce war.

That view was strengthened when a second potential scandal threatened to spin off the 'Dianagate' affair. On Saturday 29 August 1992, just five days after full transcripts of the tapes had been published, several newspapers carried stories warning that a set of highly sensitive photographs were being touted around Fleet Street.

The pictures were said to show Household Cavalry officer Major James Hewitt, mentioned by Diana in the tape, embracing her at Windsor barracks. At the Princess's request, thirty-four-year-old Major Hewitt had been given permission by the army to help improve her horse-riding skills. Now it was being suggested their relationship was rather more than that between teacher and pupil.

Everything pointed to a major scoop in the *News of the World* the following day. The pictures were alleged to have been taken by a cleaner and included one shot of Hewitt stripped to the waist as he relaxed with the Princess at Army stables. Another apparently pictured her leaving his private quarters.

As the nation awaited developments, Hewitt told one newspaper: 'I was her horse-riding tutor, that was all. I have heard rumours and read stories but that is all they are. I cannot honestly imagine anything I have done that could possibly be misconstrued.'

Diana, meanwhile, was riding out the storm at Balmoral with Charles, Wills and Harry. Palace aides, still clinging to the hope that the marriage could be saved, leaked a report that the royal couple were having a wild, fun time together. At the traditional Friday-night Ghillies Ball for 250 Balmoral estate workers on 28 August, the Prince was said to have swept Diana off her feet.

One source said: 'It was either a very good act or Charles and Di were really enjoying themselves. If the Prince was upset about those tapes he certainly did not show it. Di really let her hair down. She was the belle of the ball and was making the most of the night. The Queen looked radiant and was delighted to see them having such a good time.'

The truth was that although the Prince and Princess may have put on a united front for the Queen in the presence of her staff, they had spent their Balmoral break avoiding each other's company. At the private performance of a play one evening Diana had been studiously ignored not only by her husband but by the Queen, Prince Philip, Princess Margaret, the Queen Mother and Princess Anne. It was hardly the stuff of a happy family holiday.

At one point a few hours before the Ghillies Ball, she was spotted walking alone, head down, through a quiet fir forest on the royal estate. She was already looking forward to taking the boys back to London, leaving Charles to spend a week fishing on his own. Apart from anything else, she had arranged a secret meeting with the Nobel Prize-winning nun Mother Teresa — a woman she idolised — for the following Saturday.

As it turned out, the Hewitt photographs were so much hype. Sunday's *News of the World* carried a front-page story claiming the Princess feared she would be blackmailed over them, and that Major Hewitt had confiscated the negatives from the cleaner and arranged for them to be destroyed. 'We have not been shown these pictures and so far there is nothing to corroborate their existence,' the paper pronounced. But although there was no smoking gun, the episode was significant in the eyes of Diana and her friends. It was further confirmation that a dirty-tricks squad was active. Some-one was out to destroy her.

Charles's camp was certainly not idle in its secretive dealings with the media. The Prince, his friends insisted, 'loathed' the Princess and referred to her privately as 'Diana the Martyr'. His fury at her co-operation with author Andrew Morton's book, and its criticism of him, had only been tempered by publication of the 'Dianagate' tape, which he regarded as 'a dose of her own medicine'.

One source, said to be a cousin of the Queen, claimed: 'Words cannot convey how betrayed the Prince of Wales feels by what the Princess has done. He is deeply hurt and very, very angry over his wife's alleged conduct. In his scale of things, such conduct is so despicable it is unimaginable. Charles now loathes his wife. Even more important, he doesn't trust her as far as he can see her. The family now understand that she is a very devious and calculating woman beneath that sweet exterior and that she has the power to do them a great deal of harm.'

Time and again, those briefing the press on Charles's reaction insisted he would not stoop to her level.

However, speaking of the effect the 'Dianagate' tape had had on him and his supporters, one aristocrat observed: 'They are realistic enough to see that this is one cloud that has a silver lining. This is the first bit of proof the public has had that Diana is not necessarily the goddess they think she is. They have played the whole thing down because it doesn't suit them to have anyone question the Princess of Wales's fidelity as long as she remains a member of the Royal Family. But it has also given them the ammunition to ask the right questions if and when they need to.'

One ex-member of the royal household was more forceful. 'The Princess of Wales is a jumped-up little drama queen,' he said. 'She is no better than one of those movie stars who starts believing her own publicity.'

As Diana's behaviour behind closed doors became increasingly bizarre, staff at Kensington Palace nick-named her 'the actress' for her fine television perform-ances as the warmest-hearted woman in Britain – which were often followed by angry tirades when she returned home. 'We could never understand how she could be so nice in public and so horrible back at the shop,' said one verbally-battered servant.

Diana was well aware of this kind of hostility but refused to be cowed by it. Far from retreating in the wake of the tape revelations, she pressed home her demands for a future without Charles. During an extraordinary series of meetings with the Queen, Prince Philip and her husband, she set out her case for a legal separation, a sizeable financial settlement, unlimited access to the two Princes and retention of her title. She also tabled a request for her own royal court, operating outside the strictures of Buckingham Palace, and indicated that she would walk out on the family as soon as Wills and Harry returned to boarding school in September.

The Queen was reported to be furious at such raw nerve but realised the need for a period of reflection between all parties. She persuaded Diana to stay onside until after Christmas, when arrangements could be formalised. A date was also roughed out for an official announcement of a separation.

It was not so much a truce, more a lull in hostilities. The Queen, who for so long had been quietly sympathetic to Diana, was now deeply mistrustful of her. She decided a long-planned counter-offensive should be launched in which senior royals would freeze out Diana. Charles would be given a much higher profile. His role as a family man was to be emphasised, with as many photo opportunities as possible in which he and the boys could be seen together.

Prince Philip, meanwhile, was being characteristically forthright. At Ascot earlier in the year he had publicly humiliated his daughter-in-law by refusing to talk to her at a time when they were the only two people in the Royal Box. Later at a family summit, he branded Diana a 'fifth columnist' for leaking details of her rocky marriage to tabloid reporter-turned-author

Andrew Morton. Now as the dust from 'Dianagate' began to settle, he was bluntly telling senior members of the royal household that the family was better off without her. He reasoned that her stunning looks and popularity with the public would gradually form a wedge between the monarchy and the people.

Even the Princess's closest ally among her in-laws, Prince Andrew, was distancing himself. Andrew of course had marriage troubles of his own. But whereas he had confidence in the Duchess of York not to spill any unsavoury beans, he regarded Diana as 'a loose cannon'.

It now seems that in the late summer and autumn of 1992 there were at least two active campaigns against Diana from within Palace circles. One, which might be termed the 'official stance', was for a softly, softly approach in which it was hoped the 'Dianagate' tape would leave her to 'swing in the wind'. The other, much more aggressive, campaign was being orchestrated by powerfully-connected friends of Charles.

It was this second group which briefly became the focus of a new twist in the marriage crisis. On 1 September newspapers reported that an internal communication within the royal household, addressed to one of the Queen's closest advisers, had been leaked. The letter spoke of Diana relishing her role as a dutiful wife trapped in a loveless marriage. It spoke of the need to get Prince Charles's case into the newspapers and of how Diana was capable of destroying the monarchy. It would have been dynamite except for one major drawback. It was a transparent fake. The newspapers smelled this particular rat very early on and the story quickly died a death. The mere fact the letter was faked was cited by some as proof that a pro-Charles conspiracy was all in the imagination of the media. It proved nothing of the kind. The Charles clique was simply too worldly-wise to put anything in writing.

Despite all that had happened in previous weeks, Palace press officers were still gamely spinning the line that the royal couple had a future together. They must have been congratulating themselves on the evening of Sunday 6 September after Independent Television News screened a one-hour special documentary entitled 'Diana – The End of a Fairytale?' This programme assured its sixteen million viewers that, despite enormous strains, the marriage would survive. Presenter John Suchet asserted: 'We understand that by the time Prince Charles arrived in Scotland for an engagement on Thursday, he knew that divorce was off the agenda.'

The following day a buoyant Palace press office was determined to keep the positive images flowing. When Charles and Diana turned up with Prince Harry for his first day at Ludgrove boarding school, in Berkshire, the very fact that they 'chatted and looked relaxed' was seized upon as evidence that they were making a go of the marriage. Reporters were informed that the Waleses would be spending the night together at Kensington Palace and would be working side by side in Nottingham the following day. And, of course, plans were advancing for their royal tour together to South Korea.

If this was the official line, Charles and Diana seemed happy to ignore it! So when at Ludgrove the Prince had the perfect opportunity to be pictured in a public show of unity with his wife, Harry and William (also a boarder), he instead walked off chatting to headmaster Gerald Barber. It was a similar story the next day in Nottingham. The couple spent only a few minutes together at the Queen's Medical Centre, and even then they were several paces apart. One single, cold glance was all that passed between them. As for Korea, they didn't even bother to look at each other. They clearly had their own agenda to which the press office was not a party.

Reaction to the 'Dianagate' tape rumbled on. The day after the Nottingham trip, Cyril Reenan, the man who made the fateful recording via his scanner, issued a statement apologising to Diana. Speaking from his neat, semi-detatched house in Abingdon, Oxfordshire, the seventy-year-old retired bank manager said: 'Knowing what I do now, I think I would have tried to warn Diana her conversations were being overheard. I cannot deny there was a greed aspect to it but I regret that now. It's not as if I need the money. I'm not that hard up.'

In fact, if some royal insiders were to be believed, Princess Diana needed the money as much as Mr Reenan! Charles was said to have slashed her personal spending budget and refused to renew the lease on her £20,000 Mercedes sports car. In railing back her expenditure, he forestalled any plan she may have hatched to set up her own royal court. They would continue to share their office at St James's Palace, and Charles would continue to have an eye on her diary and daily routine.

The problem for Diana, as one observer put it, was that 'she has plenty of uninfluential friends like James Gilbey but hardly anyone with access to the wheels that matter'. Gilbey, in fact, remained in touch with the Princess throughout the 'Dianagate' furore. They agreed a 'cooling-off' period which they (wrongly) believed was long enough to allow media speculation to die down, but by early 1993 were in regular touch by phone. Pointedly, they did not favour mobile phones.

While there were some who sneered at the Princess's lack of 'big guns' at Westminster and Buckingham Palace, most of the big guns themselves knew better. True, the Princess could to an extent be marginalised during the Queen's reign and (assuming it happened) Charles's succession. But one day, perhaps not so far away, William would be King. Diana could then look forward to an immeasurably strengthened position in royal circles.

Speculation as to the succession, and indeed the whole future of the monarchy, was now rife around the world. The public in the Commonwealth and America, for so long sceptical of the British tabloids and their reporting of a royal marriage crisis, suddenly realised it was all true. For them the 'Dianagate' tape was the first proper sniff of scandal.

Constitutional experts were trotted out to interpret dusty old laws dating from the seventeenth century. Royal correspondents wearily tried to explain the implications of it all to mystified Japanese TV link men. And the pollsters had a field day trying to predict which way the 'swingometer' of public opinion was going.

In Australia the crisis was linked to an upsurge in political initiatives to turn the country into a republic. Younger Australians regarded the affair as something of a joke, a real-life soap opera which knocked TV's 'Neighbours' and 'Home and Away' into a cocked hat. An older generation, brought up to love and respect their Queen, viewed it with increasing incredulity and sadness.

In America celebrity magazines indulged in a feeding frenzy as every day brought another sumptuous feast of gossip. The magazine *Who Weekly* opined: 'Though the Palace at first insisted that the tape was a hoax ("This is not a story that we can take seriously," sniffed a spokesman) by week's end its silence, and lack of a formal denial, was deafening. Further, the

Palace's last line of defence — that the tapes do not necessarily indicate an intimate affair — hold little water in the light of the kinds of banter portrayed in the transcripts.'

The magazine went on to echo the British *Daily Mail*'s comment: 'If proved to be genuine, and by implication that means the Princess has had an extra-marital affair, the tape could prove irrevocably damaging to her marriage to Prince Charles. For the future Queen to be linked with anyone other than her husband is unthinkable.'

Back in Britain the aftermath of 'Dianagate' had produced plenty of grim reading for the Establishment in general and Prince Charles in particular. On 30 August a survey by the Twin Networks organisation showed that 59 per cent of the public would blame Charles for the marriage break-up if he left the Princess on the basis of her taped conversation. Only 43 per cent said they would blame Diana if she left him.

Worse still for the Charles camp, more than two-thirds of the 1,156 people questioned said he was responsible for her turning to another man. Three-quarters continued to regard Diana as caring and sincere.

Three months later and still the British public was backing Diana in preference to Charles. A survey by ICM revealed that 57 per cent sympathised with her, compared to a mere 12 per cent who supported him. And although more than half those questioned said

Charles should succeed to the throne even if he married again, a hefty 76 per cent thought it would be better for him to hand straight over to Prince William.

It was a trend which continued in later polls. Most worrying of all was the inference that months of scandal had severely damaged the Royal Family as a whole. One survey indicated that more than a quarter of the population believed Britain would be better off without them – double the number of five years earlier.

Bizarre though it seemed, an eavesdropped phone conversation now seemed to threaten the very existence of the monarchy. Its funding by taxpayers was put under the microscope: £60 million on security, £9 million to keep the royal yacht *Britannia* sailing, £25 million to maintain palaces, £6.7 million for the Queen's Flight and £2 million for the royal train. The Queen, known to have good political antennae in these matters, carried out a pre-emptive strike to see off some of the criticism. During a private meeting with Prime Minister John Major at Balmoral in early September, she made a discreet offer to trim down the Civil List. She also acknowledged that the time had come for her income to be taxed.

The monarchy was not without persuasive supporters. What would be achieved by abolishing it, they argued. The nation would still need a head of state. The castles would have to be maintained, banquets would continue in honour of foreign dignitaries. Why seek to punish the Queen for the shortcomings of her children?

As the debate intensified, so did analysis of Diana's role in exposing the truth of her loveless marriage. Through their media contacts, Charles's loyal courtiers made sure that pressure on her was subtly maintained. In early January 1993 his biographer, Penny Junor, warned: 'I have been told by people close to the Royal Family that Diana is still suffering from bulimia, which will add to her turmoil. She will be subjected to bouts of depression and wild mood swings.

'That combined with the lack of security from her sons, and her being branded a liar, means she will need all her strength to pull through ... there is a fragility in her life that could snap. At the moment I would say she is a desperate woman.'

The message was clear. If the monarchy were ever to fall, history would record a mentally unstable Diana as the one who chipped away the foundations.

11

The Cold War

On the night of Saturday 21 November 1992 the Queen wept as she watched her favourite home go up in flames. Fire had broken out at Windsor Castle that morning and, partly because of a delay in calling the fire brigade and partly because some of its appliances could not squeeze through the ancient gates, the blaze engulfed a large part of the historic building. The magnificent St George's Hall, scene of 600 years of state banquets, was gutted. The Brunswick Tower, Chester Tower, Star Chamber and the Queen's private chapel were also severely damaged at a cost to the reluctant British taxpayer of at least £60 million.

The greatest heritage disaster of the century seemed a symbolic end to a year in which the British monarchy had been sent reeling by blow upon blow. Yet this was not to be the end of the Queen's agony. Worse was to come.

The fire at Windsor Castle may have partly

destroyed the Queen's much-loved home, but an announcement just a few weeks later was to devastate her life. It rocked the monarchy and the nation to an extent that rivalled the abdication crisis of Edward VIII. After months of speculation, the announcement was made by Buckingham Palace that Prince Charles and Princess Diana were to separate. On 9 December the following statement was read by the Prime Minister, John Major, to a hushed House of Commons.

It is announced from Buckingham Palace that, with regret, the Prince and Princess of Wales have decided to separate. Their Royal Highnesses have no plans to divorce and their constitutional positions are unaffected. Their decision has been reached amicably, and they will both continue to participate fully in the upbringing of their children. Their Royal Highnesses will continue to carry out full and separate programmes of public engagements and will, from time to time, attend family occasions and national events together. The Queen and the Duke of Edinburgh, though saddened, understand and sympathise with the difficulties that have led to this decision. Her Majesty and His Royal Highness particularly hope that the intrusion into the privacy of the Prince and Princess may now cease. They believe that a degree of privacy and understanding is essential if their Royal Highnesses are to provide a happy and secure upbringing for their children, while continuing to give a wholehearted commitment to their public duties.

It was naïve of the Palace to believe that the statement would end the intense focus on Charles and Diana. The reverse occurred: it opened raging debates on the future of the crown, the prospect of a King without a Queen and the feasibility of two people who obviously loathed one another carrying out an officially sanctioned charade of parental togetherness and, more crucially, of royal unity.

How could there be a separation without divorce? How could Charles take the throne with Diana – or without her?

Few believed, as the Palace was later to add, that 'their continuing relationship would be better under separate domestic arrangements'. Neither could many people accept the Prime Minister's insistence that there would be no constitutional crisis. He told Parliament: 'The succession to the throne is unaffected. The children of the Prince and Princess retain their position in the line of succession and there is no reason why the Princess of Wales should not be crowned Queen in due course. The Prince of Wales's succession as head of the Church of England is also unaffected.'

There were audible gasps at John Major's suggestion that Princess Diana would one day be Queen. Several Members of Parliament later said there was no possibility of the Princess becoming Queen in such circumstances. To suggest that she would do so was a confidence trick being played on an already cynical public. How could Diana accept the title and privileges of Queen without accepting the duties that went with it? MPs said that the institution of the monarchy could not survive a King separated from his Queen. The prospect of a coronation in such circumstances was variously described as 'ludicrous', 'bogus' and 'completely out of touch'.

The newspapers were condemnatory to the point of vitriol. 'Victory for Di' screamed the tabloid *The Sun*, adding: 'Winner takes all. She wanted the kids, she got them. She wanted the cash, she got it. She wanted her staff, she got them. She wanted a palace, she got it. What a result for devious Di.' But the headline common to most newspapers said it all: 'End of a Fairytale'. The day after the announcement, page upon page chronicled the marriage that started with a kiss on a balcony and ended with cold looks and sad resignation – and all played before an audience of millions worldwide.

Public reaction to the news was best illustrated when the Queen made her first appearance the day after the announcement. As she stepped out of the official car to visit her royal bank, Coutts, in the heart of London, she was greeted by a crowd four-deep – and silent. There was not a cheer, wave, shout or cry. 'Not even a ripple of applause,' reported the *London Evening Standard*. The Queen was puzzled and hurt. The Duke of Edinburgh accompanying her looked apprehensive. By contrast, that same day, on her first public engagement since the news broke, Princess Diana smiled broadly as she attended a gala lunch at a London hotel. Her husband, on a separate engagement in the City of London, was expressionless. If Diana was the Princess who had won it all, then Charles was the Prince who looked as if he had lost everything he had ever held dear.

There was also speculation over the timing of the announcement. Was it made to allow those innocent victims, Princes William and Harry, to be given the sad news before they finished their school term? Was it, as rumours suggested, because one national newspaper had details of the statement and the Palace wanted to release an official version before it got into print? Was the statement issued at Diana's insistence to make public her own feelings? Or, more maliciously, was the intention to cast a shadow over the marriage of Diana's sister-in-law, Princess Anne, to Commander Tim Laurence that very weekend?

Diana was noticeably absent from the wedding guest list. Being a royal divorcee and therefore unable to marry in the Church of England, Anne wed in a quiet, austere, Church of Scotland ceremony at Crathie, near Balmoral. The ceremony caused other reactions, apart from Diana's absence. The Queen Mother was at first said to have refused to attend because she disapproved of remarriage after divorce. In the end, she did turn up, along with the Queen, Philip, Charles, Edward and Andrew — the latter being ordered reluctantly to leave a shooting party at the very last minute.

Certainly, there was no love lost between the Princess Royal and Diana. Soon after the 'Dianagate' tape put the monarchy under fire, it was mooted by some Palace aides that an early date for Anne's wedding might alleviate some of the flak. Anne was outraged. 'I won't bale out those two silly girls,' she told a close friend. 'I had to fight my way back after my problems — so can they.' She stubbornly postponed her original date to ensure the Palace public-relations exercise was comprehensively thwarted.

Anne's 'silly girls', of course, were her sisters-in-law. For like Diana, the Duchess of York had played a full part in the making of the Queen's *annus horribilis*. Indeed, it could be said that she started the ball rolling.

On 20 August 1992 Fergie's personal life had suddenly grabbed centre stage. The *Daily Mirror* published an astonishing set of photographs which showed her frolicking by a swimming pool in the south of France with her financial adviser, the thirty-seven-year-old 'toe-sucking' Texan, Johnny Bryan. The pictures of them lying close together sunbathing were bad enough. 'Just how much financial advice can a girl take,' cackled the media critics. What really destroyed the Duchess's already fragile public image, however, was that Princesses Bea and Eugenie could be seen in the same pictures, and in others were seen being carried by Bryan. Intimacy was one thing, but in front of the children? The British public was not impressed.

For a few days it was open season on Fergie. She and Diana were compared as the saint and the sinner and the public were in no doubt that Prince Andrew had made a Big Mistake. Fergie was labelled lazy, greedy, vulgar and promiscuous. She was accused of being a bad mother and of subjecting her servants to torrents of abuse. And when it seemed there could be nothing left to level at her, her critics rounded on yet another of her heinous crimes . . . she was too fat!

It was said that she made her cooks prepare ten different types of pasta in the evenings because she could never make up her mind which she would fancy. Her packed fridge-freezer would contain up to thirty different flavours of ice cream and such luxuries as out-of-season strawberries. It all helped make for an annual food bill of £40,000 – and fuelled the debate on whether the Royal Family was deserving of tax-payer support. Fergie, according to some experts, had cost the British people £3.5 million in the first six years of her marriage. The money had gone on providing her with personal security and on paying the bills for her official functions. Then of course there was the small matter of the Duchess's holidays: fourteen in the nine months up to her south of France liaison.

When the Queen saw the photographs of Fergie and Johnny Bryan, she was both furious and saddened. Were all her children's marriages doomed to failure?

'Those pictures have ruined my holiday,' she confided to staff at Balmoral.

The atmosphere inside the Queen's Scottish retreat, where all the senior royals had congregated as usual, varied between frosty and arctic. On Sunday 23 August, as the family prepared to leave for church, the Duchess could take no more. She and the girls made a very public exit and flew back to London from Aberdeen airport, 'into exile' some observed. It was a nightmare day for the entire Royal Family — for that very weekend the *Sunday Express* published the first hint of the 'Dianagate' tape.

Fergie had already humiliated the Royal Family publicly. But she did not stop there. She was seen dancing with Bryan at her favourite nightclub, Annabel's, and sharing a drink with him during a heart-to-heart chat in the bar of London's Sheraton Park Hotel. In the months which followed she jetted off with him to Thailand, Indonesia, Argentina, Paris and Scotland. Officially, he remained only her 'financial adviser'.

The British security service MI5 had not sat back idly while the Fergie–Bryan relationship blossomed. There were rumours of embarrassing taped conversations between the couple, of trysts at a discreet Chelsea address and of photographs of them hugging and kissing. An MI5 dossier, it was claimed, had gone to the Queen. Spymasters believed she had to know the potential damage to the future of the monarchy.

Amid all these personal and domestic problems the

Queen faced a new dilemma. Had the time at last come for her to pay income tax?

It was no coincidence that this issue surfaced at the height of the 1992 Palace scandals. With senior royals at the centre of so much opprobrium, it was inevitable that sooner or later people would ask: 'What do they actually do for their money?' Sensing the importance of remaining receptive to public opinion, the Queen jumped into paying tax before she was pushed.

It was still not an easy decision. For a start, calculating her personal wealth was nigh on impossible. The Palace put her assets as low as £50 million. Others derided this figure, saying it was closer to £600 million, with an annual income of £40 million. Whatever the truth, the Queen had no shortage of conflicting advice. One of her close friends, the constitutional expert Lord St John of Fawsley, interrupted his August holiday to warn her of the dangers of being railroaded into paying tax. Yet other avowed royalists such as the former Tory MP and historian Sir Robert Rhodes James were greatly in favour. 'Even ardent royalists now feel she should pay tax,' he said. 'It would be a wise move and the public-relations boost would be very useful.'

The likes of Sir Robert won the day. The Queen decided she must make a fair contribution and left the timing of the announcement to the Prime Minister. All she wanted was an end to the murkiest and most miserable year of her reign.

The plain facts were that despite rearing a large and proliferating family, despite raising the best-trained, most caring heir to the throne; despite being blessed with a daughter-in-law who possessed the best-known face on the planet; despite unimaginable wealth, power, prestige and majesty, the very existence of the Queen's dynasty was in doubt. She could not fail to be aware that the Princess of Wales, already indignant with righteous anger at the way she had been marginalised in royal life, was now preparing to cast herself as an avenging angel. The targets of her wrath were Charles and his lover, Camilla Parker Bowles.

12

Exhibit 'B' —The 'Camillagate' Tape

Princess Diana did not have to wait long for the revenge she sought to wreak on her estranged husband. Just as the furore over the 'Dianagate' tapes was beginning to die down, the existence was revealed of another tape-recorded conversation. This time it was not between Diana and one of her paramours; it was between Prince Charles and his lover Camilla Parker Bowles.

The tape surfaced in late 1992 – nearly three years after the conversation took place. It was offered to the *Daily Mirror*, who hinted at its contents in a story published in November under the headline 'Charles's Secret Bedtime Phone Call'. But it was not until January 1993 that the sensational, tawdry, humiliating details of the conversation were revealed when a transcript was published in Australia by the Rupert Murdoch magazine *New Idea*.

The telephone call was reportedly made on the

night of 18 December 1989 or in the early hours of the following morning. This was two weeks *before* the notorious 'Dianagate' phone conversation took place. Charles was speaking to Camilla as he lay in bed at a Cheshire mansion after completing a brief tour of Wales. The Prince was using a mobile phone to speak to Camilla at her family manor house at Corsham, Wiltshire. The eavesdropper is known to have listened for at least fifty minutes, probably until about 2 a.m., during which time the Prince read out one of his speeches. It was, however, only the final part of the conversation that the eavesdropper recorded, when the conversation became extremely personal.

In fact, the tape was spellbinding in its lewdness. The couple whispered intimacies to one another and discussed a friend's house where they planned to meet two days later. It was a day on which Princess Diana and Camilla's husband, Brigadier Andrew Parker Bowles, would be at their respective London homes. It was obviously just one of the many loving telephone conversations that Charles and Camilla had shared over the years to arrange clandestine meetings.

The couple are heard to plot and plan with military precision their regular secret assignations at the country homes of friends, among whom their affair is an open secret. For years Charles and Camilla had attempted to meet at least once a week, usually on Sunday or Monday. Camilla describes it as her 'Start the Week' tonic.

During the six-minute, 1,574-word tape,* Charles says twice that he loves Camilla; she says eleven times that she loves him. He calls her 'darling' seven times; Camilla calls him 'darling' eighteen times. He says he adores her. He bids her farewell around nineteen times.

All of which sounds very lovey-dovey. Many of their comments, however, bordered less on romance than sheer smut. The conversation turns from banality to suggestiveness at an early stage of the recording when Charles talks of cautiously 'feeling one's way along . . .'

Camilla immediately retorts: *'You're awfully good at feeling your way along.'*

Charles: *'Oh stop! I want to feel my way along you, all over you and up and down you and in and out.'*

Camilla: *'Oh!'*

Charles: *'Particularly in and out.'*

Camilla: *'Oh, that's just what I need at the moment.'*

Charles: *'Is it?'*

At this point the person making the recording speaks over the couple to record the date as 18 December (although the tape is now believed to have been recorded in the early hours of the morning of 19 December). From this point onwards, the two-way talk is rarely of anything but allusions to sexual acts. Such as Charles's comment: *'I fill up your tank!'*

Camilla replies: *'Yes you do.'*

* A full transcript is printed in Appendix 2 to this book, p. 421.

Him: *'Then you can cope.'*

Her: *'Then I'm all right.'*

Him: *'What about me? The trouble is I need you several times a week.'*

Her: *'Mmm, so do I. I need you all the week. All the time.'*

Him: *'Oh God. I'll just live inside your trousers or something. It would be much easier.'*

Camilla, beginning to laugh, asks: *'What are you going to turn into, a pair of knickers? Oh, you're going to come back as a pair of knickers!'*

Both of them are now laughing as Charles retorts: *'Or, God forbid, a Tampax. Just my luck!'*

Her: *'You are a complete idiot! Oh, what a wonderful idea.'*

Him: *'My luck to be chucked down a lavatory and go on and on for ever, swirling round on top, never going down . . . until the next one comes through.'*

The supposedly sophisticated couple are now chuckling like pre-pubescent teenagers as they develop their theme on the subject of this British proprietary name for a brand of tampons. Far from coy, Camilla suggests: *'Perhaps you could come back as a box.'*

Charles: *'What sort of box?'*

Her: *'A box of Tampax, so you could just keep going . . . repeating yourself. Oh darling, oh I just want you now.'*

Him: *'Do you?'*

Her: *'Mmm.'*

Him: *'So do I.'*

Her: '*Desperately, desperately, desperately . . .*'

Inflamed with passion, the couple then set about making arrangements for a secret assignation involving the use of friends' homes and the relocation of children and nannies. They also plan a duplicitous alibi to cover their tracks. Camilla even asks him to phone her again in the morning 'before I have these rampaging children around'.

Camilla refers to her husband Andrew only as 'A' and 'he' – as in: 'He won't be here Thursday, pray God.' It is hard to believe that 'A' is counted as one of Charles's closest friends as well as being the man he is cuckolding.

The impression the tape gives is that Brigadier Parker Bowles, who has had close friendships with other women, is unaware of the depth of the relationship his wife has with the heir to the throne. Camilla obviously puts Charles before her husband; it also seems that on this occasion she even puts him before her children.

Yet there is certainly no element of guilt in their words. They are cuckolding her husband and dismissing her children, but their greatest concern is how to arrange a love tryst at Christmas.

The logistics of their affair are immensely complicated. They cannot go to hotels or guest houses to make love. There are few people they can trust with their secret. It is Camilla alone, however, who seems to make all these complicated and devious arrangements; she is still the bossy 'prefect' that she was when a schoolgirl.

There is a more tender side to the conversation, however. The Prince has often been described as selfish. Yet in their conversation Charles seems to be as caring of Camilla as she is for him. When he says that her greatest achievement is to love him, the impression is not of arrogance but of gratitude from one who feels perhaps that he has not always been deserving of love.

It is clear that Camilla's overwhelming confidence and support are exactly what Charles needs. Her assurance gives him strength. She asks to see his next speech and praises him for his last one. She rightly tells him that he is not good at 'thinking positively'. She tells him how clever he is and what a 'good brain' he has.

Finally Camilla persuades Charles to ring off and get some sleep. But not before they have bid each other a score of farewells. As, for instance, Camilla: *'Bye. Press the button.'*

Him: *'Going to press the tit.'*

Her: *'All right, darling. Wish you were pressing mine.'*

Him: *'God, I wish I was, harder and harder.'*

Then: *'Oh darling . . . Night . . . Love you . . . Press the tit . . . Adore you . . . G'night my darling . . . Love you.'* And so on and so on *ad nauseam* before Charles finally hangs up.

*

Once the tape transcript had been published in Australia, there was a rush to get into print worldwide. In Britain, newspapers at first questioned the good taste of publishing the heir's tawdry sex talk, but in the end they broke ranks and some of them printed the full transcript of the six minutes of taped chit-chat. The contents became the topic of conversation in every bar, office and home.

The tape also provided the world with a new kind of guessing game. Who, what and where were the names and places mentioned throughout the conversation? The solution to the riddles should prove the authenticity of the recording . . .

On 18 December 1989, the Prince had been to Wales to visit a youth enterprise centre in Greenfield, Clwyd. He then presented some awards in Mold, visited an old people's home in the town and rounded off his day with a visit to a technology park at Wrexham. It is clear from their chit-chat that Charles and Camilla normally attempt to meet on a Sunday or Monday but that on this occasion they have been forced to go without one another.

The overnight location from which Charles is thought to be making the call is Eaton Hall, in Cheshire, the home of his good friend, the Duke of Westminster, allegedly then the richest man in Britain.

Other names dropped in the conversation are: 'Nancy', thought to be a nickname for the Duchess of Westminster; 'David' may be Baron Willoughby de

Broke, who has a home in Gloucestershire; 'Northmore' may be the Exning, Newmarket, stud farm previously owned by millionaire racehorse trainer Hugh van Cutsem, a friend of both Charles and Diana; 'Bowood' is the stately home of the Earl of Shelburne, Charlie Petty-Fitzmaurice, set in 4,000 acres near the Parker Bowleses' own Wiltshire home; 'Patti's Charlie' is though to be a reference to Patti Palmer-Tomkinson, who was seriously injured in the 1988 royal skiing accident and who lives with her husband Charlie on a farm at the aforementioned 'Dummer' in Hampshire.

During the conversation, Mrs Parker Bowles mentions a place apparently called 'Yaraby' and says she thought of Charles a lot while staying there. There is no such place in the English gazeteers, however. Royal insiders believe she may have been referring to Garowby, the Yorkshire home of Lord Halifax and his wife, the Countess of Halifax – coincidentally also called Camilla and coincidentally also a former escort of Prince Charles. The Countess was the first wife of Rick Parker Bowles, Camilla Parker Bowles's brother-in-law. Garowby is often used by the royals for shooting weekends.

Camilla inquires about a speech on the subject of 'business in the community'. On the following Wednesday he was to launch the Dragon Awards for City Community Involvement at London's Guildhall. He had already been working on a controversial speech which he was to deliver on the Tuesday when presenting the Thomas Cranmer Schools Prize at St James Church in the City of London. In the speech, he would attack the Church of England for the 'banality, cliché and casual obscenity' of the language in the new prayer books. Charles was to add pointedly: 'The word of God is supposed to be a bit over our heads. Elevated is what God is.'

So the proof was there . . . the tape was genuine. But was it doctored?

During the conversation, Mrs Parker Bowles refers to the birthday of her son Tom and says the house will soon be full of 'rampaging children'. The birthday is 'tomorrow'. However, Tom Parker Bowles's birthday is 18 December – the day leading up to the night when the call was allegedly taped . . .

If the 'Camillagate' tape was broadcast after it was initially recorded, it would fit the same pattern as Princess Diana's conversation with James Gilbey.

Suddenly the question on everyone's lips was not 'Is the tape genuine?' but 'Who's behind it?'

The tape, which had at first provided no more than riveting reading, now produced a serious debate about both the moral probity of the heir and the morality of those spying on his private moments. For the timing of the bugging raised the same ominous questions that had arisen at the time the 'Dianagate' tapes were published: Who made the recording and for what purpose was it released? Just who was bugging the future King and Queen of Great Britain?

The 'Camillagate' tape was, just like the 'Dianagate' tape, of high quality. That seemed to rule out casual eavesdroppers. Indeed, experts said there was 'a million-to-one chance' of amateurs taping love conversations involving Charles, Camilla, Diana and Gilbey over a two-week period. They believed that, as with the 'Squidgy' tapes, this too was a rebroadcast of a previously-bugged telephone conversation. And this time, because of the amazing 'coincidence' of two sets of recordings being made only a fortnight apart, newspapers were more ready to accept that the security services must be behind them.

So how did the tape come to be published at a time when it would most damage the Prince of Wales?

It took a good few weeks for the full, tangled tale of the mysterious tape to come to light. It appeared that in the autumn of 1992 a mysterious caller telephoned the *Daily Mirror*'s offices in Manchester, followed by a series of clandestine meetings by *Mirror* reporters and executives with a man who insisted that his identity be kept secret. He said he was no more than a radio amateur.

The *Mirror* editor at the time, Richard Stott, assigned the newspaper's chief reporter and royal expert, Harry Arnold, to investigate the informant and his tape to establish whether both were authentic. The man told Arnold that he had cut into a Cellnet conversation using a simple radio scanner. Arnold found that this particular model, a 'Realistic' from the Tandy chain of electrical stores, cost only a modest £200.

The newspaper also telephoned Mrs Parker Bowles to get her voice on tape; a voice expert quickly confirmed that the recordings were of the same woman. It was also obvious to experts that Prince Charles had been speaking on a mobile phone. At one point, he talks about 'pressing the tit' to turn the handset off. The paper discovered that Charles had been staying in Cheshire on the night of 18 December, not far from the home of their radio man.

The *Mirror* believed their informant. They were sitting on one of the scoops of the century. When Stott was presented with Arnold's findings, however, he decided against publishing. He said later: 'The tape was made by a very ordinary member of the public. I believed it to be genuine. But it seemed at the time that the Prince and Princess were making an attempt to get their marriage working again. I didn't want the *Mirror* to be accused of rocking the boat.'

A month or so later, when it became clear that the marriage was still in total disarray, Stott changed his mind and decided to publish a series of articles based on the evidence of the tape without revealing its contents in full. Only on the fourth day of the series were any of the more alarming details of Charles's infatuation revealed, and even then the words were edited to him telling his beloved: 'I love you, I adore you.' To Stott's astonishment, however, his deadly Fleet Street rival *The Sun* matched the *Mirror*'s stories day by day and fact for fact – seemingly demonstrating that they also had a copy of the damaging recording. The *Mirror* refused to say whether they had a copy of the tape but it was understood that at least four transcripts were made by that newspaper and all were deposited in the editorial safe. Did one go astray, as Fleet Street gossip had it? Just how many copies of the tape were there?

In early January 1993 – eight weeks since the *Mirror* reports and at a time when the transcript had still not been published – a series of phone calls to the British media from a man in Norway provided the first hint that the full 'Camillagate' scandal was at last about to break. At least one meeting was arranged with newsmen at Amsterdam's Schipol Airport when a transcript was made available. The scene was further confused when John Cook, a freelance journalist from northern England who regularly supplied stories to the American magazine *National Enquirer* among other publications, offered to sell copies of the tape to anyone interested for upwards of £10,000. How the tape got to Australia has never been made clear.

What was clear, however, was that someone had gone to an awful lot of trouble to ensure that the slow, ticking time bomb of the 'Camillagate' scandal was eventually triggered to explode. The question 'Who?' was swiftly answered by an angry chorus . . .

Lord Rees Mogg, former editor of *The Times* and one of the most influential figures in the British media, said of the tape: 'There are obvious parallels between the Camilla and the Squidgy recordings. This is way beyond what could have been achieved by amateurs. If it were that easy to do, newspapers would be full of cricketers slagging off team mates over the car phone or one showbiz star gossiping about another. It just doesn't happen like that. No one in the press has the time or resources to conduct something like that.'

He called for a governmental inquiry. 'It should centre on the role of MI5,' he said. 'I find it difficult to believe that they were not in some way involved.'

The head of one major security firm with knowledge of MI5 operations said: 'This was never the work of an amateur. It is just possible that Princess Diana's calls could have been picked up by chance. But now we are being asked to believe that, two weeks earlier, someone coincidentally heard an equally damaging call from Prince Charles. It's just too much to believe.'

Another influential commentator, Sir John Junor, said in the *Mail on Sunday* that the recording of both the 'Dianagate' and 'Camillagate' tapes only a couple of weeks apart was 'just too big a coincidence to be believable'. He went on: 'Somewhere there just has to be a highly skilled operator at work, acting with malice. And isn't it extraordinary that, even though such conversations have done such harm to the monarchy, nothing is apparently being done to discover just how they became public knowledge at all.'

Telecommunications expert John Nelson, who had also analysed the 'Dianagate' tapes, said of the Camilla tape: 'The odds are overwhelmingly stacked against this conversation being recorded by someone with a scanner.'

Royal expert and archivist Margaret Holder said: 'MI5 have long had a file on Prince Charles's private life with Camilla. The reports are made routinely by officers of the Royal Protection Squad and passed up the line. MI5 has to know about the Prince's movements and his friendships for reasons of security. Everybody who gets close to the royals is screened, so they obviously need to know about any clandestine meetings, overnight stays and visits to isolated houses where Charles could be vulnerable to terrorist attack or kidnap.'

Downing Street immediately rebuffed all calls for official inquiries into the workings of their various 'secret squirrels' – but the taint upon MI5 and other government security arms would not go away. As well as MI5, the Special Branch was put in the frame by the British press. Both groups maintain discreet surveillance on the royals' private lives, keeping tabs on their movements for their own safety and in the interests of state security. But would any agency gleaning such sensitive information really pass it on to journalists or members of the public?

The only other organisation in Britain with the expertise and technology to bug telephone calls on such a large and targeted basis is the Government Communications Headquarters at Cheltenham, Gloucestershire, the top-secret listening base which works closely with America's National Security Agency.

Suspicion was directed towards GCHQ by a former member of MI5's sister organisation, MI6, who said the tape had seemingly been enhanced and rebroadcast in the region of known radio hams. The ex-MI6 officer, James Rushbridger, author of *The Intelligence Game* (and who was found hanged at his West Country cottage a year later), added: 'The tape is most likely the work of an employee of GCHQ where many of the staff were upset when they lost the right to trade-union membership. By pressing a button at GCHQ, a worker can listen to Boris Yeltsin on his car phone. Press another button and it's Prince Charles. It's as simple as that.'

Denials of government involvement were categoric from all quarters. But few believed them – and for the first time Members of Parliament did not believe them either. They called for a full investigation into the snooping. Unsurprisingly, the government steadfastly refused. The Home Secretary, Kenneth Clarke, dismissed such suspicions as being 'extremely silly'. However, his snooty stance was at odds with security chiefs who swiftly launched their own individual investigations. Every officer who could possibly have been involved in bugging royal calls was rigorously interviewed. An extremely senior source stated: 'The possibility of a rogue influence within the service cannot be discounted until the truth is known. MI5 has been looking at this for some time.'

The investigations may have provoked a great deal of hot air among the pressmen and politicians but it also produced a lot of hot collars among the royals and their courtiers. Both the Prince and Princess of Wales had been individually supplied with transcripts of the tape by friends to forewarn the couple about the looming crisis shortly before its publication. According to Charles's biographer, Penny Junor, the reaction of the Prince was that he was 'shattered – dying inside'. Of Diana, she said: 'Mentally, she is very fragile. She is feeling terribly down, unloved and alone.'

The Princess herself let it be known that she was 'sickened and appalled' by the language on the tape. What most infuriated Diana was that it had taken so long for public confirmation of the existence of Charles's 'other woman'. Diana's pride was also injured by the knowledge of the passion which her husband could display to another woman while being icily cold towards his own wife. She was also reported to feel betrayed by people she had considered her friends. Even she had not been fully aware of the extent of unquestioning loyalty which a tight circle of supporters had shown her husband in keeping his long-term romance under wraps.

Diana's copy of the transcript was given her by a friend who was supplied with it by Michael O'Mara, publisher of Andrew Morton's book *Diana, Her True Story*. Mr O'Mara said: 'I understand that the Princess found it smutty, lewd, coarse and unpleasant. Although she knew about the relationship, it still came as a terrible body blow to see the whole thing written down in black and white. Whatever is said, Prince Charles is still her husband and the father of her children. She had to choke back the tears when she read the transcript.'

One of her inner circle revealed: 'She cannot believe how he talks to Camilla. If she ever had any doubt about how deep the relationship had gone, those doubts no longer remain. The most upsetting aspect for the Princess was reading the succession of names mentioned on the tape. They were people she thought were friends of both of them. Now she has learned that they were all lying to her. It has crushed her.'

As the Princess relayed her thoughts through friends to eagerly scribbling newsmen, the 'other woman' in the scandals, Mrs Parker Bowles herself, disappeared from her Wiltshire home and went into hiding – no doubt tipped off about the looming crisis by her royal lover. Her cuckolded husband, Brigadier Parker Bowles, remained loyally on duty at Aldershot.

Prince Charles was already in hiding – safe from public humiliation in the wilds of Scotland. He had already called an emergency summit to attempt to quantify the damage caused by the 'Camillagate' crisis, summoning an inner circle of his closest friends to join him at Balmoral and help him decide how badly his reputation had been tarnished. Charles asked his trusted cousin Lord Romsey and wife Penny, plus skiing friends Patti and Charlie Palmer-Tomkinson (who were mentioned in the tape itself) to join him in a weekend council of war at Birkhall, the Queen Mother's private home on the Balmoral estate. Their advice may well have been summed up by another of Charles's chums who said off the record: 'The tape was a sword of Damocles hanging over him. The worst is now over. Things can only get better.'

His optimism might have seemed short-lived, however, when the Charles 'summit' learned the reaction of the hierarchy of the Church of England, which could one day have the Prince as its head as 'Defender of the Faith'. The criticism was launched by Britain's second most senior churchman, the Archbishop of York Dr John Habgood, who called for a nationwide debate on whether the Church and the monarchy should split after 460 years. Dr Habgood said on BBC television: 'Looking back over history, the nation has been extraordinarily tolerant of all sorts of behaviour by its monarchs. But tolerance has its limits. I would not want to say myself where those limits lie.' The Archdeacon of York, the Venerable George Austin, declared: 'The Queen could die tomorrow, which would raise all sorts of problems. It would make it very difficult if Charles wanted to divorce and remarry. Those in positions of power and responsibility in Church, state or monarchy have a duty to conform to the standards they are meant to uphold.'

Another unforeseen reaction came from members of the public who wrote to the newspapers' own watchdog body, the Press Complaints Commission, to seek a formal investigation of the tape and the admonishment of papers which published the transcript on the grounds of 'unwarranted intrusion'. The PCC received about a dozen complaints and was bound to act on them in some way. However, Buckingham Palace told the commission that Charles did not wish to become involved in an official inquiry. Camilla confirmed this, thus removing what would have been another juicy slab of copy in every British newspaper as they gleefully reported on their own 'misdemeanours'!

The 'Camillagate' scandal was the most humiliating blow so far in the sorry saga of the heir's marriage. What the crisis did achieve, however, was a balance to the history of cheating and lying by both sides within the royal marriage. If the 'Squidgy' tapes revealed Diana as a bored, vain and sometimes vacant wife seeking male companionship on the side, the Camilla tape equally exposed Charles as a seeker of telephone sex with a rather smutty turn of schoolboy language. The boot was now on the other foot. It was Diana who was beginning to regain the moral ground. She at last had the 'ammunition' to forge a deal in what now looked like being the messiest divorce and custody case of the century.

Diana now felt totally vindicated in everything she had claimed about the sick and sorry nature of the family into which she had married. She realised that she might never be crowned Queen ... but equally her husband had been so compromised that she began to believe that he might never be crowned King.

In private and among her closest friends, the Princess was jubilant about the public opprobrium being heaped upon Charles. For if the truth be known, Diana had long decided that it mattered little whether or not she became Queen. More important to her was her determination that the husband she hated should never be King. It was her eldest son William whom she desperately wanted to be crowned the next British monarch. And at this ill-fated moment in history, it now looked as if she would get her way.

The fight was now on between Charles and Diana, not just for the hearts and minds of the nation, but for the hearts and minds of their own children: the heirs William and Harry.

13

The Other Woman

Looking her age, a lack of poise and style giving her a frumpy, old-fashioned appearance and with a face that could by no means be described as attractive, she has become one of the twentieth century's most controversial scarlet women.

Incredibly, throughout years of open vilification and accusation, Camilla Parker Bowles has publicly never once spoken a word or acted in such a way that would betray the dark secrets she holds.

For this is the woman who longs to be married to the heir to the throne, who yearns to be Queen of England. This is also the woman who humiliated 'Darling Diana', the beautiful, perfect royal wife before her adoring world public, who was always in the shadows-waiting, waiting to reclaim the man she loved then lost. But most important of all, this is the woman who sabotaged a royal marriage – and willingly and knowingly changed the course of British royal history.

Camilla Parker Bowles didn't always have the looks or the determination that earned her Princess Diana's nickname of 'The Rottweiler'. Born Camilla Shand on 17 July 1948 at King's College Hospital, London, she grew into first a cute, snub-nosed tot, then a sophisticated debutante who was always destined to marry well. Her background had her well groomed for just this future.

Her father, Major Bruce Shand, was a low-profile British officer who none the less had twice won the MC and who had been a prisoner of war. Her mother Rosalind came from the Cubitt building family. There was the Shands' London home and there was the family estate in Plumpton, Sussex, venue for Conservative Party fetes and haven for the hunting and shooting set. Camilla went to school first at Dumbrells, a stark place for little girls and boys three miles from her country home, and then, when she was ten, to Queen's Gate School in Kensington. The London school was a delight for Camilla, relieved to be away from the strict, Victorian regime of Dumbrells. Here at last, the hockey-playing, athletic young girl found the freedom to grow up and into the fun circle of society. It was also accepted that here was the springboard to launch young ladies into the company of suitable husbands. The school was proud of its reputation for providing wives for 'half the Foreign Office'.

Like many of her breed, Camilla did not shine academically. She did not sit any A-level exams at school. But unlike many of her friends, neither was Camilla a rebel. She never dressed outrageously, preferring sensible clothes. Some, rather cruelly, have said that Camilla was born wearing twinset and pearls. One old girl, Lynn Ripley, recalls: 'She has not even changed her hairstyle. She seems to be identical now to then.' Lynn tactfully described the young Camilla as 'the coolest girl in the school'.

Others do not have such kind memories. 'I'm not surprised she's ended up doing what she has done,' says one, referring to Camilla's involvement with Prince Charles. 'She was a bully, a horrible girl. I was terrified of her. She made my life hell.'

Camilla left Queen's Gate in 1964. Now the search for a suitably placed, suitably rich husband began in earnest. In true debutante tradition, she went straight to finishing school in Switzerland and Paris to learn the art of table-laying, flower-arranging, a smattering of French and all the little niceties that make up the perfect society hostess.

The husband-bagging season began six months later in March 1965. Camilla was seventeen when she gave her very first cocktail party in Knightsbridge. Never a serious competitor to the lovely young things that flitted from party to party in their figure-hugging evening dresses, Camilla was selective about which gatherings she attended. Hence, while fellow, blonde social butterflies were photographed regularly for the glossy magazines and diary columns, Camilla was socialising quietly with close friends. No one could have guessed that forty or so years later Camilla Shand would be relentlessly hounded by newspaper photographers.

Quietly, at eighteen, Camilla discovered sex. Old Etonian Kevin Burke was her first serious boyfriend. He remembers her as 'sexy and attractive, never tongue-tied or shy'. Kevin adds that it was 'real young love'. It was Camilla who called a halt to their relationship.

Camilla was enjoying a bachelor-girl life in the debutantes' haunt of Chelsea. Like others in her circle, she had found stopgap work as a secretary until husband material came along. She lived in Chelsea's Ebury Street, in a two-bedroom, ground-floor flat shared with Virginia Carrington, daughter of Lord Carrington, Foreign Secretary of Prime Minister Margaret Thatcher. Camilla's boyfriends included Robert Hambro of the merchant banking family. It was Robert who took her to the party where she first met Andrew Parker Bowles.

Parker Bowles was a dashing young officer who was well known on the debutante dating scene. He was a popular and glamorous figure from a rich, land-owning Berkshire family. It was a family with influence – and with royal connections. His father Derek, a Jockey Club steward, was one of the Queen Mother's closest friends. As was to be proved many years later, loyalty to the Crown was already in the Parker Bowles blood.

Brought up at Donnington Castle House, near Newbury, Berkshire, Andrew, a staunch Roman Catholic, was educated by Benedictine monks at a leading public school, Ampleforth, in Yorkshire. He then went on to Sandhurst and was commissioned into his father's regiment, the Royal Horse Guards ('The Blues'), and became their adjutant after they merged with the First Royal Dragoons to become the First Blues and Royals.

Andrew was horse-mad. He almost killed himself in 1967 when he suffered a fall at Ascot, splintering his ribs and puncturing a lung. Two five-inch metal rods were inserted in his spine and have never been removed. The accident did not deter him from racing. In 1969 he completed the gruelling Grand National at Aintree on his own horse, The Fossa.

Andrew Parker Bowles and Camilla Shand had first met in 1966. They were attracted straight away and started seeing each other on a regular basis. Nevertheless, neither gave up dating other people. He still escorted girlfriends such as Lady Caroline Percy, eldest daughter of the tenth Duke of Northumberland, to dinners and parties. He pursued one of her friends, Lady Amabel Lindsay, as well as Princess Anne, then aged twenty, with whom he shared a passionate love of horses. There was no possibility of marriage, however, because he was a Roman Catholic.

Friends have told a story (possibly dating from an even later stage of their relationship) about an occasion on which Camilla let herself into Andrew's west London bachelor apartment – to find Andrew with a blonde.

Andrew and Camilla were often separated by his various postings – and when he was away, life continued much as before for the debby Miss Shand. It was only after Parker Bowles's own younger brother Simon had himself dated Camilla that Andrew seemed to wake up to the fact that Camilla was suitable marriage material. Brother Simon acted as matchmaker and brought Andrew and Camilla together again. This time, the twenty-seven-year-old officer seemed totally smitten.

While their friends saw marriage as an obvious outcome for the couple, Camilla continued to keep in touch with her old flames. She was nevertheless saddened when Parker Bowles was posted to Hobart Barracks, Detmold, near Hanover in Germany, in 1969. It was Parker Bowles's absence that encouraged Camilla to socialise as a single woman once more. And it was during this same absence that she met Prince Charles for the very first time.

That meeting between the Prince and the commoner, at a polo match at Windsor in 1971, was to set the scene for the Royal Family's most sensational chain of events since the abdication. He was heir to the throne. She was a woman with a sexual past. And while the

Palace old guard were prepared sniffily to turn a blind eye to what they saw as just another romance for the Prince, it would never give its blessing to marriage. Camilla and Charles may have been two young people destined to fall in love but they were also destined for a love forever cursed. They could never be man and wife. Camilla was to go down in history as yet another infamous royal mistress.

Camilla and Charles were both twenty-three when they met. He was immediately besotted. Shy and awkward, the young Prince had difficulty relating to women but the bubbly Camilla made him feel attractive and entertaining. She was at ease with him. They laughed easily together. Charles could sense her sexual presence. She made him feel manly. Some weeks later, the couple went to the London nightclub Annabel's together . . . and that night, their love affair began.

A friend who knew both Charles and Camilla said: 'From the moment they met, it was clear that there was something special between them. Charles was fresh from Cambridge University and very wet behind the ears. She was vivacious, bubbly, charming and altogether far more worldly than him. Yet they could converse with one another in a way that was unique. She addressed the heir to the throne with a frankness that no one else dared to do. They were simply very good friends. It was also clear to some of us that they were also having a great time in bed together.'

Charles fell desperately and hopelessly in love. But

while he was naïvely mapping out a future for them together, Camilla was worldly-wise enough to feel uneasy. She loved Charles with a passion. She also knew she could never be his wife. Charles talked of marriage. He even proposed marriage to her at his uncle Lord Louis Mountbatten's Broadlands estate in 1972.

Mountbatten's former valet John Barratt said: 'Camilla had no desire to be his Queen. She was from an aristocratic background herself; she knew precisely what being his wife would mean. Camilla didn't want that life for herself. She preferred to stay out of the public spotlight.'

As another friend recalls: 'The secret of Camilla is that she loves Charles the man. She did not fall in love with the title, the prestige, the position or the job. That was Diana's mistake, not hers.'

When Camilla heard Charles's stumbling attempt at a proposal on a wintry day in the sanctuary of Broadlands, she realised that things were getting out of hand. She countered the Prince's ardour by making a joke about their relationship – reminding her lover that she was the great-granddaughter of Mrs George Keppel, mistress of Edward VII.

It was an unhappy and confused Charles who set out to sea with the Royal Navy in 1973. The announcement just a few weeks later that Camilla was to marry Andrew Parker Bowles left him devastated. Despite desperate calls to Camilla over the next few months,

Charles could not win her back. Within six months, Camilla became Mrs Parker Bowles. The bridegroom was by then a major and the wedding took place at the Guards Chapel. The Queen Mother, Princess Anne and Princess Margaret attended the reception. Charles sent a telegram. His lover may have married someone else but Camilla would still always be his.

Thus began a bizarre state of affairs. Andrew and his bride made their home at Bolehyde Manor near Chippenham, Wiltshire. From there, Camilla and Charles communicated constantly. He was godfather to the first Parker Bowles child, Thomas Henry Charles, born in December 1974. Four years later, Camilla gave birth to a daughter, Laura. Throughout, Camilla remained Charles's confidante, watching from the wings as he took up with one girlfriend after another, advising him on matters of the heart and listening intently as he talked of his hopes and plans and preparation towards one day being King.

Charles's schedules and Camilla's determination to make her marriage work meant they met far less than Charles would have liked. But there were long spells when Major Parker Bowles was absent on duty. In the Army, Andrew was making a name for himself as a cool customer with his men, but also as a cool leader under fire. He had, after all, commanded an armoured squadron in Londonderry, Northern Ireland, at the height of the IRA troubles.

Things might have been hot for Parker Bowles, but

the relationship between his wife and Prince Charles was also hotting up again. Camilla made elaborate plans – with an almost military precision that her husband would have admired – to create special times when she and Charles would be reunited for more than just a few hours. Camilla was a frequent guest at Birkhall, a secluded house on the Balmoral estate. When apart, there were almost daily telephone calls between the two. It was rare that Charles would make a decision on anything, no matter how trivial, without first consulting Mrs Parker Bowles.

Fate sometimes drew Charles and Camilla together publicly. In 1987 Parker Bowles was promoted to colonel and took up another post: that of Silver Stick in waiting to the Queen. This kept him at Buckingham Palace during state visits, his duty being to wait on the monarch holding a silver-topped walking stick. Then in 1979 Parker Bowles became an aide to Lord Soames, who was appointed the last Governor-General of Rhodesia (later Zimbabwe). By coincidence, Prince Charles made a visit to Rhodesia and was greeted by Camilla and her husband.

Camilla was Charles's desperately-needed soul mate that same year when the IRA blew up his beloved Uncle Dickie, Lord Louis Mountbatten. He turned to her when the grief was too much to bear. He knew that while his father would see tears as a sign of weakness, with Camilla he could sob his heart out while she held him in her arms. The loss of his uncle meant Charles had only one person left in the world whom he could trust: the married Camilla Parker Bowles. A broken Charles even begged Camilla to leave her husband.

Charles was now within months of meeting the woman whom fate — and royal protocol — would decree as his wife. In fact, marriage to the shy, plump-cheeked Lady Diana Spencer was the last thing on Charles's mind when they first met. But there was pressure from the British public, anxiously holding their breath for their future King to find himself a wife. There was pressure, too, from Charles's parents, especially Prince Philip. And then there was Camilla who, fearing that because of her Charles would never fulfil his royal obligations to marry, actively encouraged the relationship with Diana towards a fairytale wedding. Camilla, and indeed her husband, became an established part of Charles's wooing of Diana. It seemed the couple were always present at gatherings of Charles's closest friends. They were later always on the guest list for more formal functions when Charles wanted to show off his young bride.

If Diana sensed the obvious intimacy between Charles and Camilla, she chose to ignore it. In the early days, she was too head-over-heels in love with her Prince to let even the slightest doubts mar her happiness. And Charles acted very much the attentive suitor. It would have devastated Diana to realise just to what extent her relationship with Charles was discussed between the Prince and Camilla in private hours together. Looking back, Diana must often wonder how she could have missed those looks between them, those secret smiles, and often just a subtle touch. Camilla even took Diana in hand to groom her as a suitable wife for the heir to the throne. When Diana made her first public appearance at Ludlow racecourse in 1980, Camilla was by her side. It was to Camilla that Diana turned for 'older sister' advice. Every word was relayed back to Charles with relish.

Camilla secretly enjoyed watching the romance with Charles and Diana develop. She felt she was controlling it. Camilla knew before anyone else that Charles was going to propose to Diana. In fact, Camilla and Charles had decided on the proposal together as they sat, he with his head resting on her shoulder.

'Well, we've decided what you should do,' joked Camilla. 'Now perhaps you ought to fill the Queen in on it. We're buggered if our plans don't meet her approval!'

Charles left Camilla's side just hours before his engagement to Diana was officially announced on 24 February 1981. Two weeks later, Camilla invited Diana to have lunch with her and asked her if she would be going hunting with Charles. Diana innocently told her no; a riding accident as a child had put her off horses. Fate was providing her with the perfect chance to meet Charles without Diana being around.

It was only as Diana's wedding date drew nearer

that she realised the true extent of Camilla's hold over Charles. The phone would ring as she sat with her fiancé in his private quarters discussing the marriage. It was almost invariably Camilla on the line. The look on Charles's face as he spoke to this 'other woman' worried his young wife. Diana's worst fears were confirmed when she heard Charles saying down the phone: 'No matter what happens, I will always love you.'

Diana was increasingly made to feel she was an outsider, not only during these calls but now increasingly in Camilla's presence, too. It was as if Camilla had successfully completed the mission to find Charles a suitable marriage mate but now no longer wanted much to do with the girl she called 'The Mouse'.

Camilla and Andrew Parker Bowles were guests at Charles and Diana's wedding in July 1981. Before the event took place, Camilla had changed the game rules. She told Charles that his marriage meant sex between them had to stop. That although she would always be there for him, they had to cease being lovers. It was almost as if she was testing Charles to see just how committed he was to a marriage that had in all essence been arranged for him. The confused heir reluctantly agreed to Camilla's love-ban.

She smiled as she slipped a small package into his hand. 'My wedding present, darling,' she said. The parcel contained cufflinks. But Camilla's real wedding present was what followed. Their final, bitter-sweet, emotional, sexual parting ... just two days before Charles walked down the aisle with Diana.

Diana knew almost immediately that she had made a disastrous mistake. On honeymoon, she still suffered the eating disorder, causing her to make herself sick after meals, which had worsened soon after her engagement to Charles. All was not well aboard their floating honeymoon 'hotel', the royal yacht *Britannia*. Diana knew her husband's thoughts were elsewhere. The Princess bride was present when, looking through his diary, Charles accidentally let two photographs of Camilla fall from the pages.

Camilla could not resist mischievous phone calls to Charles on his honeymoon; neither could Charles resist calling Camilla. It was the couple's pleasure of shared intimacies over the phone which was to be the subject of the scandalous so-called 'Camillagate' tapes in future years. It was also what helped bring about the end of Charles and Diana's marriage. For Diana still trembles at the memory of the first time she ever pressed the redial button on Charles's private phone. It was Camilla's voice that answered. It was always, it seemed after that, Camilla's voice that answered.

Publicly, Charles and Diana enjoyed the fairytale marriage that stirred the hearts of their subjects. Privately, both knew their relationship was built on shaky ground. That glorious wedding was the happiest moment they were to know. For the first year, both tried hard to feel as newlyweds should. And appearing among the crowds on foreign tours, official visits, galas and walkabouts, Diana glowed. Seen out by their adoring public, the royal couple acted their roles perfectly. A discreet touch or comforting glance from Charles was all the confirmation needed that the heir to the throne and his future Queen were blissfully happy together. But behind closed doors, the rows had begun in earnest.

Quite simply, Diana could not tolerate the constant presence of Camilla. No matter how much she tried, Diana was unable to extricate her husband from the hold Mrs Parker Bowles had on him. What cut her even more deeply was the realisation that Charles needed Camilla and still desperately desired her.

Just over a year after their wedding, Charles confessed to Diana in a raging argument at Highgrove that he remained close to Camilla. He stormed that he had 'no intention of giving her up – ever!' (Although this was nothing compared to the worldwide humiliation Diana was to suffer much later when Charles revealed in his authorised biography that, when he married, he had not loved Diana.)

Diana did what the nation expected of her. She gave birth to a son, Prince William, in 1982. Camilla was one of the first to hear the news; Charles telephoned her personally immediately after the birth. However, the arrival of a child did little to reconcile the parents as true man and wife. The behind-the-scenes clashes continued. Sometimes they were about

Diana's reluctance to conform to royal rules. Most of the time they were about the woman described as a cancer in the Waleses' marriage: Camilla.

Indeed, an infamous, public upset later that year was said to be down to the Princess's love rival. Diana was absent from her husband's side at the Remembrance Day Service at London's Albert Hall. An embarrassed Charles explained his wife's non-appearance by saying she was ill. But five minutes later Diana turned up. In fact, before setting off for the service, the royal couple had started to argue about Diana's mood swings. It had developed into a monster row about Charles's clandestine meetings with Camilla.

It was through mutual friends to whom Diana was confiding her marital troubles that the sad Princess heard that all was not well with the Parker Bowleses' marriage. Andrew, it was rumoured, was enjoying the company of other women. There had been an extra-marital relationship six years after the Parker Bowles wedding. The involvement was when Andrew had served as ADC to Lord Soames. As Commanding Officer of the Household Cavalry, based at Hyde Park barracks in Knightsbridge, Andrew spent much of his time in London while Camilla stayed in the country. Parker Bowles may, in later years, have been described as a man willing to 'lay down his wife for his country', but he was hardly the faithful, wronged husband many believed him to be.

Charles and Camilla, both now desperately insecure

in their marriages, found it harder not to be drawn together sexually. The need to be with each other whenever possible was growing. Diana meanwhile was determined to make something of her role as Princess of Wales. She knew that keeping a high profile as patron of many charities and being seen as a supportive wife was important in her bid to retain public loyalty. It was more through duty than disposition that she still slept with Charles. But Camilla was again one of the first to be told when Diana gave birth to her second son, Prince Harry, in September 1984.

As Diana tried to come to terms with 'baby blues' and the pressures of both her unhappy marriage and royal bureaucracy, Charles increasingly found his young wife intolerable to be around. Another year was to pass, however, before in 1986 he resumed a physical relationship with Camilla. Charles's and Diana's intimate side of marriage was now over. The husband-and-wife togetherness was now a charade. And as Camilla once again hungrily devoured Charles both physically and mentally, it became increasingly difficult to keep their affair secret. Camilla and Charles relied on their closest friends to keep silent, to cover their tracks — and often to provide the opportunities and venues for the lovers' meetings.

'Safe houses' were carefully selected. These included Stourpaine House, home of Camilla's married sister, Annabel. The secluded home just outside Blandford Forum, Dorset, was an ideal location for undisturbed, illicit rendezvous. Other friends provided secret meeting places. Charles's close friend Charles Palmer-Tomkinson and his wife Patti made Dummer Grange, in Hampshire, available. The Duchess of Devonshire extended an open invitation to Chatsworth, her seventeenth-century mansion in Derbyshire. Two other hideaways were to become particularly significant in Camilla and Charles's illicit affair: Eaton Lodge on the Duke of Westminster's 13,000-acre Cheshire estate, from where Charles made the infamous 'Camillagate' phone call to his mistress, and Garrowby Hall, Pocklington, the Yorkshire home of the Earl of Halifax. Garrowby Hall was one of the meeting places mentioned on the 'Camillagate' phone call.

In 1990 Camilla and her husband moved to a 500-acre estate, Middlewick House, at Corsham, Wiltshire. The move meant Camilla was now just a short drive away from Charles and Diana's Highgrove home

Camilla's role in Charles's life became increasingly close and more and more open; she was taking over from Diana as Charles's social escort. Camilla at one point firmly ensconced herself as the lady of the house at Highgrove, even greeting weekend guests. It was Camilla who took Diana's place at the Highgrove dinner table, enchanting diners with a conversational mix of intellectual debate and earthy humour. By virtue of the close friends invited to these gatherings, it was rare that Charles felt he had to explain the Princess's absence. But if the need arose, he would matter-of-factly state that Diana was in London fulfilling her own social commitments.

Diana knew Camilla was taking over her home — and successfully taking over her husband. But she was still sickened on one occasion when she returned to Highgrove to discover obvious evidence that Camilla and Charles had slept together. It was usually senior valet Ken Stronach's job to ensure the Prince's bedroom gave no clues to Camilla's recent presence. Such subterfuge did not always work, however. Ken Stronach's former wife Brenda recalls: 'One night there was a hell of a panic. The Princess called Highgrove to speak to her husband after midnight. She was told he was in bed and couldn't be disturbed. But she obviously suspected something because she called him on his mobile phone and he answered it while being driven back from Mrs Parker Bowles's home.'

The unworkable marriage of Charles and Diana was now attracting serious attention from the media. Newspaper reports of their public appearances and royal tours focused on the hostile atmosphere between them, of Diana's sullen looks and the telling distance they kept apart. There were separate holidays. There were the times they arrived separately to visit their sons at school. Speculation was rife about where Charles went and what he did out of 'official' hours.

What was not speculation, however, was what happened when Charles broke his arm in a polo accident in 1990. Although Diana dutifully visited her husband in hospital, it was Camilla Parker Bowles who nursed Charles at Highgrove and Balmoral. And it was Camilla who accompanied him on a painting trip to Florence a year later. Knowledge of the explosive relationship between Camilla and Charles was no longer confined to an inner sanctum of royal friends. It was now public knowledge.

But confirmation was to come in a particularly sordid, sensational way when transcripts of the 'Camillagate' telephone conversation were published, littered with late-night murmurings and explicit, sexual declarations.

When challenged, Camilla Parker Bowles kept her lips sealed. She made one public appearance shortly after publication of the transcripts and, as always, strode purposefully through the crowds, giving no indication of her thoughts. Suggestions that Charles had severed all links with his mistress were fed to a disbelieving public. Everyone now knew that Camilla was the Prince's 'unfinished business'.

The official separation of Charles and Diana was announced in December 1992 by Prime Minister John Major. The world sat back and waited to see where — and to whom — this separation would lead. There was no doubt that Camilla was still the clandestine love of Charles's life.

There was another separation at about this time — one that was not announced in a blaze of publicity. It was the secret separation of Andrew and Camilla Parker Bowles. They had long been living a lie.

They no longer slept together. Camilla had her Prince; Andrew had his ladyfriends. Yet they still maintained the charade of a happy family in order to protect their children. Often photographed strolling with Camilla in the grounds of their home, Andrew had always stood firmly by his wife. When cornered by the press he would deny any impropriety by his future sovereign, Charles. In 1992 when stories about Charles and Camilla were first published, he insisted: 'No, it's not true. How many times do I have to spell it out? It's pure fiction.'

Fiction, however, it certainly was not. Parker Bowles and his wife were living a total lie. He lived largely in London, seeing his own ladyfriends (as we shall later learn), while Camilla became a virtual recluse at their Wiltshire home. There were rare, tantalising occasions when she was photographed with her husband at Middlewick House — her appearance usually unkempt, her demeanour dowdy as the telephoto camera lenses captured her momentarily fleeting figure.

Comparisons between Camilla, the plain, middle-aged unfaithful wife, and Diana, the beautiful, tormented Princess, were obvious. And perhaps cruel. Only Charles fully understood the magnetism of a woman who for over twenty years has been his mentor and lover.

The notion that Camilla would shape the course of royal history by being as inseparable from Charles as Wallis Simpson was from Edward VIII may once have sounded too sensational to consider. But the woman who had already played a part in smashing the marriage of England's future King and Queen now had little to lose in making her romantic intentions clear. For Charles, having sullied his path to the throne, now had only his loyal mistress to turn to.

Either waiting in the shadows – or waiting to take what she felt was her rightful place in his life.

14

The Phoney War

With the Waleses' sham of a marriage at last exposed publicly, Diana felt free to cast off the chains of the last seven unhappy years. She was determined to rediscover something of the girl-about-town lifestyle which she had relished all too briefly before her engagement. It was hardly an attempt to recapture her youth – the trauma of the previous twelve months had left her too wary and careworn for that – but she could at least prove herself capable of surviving without the suffocating influence of Buckingham Palace.

Her needs were threefold. First to get out socially with trusted women of her own age and outlook. Secondly to canvass an unofficial 'star chamber' of older female friends who could lend her wisdom and experience in plotting tactics for an inevitable pre-divorce phoney war with the Palace. And finally to be escorted to private functions by men. They had to be 'safe' men, usually married, often older, invariably charming and unwaveringly discreet. It helped if they also had understanding wives who recognised there was nothing sinister in the Princess's enjoyment of male company.

Diana's 'walkers', as they were known, could fulfil one other useful function. If she were to meet someone to whom she was strongly attracted, and if she did try to meet that person regularly, the relationship would excite less interest if it could be suggested the consort was merely one among many. Charles had, after all, already accepted that she would eventually remarry following divorce. She saw no harm in enjoying the feeling of being courted again. Flirting had always come naturally to her!

So who were the 'walkers' and how had they earned their privileged position?

Easily leading the field was Old Etonian Oliver Hoare, unusually among the 'walkers' also a close friend of Prince Charles. More about this seemingly innocent friendship later. On one occasion, photographed with Diana returning in her car to Kensington Palace, he rang the Prince to assure him that nothing untoward had taken place. He had merely been escorting the Princess and two of her close girlfriends on a dinner date. Throughout 1993 and 1994 Hoare, described as a happily married man, remained a regular dinner guest at Kensington Palace.

Another married man and Old Etonian favourite was businessman Dr James Colthurst, a former radiologist. He had known Diana since she was a fresh-faced teenager on the Swiss ski slopes and called on her regularly during her brief bachelor-girl days in London. As her marriage fell apart he was a regular lunch guest at Kensington Palace, though he shunned the prospect of meeting at fashionable restaurants or clubs.

Among the Princess's highly eligible bachelor consorts at this time was William van Straubenzee, forty-one. He had been a platonic friend for almost two decades and one she regarded as totally trustworthy. She would meet the City investment manager, nicknamed Willie or Straubs, for tennis on Saturdays, lunches at San Lorenzo, quiet dinner parties and the odd country weekend.

Another tennis partner was bachelor Simon Slater, a successful restaurateur in his forties whom Diana would meet on the frequent occasions he would try to chat up her friend Kate Menzies. 'Slates', as he was known, would occasionally cook for her – but only when Kate was also present.

There were older consorts too. Like her long-time family friend Roger Bramble, a sixty-two-year-old Westminster city councillor and former Lord Mayor of London. Like fifty-four-year-old Christopher Balfour, the sporting, bridge-playing intellectual who was a big name in the City. Like Lord Rothschild, fifty-seven, of Rothschilds merchant bank, who introduced her to heavyweight international statesmen such as Henry Kissinger. And there were much-publicised lunch dates with TV personality and newspaper columnist Clive James, fifty-four.

Father-figures were all very well. But if Diana were to re-enter the London scene fully, she would need some youthful exuberance around her. Among Diana's young female friends — BFs (best friends) in Sloane-speak — a handful of women stood out. Foremost among these was Kate Menzies, whose Scottish father John was the self-made millionaire behind the Menzies chain of newsagents. Described by her friends as possessing 'the best address book in town', she took it upon herself to oil Diana's rusty social life. Reliable young men and discreet women would get a phone call from the thirty-three-year-old blonde telling them to turn up at some fashionable West End restaurant such as Pontevecchio. 'You know the score,' Kate would say, 'and no gatecrashers please.' Those who received such a call would refer to it wryly as 'The Summons'.

It was Kate who in January 1993 persuaded Diana to join her for a night out at the movies. Diana paid for the seats; Kate paid for the popcorn. Then they settled back in the Fulham Road cinema to watch Whitney Houston and Kevin Costner in *The Bodyguard*.

The two other members of the party that night were Julia Samuel and Catherine Soames. Julia, thirty-three-year-old daughter of James Guinness CBE, had a reputation for being among the liveliest members of the Princess's close circle. Because she was also a Kensington resident, it was easy for Diana and her to

meet regularly. Catherine, the thirty-five-year-old heiress to Hong Kong-based conglomerate Jardine Math-
eson, was a long-time friend. It was she who had
accompanied the Princess with Wills and Harry on
their Caribbean holiday a few weeks earlier. The two
women were also regularly seen playing tennis together at the west London Vanderbilt Club.

As it happened, neither Julia nor Catherine was a
stranger to Charles. Julia's younger sister Sabrina was
one of his old flames, while Catherine's ex-husband,
Tory MP Nicholas Soames, had been Charles's equerry
back in the early seventies. Charles had even been best
man at the Soameses' wedding.

The success of the Fulham Road jaunt was followed
on 11 February by another Kate Menzies-inspired
evening. It was almost as though Diana was trying to
spell out to the world that she was now a new
woman, with her own agenda and her own lifestyle.
This time the venue was the Royal Opera House,
Covent Garden, to see a performance of Stravinsky's
Firebird. The two women and another mutual friend,
Lulu Blacker, later left in a grey minibus. Judging by
Diana's relaxed smile, there would be a few more of
these girls' nights out.

One friend of Kate's observed: 'Katie is gloriously
single. She is not the sort of friend who allows you to
wallow in self-pity. What she does is give you a huge
kick up the pants. I know for a fact that Diana is
immensely grateful to Katie for doing that.'

So much for the younger set and their efforts to rehabilitate Diana on the London social scene. What role had her older female friends mapped out for themselves? One of these women in particular, Lucia Flecha de Lima, was soon taking the lead as both mother-figure and adviser.

Lucia, the fifty-two-year-old wife of Brazil's UK ambassador Paola Tarso Flecha de Lima, first met Diana at a cocktail party in 1990. They took an instant liking to each other and in April 1991 the friendship was sealed when the Flecha de Limas accompanied the Waleses on an official tour to Brazil. At that time Diana was at an all-time low point in her marriage; 'dissolving in enough tears to drown herself at every possible moment', was how one friend put it. In Lucia she found a sympathetic ear and a shoulder to cry on. Now, as she rebuilt her life, it was Lucia to whom she naturally turned for advice.

Another of these older friends ('women of substance' the *Daily Mail* called them) was the Lebanese-born wife of Arts Council chairman Lord Palumbo. Hayat Palumbo, forty-one, had known Diana since 1986 when her marriage brought her into royal circles. She knew all about the trauma of divorce — she had been through it with her first husband, tycoon Elil Kalil.

Finally there was the Hon. Rosa Monckton, thirty-nine-year-old managing director of the high-class jewellers Tiffany's. Rosa came from a family which had been embroiled in royal scandal: her grandfather, the first Viscount Monckton of Brenchley, actually drafted King Edward VIII's abdication speech in 1936, and was the only Crown official invited to witness his marriage to American Wallis Simpson. Rosa met Diana through Lucia Flecha de Lima and the two became close very quickly. The Princess admired her energy and forthright business manner and felt she could trust a fellow member of the aristocracy. But Palace aides saw it differently. There was much tut-tutting at the fact that Rosa was married to a journalist, Dominic Lawson, editor of the arch-Tory magazine *The Spectator*.

It was these three women, more than anyone else, to whom Diana turned for advice throughout her 1993 phoney war with Buckingham Palace and the sniping from Charles's friends which accompanied it. She would need all the wise counsel she could get. The dirty-tricks brigade remained active.

Nothing illustrated this better than the circumstances surrounding her first solo foreign tour. On 2 March Diana was due to fly to the mountain kingdom of Nepal along with the British Government's Overseas Development Minister, Baroness Chalker. In contrast, Charles would be enjoying the thrills of powder snow at his beloved Swiss ski resort, Klosters. Some royal observers expressed surprise that there was no Buckingham Palace briefing on her plans and itinerary. Had not the press been called in only the other week as Charles had prepared for his tour to Mexico and the US? Could it be that the Palace didn't want to assist

Diana to hog the limelight after the Prince's trip had excited so little coverage back home?

The answer soon became clear. The Palace seemed to have done everything in its power to downgrade her visit. Some cynics even suggested the Nepalese were terrified in case they appeared to give her too warm a welcome. They had offered to play the British national anthem to greet her on her arrival, only to be informed politely by the Palace that it would be inappropriate. Instead, poor Diana was treated to a motley selection of Spanish tunes followed by the somewhat unfortunate choice of 'Colonel Bogey'.

There were several other subtle snubs engineered by the British side. Diana was not to dine with King Birendra and Queen Aishworya. She was not to stay at their palace, but in the faded residence of the British ambassador at Katmandu. She would get no senior political escort; the tourism minister would suffice. Her private secretary, Patrick Jephson, could not attend through illness and she would not be accorded a deputy. She would have no official lady in waiting; her sister Lady Sarah McCorquodale fulfilled that role. She would not have her personal driver, Simon Salari, nor her chef, Mervyn Wycherley. Most significant of all, for the first time since her marriage she had begun a royal tour on commercial airlines rather than an aircraft of the Queen's Flight. One aeroplane was with the Duke of Edinburgh in the Caribbean, one was on stand-by at home for the Queen, and the third was said to be 'undergoing maintenance'.

Diana must have mentally prepared herself for all this well in advance. What she could not have anticipated was the shock awaiting her in that morning's London newspapers.

'Love Tape Will Stop Diana Being Queen', screamed *The Sun* headline in a report which told how the Australian TV show 'Four Corners' had broadcast a previously unreleased section of the 'Dianagate' tape (see Chapter Eight and Appendix 1). In her conversation with James Gilbey, Diana insists: 'I don't want to get pregnant.' Gilbey replies: 'Darling, it's not going to happen.'

According to a source close to the Princess, the conversation was no more than a tease, an exchange between friends who were to an extent fantasising about an impossible dream. 'One part of Di wanted to leap head-on into a proper relationship to compensate for the emptiness in her life,' said the source. 'But the other urged caution because of her position.'

Whatever the truth, this latest development was a cunning sideswipe at Diana as she waited nervously for what lay ahead in Nepal. Could the timing of the tape's release have been coincidence? Pro-Charles courtiers at the Palace were gleefully rubbing their hands. They had quietly been dropping hints for weeks that the Princess's trip would be a public-relations disaster. Now a key battle had been won and they had surely been proved right. Press interest would move away from her present duties, back to her past indiscretions.

That at least was the theory. But not for the first time, the St James's Palace office of the Prince of Wales woefully underestimated Diana's resilience and the media's love affair with her. Within hours of stepping off the plane Diana was touring the Nepal headquarters of Voluntary Service Overseas. As she examined carpets woven by the Untouchables she asked: 'Does this beautiful work take for ever? Does it increase their self-esteem?' Around her the fifty-five-strong press pack jostled and clamoured for photographic positions. The Nepalese escorts could only look on in bewilderment. Had not the Palace told them Diana's visit was to be 'low-key'?

That very afternoon there was another royal photo opportunity which the Palace had hoped would steal the Princess's limelight. The Prince of Wales had let it be known that he would be available for photographers on the ski slopes of Klosters. Only one turned up. 'Where is everyone?' a baffled Charles asked his mountain guide Bruno Sprecher. The answer was not given, though it must have been obvious. They were in Nepal following a glamorous, popular Princess who was doing interesting, newsworthy things. In the phoney war, Diana's shots were hitting the mark.

It didn't end there. When Diana visited the Anandaban leprosy hospital (part of the London-based Leprosy Mission International organisation, of which she is patron) she sat on each bed, shook hands, and gently stroked each damaged limb. In fairness to her, this was not merely a public-relations stunt. She genuinely believes she can help heal the sick, as she had intimated in the 'Dianagate' tape. Nevertheless, she must have known the blanket coverage she would get in the media at home. Contrary to all the Palace predictions, her first solo tour had been a stunning success.

Having seized the initiative, the Princess was not about to let it drop. Over the next two months she seemed rarely out of the headlines amid an avalanche of positive publicity. It would all subtly strengthen her position when it came to thrashing out a favourable divorce settlement. Meanwhile, an outsider could have been forgiven for suspecting it was she, not Charles, who was heir to the throne.

One of these PR coups came on Sunday 21 March when the *News of the World* pictured her on its front page with young runaways alongside the headline 'Diana Got My Mum Back'. The story went on to reveal how for months she had been quietly working with homeless teenagers at London's Centrepoint hostel, sharing cosy late-night chats over coffee and biscuits. Only a few days earlier she had told a London conference on housing children that many runaways had 'lost their dreams'. Perhaps also striking a personal note she went on: 'The persons they were had virtually disappeared. Any possibility they saw of pulling their lives back together was being destroyed by the struggle to survive from one day to the next.'

Two weeks later the focus switched from 'Caring

Diana' to the 'Cold Hearted Palace'. Diana had desperately wanted personally to console the parents of Warrington IRA bomb victims Tim Parry, twelve, and Jonathan Ball, three. She had hoped to attend the 7 April memorial service to them and when the Queen refused she felt bitterly upset. Prince Philip was to represent the Royal Family. It would be unprecedented, the Palace claimed unconvincingly, for two senior royals to attend a private memorial service.

Diana decided this was further proof of an attempt to marginalise her and promptly retaliated by ringing up Wendy Parry to apologise for not being able to attend. 'As a mother myself, I know what you are going through,' Diana told her. 'I would like to be with you just to give you a big, big hug because we are all as heartbroken as you.'

Whatever the motives of the Palace, they had backfired badly. John Junor, writing in the *Mail on Sunday*, observed that the Princess's phone call 'was a warning deliberately and calculatingly aimed at Buckingham Palace'. He added: 'It was saying in language the Palace would understand that the Princess of Wales does not mean to be pushed into the background and that if an attempt is made so to do then she will find means to make public her displeasure, as she did by that phone call.'

Columnist Julie Burchill, in the same paper, went further. She wrote:

'I wonder if Wendy Parry and Maria Ball found the presence of Prince Philip, that notorious fountain of human warmth, at the memorial service for their sons either a comfort or a boost. Somehow I doubt it and I find the choice almost an insult . . .

'This episode will bring shame not on the Princess of Wales but on the Windsors themselves. Those phone calls were utterly in character; Prince Philip's attendance is not. Day by day, despite their pathetic PR efforts, the Family seems more and more to be the most unnatural, destructive and loathsome family since Charles Manson's homicidal gang of the same name.'

Barely three weeks passed before Diana was back on the front pages. It seemed she was now on a relentless crusade to push her husband into obscurity.

This time she chose a conference on eating disorders publicly to acknowledge her own bitter experience of the slimming disease bulimia nervosa. She told how sufferers went through a 'secret spiral of despair', how they regarded their condition as a 'shameful friend' and how the roots of it could often be traced to their unhappy childhoods. Significantly, bearing in mind how bulimia struck her worst at the height of her marriage difficulties, she went on: 'By focusing their energies on controlling their bodies, they had found a refuge from having to face the more painful issues at the centre of their lives. A way of coping, albeit destructively and pointlessly, but a way of coping with a situation they were finding unbearable. An expression of how they felt about themselves and the life they were living.'

It was a powerful speech and it marked a new confidence in Diana's public life. At last she had taken a highly personal problem and aired it openly. That night she looked dazzling in an off-the-shoulder peppermint gown and tiara as she smiled and waved to crowds outside a formal reception for the Portuguese foreign minister, Jose Manuel Durao Barroso. Charles arrived alone looking moody and miserable. He was losing the phoney war and he knew it. Thankfully, convention dictated that tonight he would not be sitting anywhere near his wife.

Perhaps it was jubilation at the sense of her new-found freedom, or simply because she had promised herself a holiday in Paris during the dark days leading up to the separation announcement. Either way, on the first weekend of May, Diana suddenly packed her bags and headed off for a carefree break in Paris with Lucia Flecha de Lima and Hayat Palumbo, the Palumbos' private jet having been commandeered for the trip. Diana's favourite royal detective, Ken Wharfe, accompanied them and the four stayed in the Palumbos' beautiful town house at Neuilly, close to the Bois de Boulogne.

This was a weekend jaunt encouraged by Lucia, who recognised that a change of scene was vital to ensure her friend's rejuvenation. Diana was determined to enjoy it. On Saturday she played the tourist, shopping for the choicest designer labels, gazing in awe at Notre Dame and lunching in Marius et Janette where fellow diners included French heart-throb actor Gerard Depardieu. Depardieu, who had met her once before at a royal film premiere in 1992 (he told her at the time that he did not speak English), strode across from his table and gallantly kissed her hand. Diana revelled in the moment.

The following day the three women jumped into their hired Renault Espace to visit the huge Matisse exhibition at the Pompidou Centre. From there it was dinner amid the sumptuous surroundings of the Ritz before a leisurely drive back to the airport. The trip had been yet another way of asserting her independence. Her message to the Palace was clear: whatever their intentions for her, she intended to be a free spirit.

Another example of this could be seen in an analysis of her official engagements on the Royal Court Circular. In the year to mid-August they fell by 101 over the previous twelve months. Further proof of her downgrading? Perhaps. But it was also the case that Diana was increasingly handling her own diary, attending charity meetings and events that would not necessarily qualify for a listing in the Circular. She certainly had no shortage of offers: 2,000 invitations for the second half of 1993 alone. Her subtle move to greater independence was emphasised by the elegant letterhead on her writing paper, a capital 'D' interwoven into a crown.

There was also her subtle attempt to strike up an alliance with the Prime Minister, John Major. In July he made a secret eighty-minute visit to Kensington Palace to be told by Diana that she did not wish to be sidelined and that she would welcome any role as a roving ambassador for Britain. It was a theme she would repeat at a second meeting in October.

The Major–Diana relationship was a convenient arrangement for both of them. She needed powerful friends in Whitehall and Westminster capable of protecting her against the Machiavellian workings of the Palace. He needed to hitch his wagon to hers in the hope that her charisma and popularity would lift what was, at the time, his own dire, grey image. Neither had forgotten his words to the House of Commons, later repeated and reinforced, to the effect that he hoped she would one day become Queen.

The spring and summer of 1993 had seen Diana bounce back from the humiliations of That Tape. Even so, there were occasional glimpses of the underlying stress in her life and of her short temper. In early August, as she escorted Princes Wills and Harry from a showing of the film *Jurassic Park* at a London cinema, she sprinted towards one of the royal photographers, Keith Butler, and yelled: 'You make my life hell!' The outburst was put down to her protective instincts for her children, who were said to be frightened at the end of the film. But maybe she also sensed a change in her fortunes with talks on divorce ready to begin at any time between the opposing teams of lawyers. No wonder she decided on a weekend away from it all with Willie van Straubenzee and some other friends at eighteenth-century Floors Castle, Kelso, home of the Duke and Duchess of Roxburghe.

In fact the approaching autumn would herald a series of reverses for Diana. First, and most intriguingly, came the sudden departure of her loyal detective Ken Wharfe at the end of October. He had been hand-picked by Diana as a trusted member of staff and had become something of a father-figure to the young Princes. He had swum with them in the Caribbean, snowballed them in the Alps, sat alongside them through the theme-park thrills of Disney World, Thorpe Park and Alton Towers, and stood in for the Prince during the 100-metres fathers' race at the boys' school sports day. Both Wills and Harry were devoted to him.

Why did he leave? The official version was that he had been unhappy in his position for some time and had been making discreet inquiries about a new job abroad, possibly in America. But other observers pointed out that his cordial relationship with Diana had cooled since she had become a royal outsider. Had her once-unswerving trust for him now been replaced by suspicion? He had himself once prophetically told a junior colleague: 'Once you start slapping on the sun cream with the rest of the royals you are out.'

Another setback to the Princess's personal life came
with the so-called 'Peeping Tom' pictures of her working out in a leotard at a west London fitness centre.
The photographs which appeared in the tabloid *Sunday
Mirror* and *Daily Mirror* newspapers angered her more
than any coverage either before or since. Even the
'Dianagate' tape had somehow not invaded her privacy
to the same extent. She vowed vengeance, even if it
meant taking the matter to court. (In fact, having
played a close 'poker hand' for sixteen months, the
Princess won her victory and her vindication when the
newspaper group apologised and settled the case only
days before the date set for the hearing, in February
1995.)

The backdrop to all these frustrations for the Princess throughout the latter part of 1993 was the constant reminder that, after months of lying low, Charles
was again seeing his mistress, Diana's loathed rival
Camilla Parker Bowles. On Wednesday 3 November
the two women came face to face for the first time
since the 'Camillagate' tape exploded on to the public
scene the previous year. At a memorial service for the
Earl of Westmorland held in the Guards Chapel, Wellington Barracks, Knightsbridge, Camilla stood staring
resolutely at the floor as Diana swept past her. There
was no exchange of glances. Charles, wisely, had
found a pressing engagement in Dorset to keep him
away.

The previous day, the Princess had rushed out of a

London theatre in tears complaining of a severe migraine. Some tried to suggest she was still upset at the departure of Ken Wharfe, although as she had known of his intentions for some time, this was stretching credulity. In fact, according to friends of Diana, her tears stemmed from the realisation that Charles's courtiers were intensifying their plans to wear her down and chip away at her public image. At a meeting with her husband in Buckingham Palace at the end of November she told him she planned to announce her withdrawal from public life. Charles argued with her, suggesting she should phase out her public duties gradually. Predictably, it made no difference.

Charles knew he would be accused of jealousy, of forcing Diana out because he could not take the competition. But he could live with such taunts. The important thing now was that, for the first time in years, Diana would be off centre stage. The phoney war was over. The battlefield ahead lay in the divorce courts.

15

The Empire Strikes Back

On Friday 3 December 1993, the Conservative Party peer Lord Archer was chauffeured into Kensington Palace for a hurriedly-arranged meeting with the Princess of Wales. Later that morning he was to be master of ceremonies at a lunch for one of her charities, the Headway National Head Injuries Association. She would be guest speaker and, for reasons at which he could only guess, Diana wanted to brief him personally on her speech.

Impassively, Archer listened to what she had to say. According to some sources he made a gentle attempt to change her mind; 'a sort of backs-to-the-fireplace chat' was how one put it. It made no difference. The culmination of weeks of discussions with Charles, the Queen and Prince Philip was upon her.

At the lunch, held in the Hilton Hotel, Park Lane, London, Diana had to wait nearly three hours before she rose to speak. In that time she ate little — an avocado and mozzarella salad, consommé, a bite of Christmas pudding – and sipped a mineral water as she watched the carriage clock she had donated go for £6,000 in a charity auction. Finally, the moment arrived and slowly, deliberately, she launched into her momentous speech:

It is a pleasure to be here with you again, sharing in the successes of the past year. Headway has grown into an organisation which is improving the quality of so many lives. I am so proud of the work you have achieved. In the past twelve years I can honestly say that one of my greatest pleasures has been my association with people like you. During those years I have met many thousands of wonderful and extraordinary people, both here and around the world – the cared-for and the carers.

To the wider public, may I say that I have made many friends. I have been allowed to share your thoughts and dreams, your disappointments and your happiness. You also gave me an education, by teaching me more about life and living than any books or teachers could have done. My debt of gratitude to you all is immense. I hope, in some way, I have been of service in return.

A year ago I spoke of my desire to continue with my work unchanged. For the past year I have continued as before. However, life and circumstances alter and I hope you will forgive me if I use this opportunity to share with you my plans for the future, which now indeed have changed.

When I started my public life twelve years ago, I understood that the media might be interested in what I did. I realised then that their attention would inevitably focus on both our private and public lives. But I was not aware of how overwhelming that attention would become; nor the extent to which it would affect both my public duties and my personal life, in a manner that has been hard to bear. At the end of this year, when I have completed my diary of official engagements, I will be reducing the extent of the public life I have led so far. I attach great importance to my charity work and intend to focus on a smaller range of areas in the future. Over the next few months I will be seeking a more suitable way of combining a meaningful public role with, hopefully, a more private life. My first priority will continue to be our children, William and Harry, who deserve as much love, care and attention as I am able to give, as well as an appreciation of the tradition into which they were born.

I would also like to add that this decision has been reached with the full understanding of the Queen and the Duke of Edinburgh, who have always shown me kindness and support. I hope you can find it in your hearts to understand and to give me the time and space that has been lacking in recent years.

I could not stand here today and make this sort of statement without acknowledging the heartfelt support I have been given by the public in general. Your kindness and affection have carried me through some of the most difficult periods – and always your love and care have eased that journey. And for that I thank you, from the bottom of my heart.

It was a bombshell of a speech, reinforced by a hint of tears, and it instantly refocused the world's gaze on the Waleses' troubles. Had Charles pushed her out? Was her decision the product of some shady deal done in the run-up to formal talks on divorce? Or had she, as she hinted, finally grown weary of the media attention? One thing is certain. Her relationship with her husband was as acrimonious as ever. In mentioning the support of the Queen and Prince Philip, it would have been possible for her to strike a conciliatory note by adding the three words 'and my husband'. She did not. He was still the enemy.

Before looking in detail at the way Diana handled her announcement, it is worth briefly assessing Charles's year . . . and the doomed attempt by 'neutrals' to patch up a reconciliation.

The Prince had begun with a brace of foreign tours, including the United States and Mexico. The US trip was distinctly uninspiring, and occasionally downright embarrassing. One TV presenter even contrived to call him the 'Phone-Sex Prince'. But in Mexico, accompanied by his latest biographer Jonathan Dimbleby and a BBC documentary film crew, he seemed to be coming to terms with his new bachelor lifestyle. Observers noticed he beamed broadly in many photographs and seemed to have rediscovered his sense of humour. In fact, this was the start of a roller-coaster ride across the Prince's emotions.

Back in the UK it became clear to him that the Princess was not going to fade away quietly, even though on the odd, acrimonious occasions they met he did his best to encourage her to reduce her public exposure. As seen in the previous chapter, Diana merely scored hit after hit in the spring and early summer, reducing her husband to something of a royal also-ran in the media.

It meant a return to the 'Moody Charles' scenario, one in which he could not fully indulge his passion for Camilla Parker Bowles (they had agreed to scale down their illicit meetings until the 'Camillagate' furore had properly died down), in which there would be anguished phone calls to his mistress, with her demanding to know his intentions, and in which he regularly bickered with his wife over custody of the children.

Friends described him as being racked with self-doubt and even questioning his status as heir to the throne. He found it hard to understand why his wife had not remained at his side and could not come to terms with the suffering and embarrassment that his lover had endured since the 'Camillagate' tape surfaced.

In public he still stubbornly stuck to the issues closest to his heart – urban decay, farming, the environment – even though he was beginning to see that they could never match those Diana espoused: sick children, battered wives and AIDS victims. In keeping with his upbringing, he refused to pour out his problems, even to close friends. When they would ask whether he had enjoyed a particular itinerary, he would reply that it had been a 'good day' or a 'learning day'. Perhaps there was a touch of tongue in cheek about this, but it rammed home the point: the Prince of Wales was not the type to acknowledge a 'bad day'.

It says something for the character and optimism of the Queen's senior courtiers that, even at this desperately late stage of the marriage, hopes of a reconciliation were still being nurtured in one quarter. Throughout late summer 1993 'Project Zenda', as it was code-named, tried to keep the Waleses on speaking terms in the belief that a salvage operation was possible. Diana herself was code-named 'Flavia', the heroine of Anthony Hope's Ruritanian romance *The Prisoner of Zenda*. Flavia was blessed with beauty, grace, intelligence and was loved by all except the one person whose love she craved – her husband, the King.

When the Queen's political adviser, the influential Whitehall fixer Sir Gordon Reece, told Diana what was planned, she was enthusiastic. She insisted she wanted a reconciliation for the sake of the Queen, the country and her boys. Sir Gordon believed she also desperately wanted it for herself. For despite the humiliations of 'Camillagate', Diana would have taken him back. Lucia Flecha de Lima, the adviser closest to her heart, was not only supportive but actively encouraged Diana to be imaginative in her responses. However Lucia did agree with her friend's demand that Charles should pledge never to see Camilla again.

In August, the month during which media interest was traditionally at its quietest, 'Operation Zenda' was launched. The plan was slowly to bring the Prince and Princess back together, starting with some carefully selected public functions and progressing to a short foreign tour. The rebuilding would continue with a family weekend or half-term holiday, and afterwards the Prince would be encouraged to spend a couple of nights a week at Kensington Palace in a separate bedroom. Throughout it all, there was to be no 'talking up' of reconciliation. The Waleses would not be bounced into anything.

The friends and advisers working with Sir Gordon believed there was a chance. But they were up against other, equally powerful forces within the Palace machine. 'Why risk it?' these courtiers asked. 'What if we end up with a second split? Would that not be another huge blow for the House of Windsor?' One of the Zenda group, the supremo of Associated Newspapers, Sir David English, explained this antagonism to readers of the *Mail on Sunday*:

They were in the Palace and their view was that the best thing for the country was for the split to become permanent. They had spent hours listening to Prince Charles peevishly complaining about Diana hogging the limelight and leaving him in the shade. They had fed his jealousy and anger by agreeing with him that the Princess had too many friends in Fleet Street ... The Prince wavered. The Queen spent much time talking to him. But the simple fact was that he had never felt about Diana the way she did about him. To take part in an illusion, he felt, was morally wrong. But if the country wanted it? Still morally wrong. What point would be served, he would ask. And so again for Diana – rejection.

While others fought to save the marriage, Charles was laying the foundations on which to rebuild his public stature. Slowly there were signs of a new broom at St James's Palace. Professional image-makers had begun moving into the press office, men such as the new press secretary Allan Percival, who was known for his blunt-speaking approach. Staff were quietly warned to be more circumspect in their dealings with the media. Less cheery greetings and gossip and more formal, businesslike responses were the order of the day. There was even a rumour that taps had been carried out on phone lines to flush out any moles in their midst.

Within a few weeks of the separation, Charles's

team had been beavering away to develop a strategy aimed at improving his poor public standing. They analysed hundreds of press cuttings and TV footage going back fifteen years and concluded that his image was at an all-time high in 1980, the year before his marriage. Then he was perceived as the all-action Prince, the sporting go-getter, the man of vision who could still drink at the bar with the best of them. In short, the natural heir to the throne.

Alongside this it was agreed that Charles should follow the example of his sister Anne. At the height of her marriage problems she told the Queen: 'I'm going to work my way out of trouble.' Now he would do the same. A packed diary would help him forget his post-separation trauma and the memory of 'Camilla-gate', an event which he believed had humiliated and ridiculed him around the world. He was urged to adopt a softly, softly approach, irrespective of the spring and summer headlines cornered by Diana.

According to one of his closest confidantes: 'His aides told him to stand back and let Diana do whatever publicity stunts she wanted. They knew she would eventually burn herself out, and very slowly they were being proved right. Charles realised the only way to re-establish himself as a serious, respectable figure was to carry on quietly with his day-to-day work. His aides convinced him that in two years' time people would be willing to forgive him for "Camillagate", provided he carried on as if nothing had happened.'

By October, Charles could see hard evidence that this was wise advice. Diana's one-day trip to Belgium attracted the interest of only a handful of pressmen, whereas only months previously Buckingham Palace would have been fighting off applications to join her. Charles's renaissance had brought about her own fall from grace. Apart from anything else, editors were suffering a form of Diana-fatigue. They were simply tired of seeing her face in their papers.

The Princess herself summed up her feelings when she revealed to one companion: 'I just want to be more like my mother. Staying in the public eye is not worth the pain it's going to cause.' It was an astonishing statement from a woman who epitomised London Society. Her mother Frances Shand Kydd lived like a virtual recluse at a remote Scottish homestead.

It was not just the publicity initiative of early 1993 which had worn her down. Behind the scenes there were intense discussions within the Royal Family regarding the young Princes' futures and the forthcoming divorce settlement. Interwoven with all this was a continuing friction between the royal couple, stemming from Charles's conviction that she was still trying to upstage him. He cited her appearance at the Remembrance Sunday parade in Enniskillen, scene of one of the IRA's most appalling slaughters, as further evidence of this.

It was the Prince though, rather than his wife, who was insisting on a move towards divorce. At one point during the Zenda project she had even offered to take him back at Kensington Palace, on the proviso that they would have had different bedrooms. He refused, fortified by Camilla's her-or-me ultimatum. When Diana told him of her plans to leave public life his reaction was scathing. He could not see the point in making any dramatic announcement. Why could she not just scale down her appearances gradually if she felt the need? Predictably, she ignored his cajoling. She suspected his real concern was to dodge the blame for appearing to have forced her out.

One acidic exchange between them summed up the hostility. He told her she was making a bad choice. Quick as a flash she hit back: 'I made a bad choice when I got married. Another won't matter.'

The Prince's negative response to his wife's proposal is certainly curious. According to her camp, only a few months previously he had demanded she remove herself and eschew royal privileges. One friend, speaking on the day of Diana's announcement, said: 'He was obsessed about the royal train and kept telling her that it should no longer be available to her. Recently, his only concern has been her decision to spend part of Christmas at Sandringham with the Royal Family. He got it totally out of proportion, complaining that everyone would think there had been a reconciliation when there wasn't.'

The Princess made up her mind on the 'resignation' speech only a month or so before delivering it. She was concerned that her office was about to hold its six-monthly diary meeting to plan her engagements for the coming year. Rather than have to start cancelling dates, she decided it would be better to make clear in advance that she could not accept any. One possible date for the speech in November had been ruled out because it clashed with a meeting with her children and she felt it would spoil their day.

On Wednesday evening, 1 December, Diana met the Queen and Prince Philip and explained what she intended to do. Though saddened, they gave her unequivocal support, asking only that she think carefully before turning her back on state occasions. She also spoke to Prince Charles by phone and he again queried the need for her to make the planned statement. The conversation only stiffened her resolve.

In the final hours, however, she did make some concessions, almost certainly at the personal behest of the Queen. She agreed to maintain her association with five regiments for whom she was colonel-in-chief: the Princess of Wales's Royal Regiment, the Princess of Wales's Own Regiment, the Light Dragoons and two Commonwealth regiments. She also accepted that there would be some low-key charity work in public, although she insisted most of it would take place behind the scenes.

What is clear about the whole episode is that Diana's relationship with the Queen, distinctly cool and even hostile throughout the upheavals of 1992, had survived intact. She had always been prepared to approach the Queen directly for a heart-to-heart chat, pouring out her troubles and confiding her fears that the world was against her. It didn't matter if the monarch was busy. Diana would simply ring up the Queen's page and make an appointment, making clear she was prepared to wait if necessary. The Queen, for her part, saw these *tête-à-têtes* as an important part of Diana's learning process, although she often felt exhausted by the time they were over.

So what was behind the Princess's announcement? It was time to round up the usual suspects.

The pressure of constant media attention was, predictably, the first theory out of the bag. The *Daily Mirror*, which with its Sunday sister paper had so infuriated the Princess by publishing sneak pictures of her working out in a gym, now printed a front-page story calling on all editors to respect her privacy. Under the headline 'Diana: We'll Leave Her Alone', the article concluded:

Diana now deserves to be given the time and space she so desperately needs. She is far too valuable to British public life and scores of good causes to be lost to them forever. Yet most of all she is entitled to have the spotlight dimmed for her own sake. To be treated when she is off duty, not as the Princess of Wales but simply as herself.

If she read the article, Diana must surely have permitted herself a wry smile!

Political reaction was more forthright. Conservative MPs, many of whom were deeply resentful at what they perceived were regular broadsides from Charles against the government, reckoned they knew a conspiracy when they smelled one. And Diana's resignation positively reeked.

One of these MPs, Terry Dicks, said: 'This is her only way out. The royal mafia has won. They are pushing her out. Anyone who takes on the Firm is bound to lose. Look what happened to Fergie. When the Prince of Wales said he wanted to be an ambassador I said at the time, and I will repeat today, that she would make a far better ambassador than him. And she would have made a far better Queen than he will make King.'

Another Conservative, Sir Nicholas Fairbairn, observed: 'She is not moving out of public life. She is being pushed by the bureaucratic thugs who go under the name of courtiers. Poor girl. They are brutalising her.'

Others were more defensive of Charles. 'I don't think there should have been a highly emotional speech which creates the impression that the Princess of Wales has come under pressure from the House of Windsor,' said James Hill, secretary of the Conservative Backbench Constitutional Committee. 'I think it should have been done a little more quietly.'

After the love has gone. Charles and Diana in India, 1992.

Above: Secret boyfriends (clockwise): James Gilbey,
Oliver Hoare and James Hewitt.

Cold war: Diana's marriage is in crisis as she visits South Korea in 1992.

Above: Proud mother: Diana with Princes William and Harry on a night out in 1991.

Opposite: I quit! Diana in 1993 – the year she announced she was giving up public life.

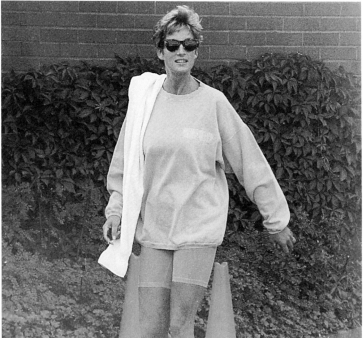

Above: Action girl: Diana puts on a brave face as 1994 ends in discord and scandal.

close relationship with a man, this was dismissed by most observers. One seasoned diarist, Nigel Dempster, described it as a 'crass invention', adding that 'there is no man, new or old in the romantic life of the Princess of Wales'. But was he right?

While Diana could no longer court publicity, she had no intention of turning into a royal vegetable. Already, plans were advancing for her to set up her own international, independent charitable foundation. Some of her more mischievous friends were calling it the 'Princess's Trust', a sly sideswipe at the Prince's Trust charity so dear to Charles's heart. The path Diana had mapped out for herself would effectively take her into the boardroom. She would shun any notion of becoming a figurehead and would instead lead policy-making, planning, and future philosophy.

There would also be some work in the field, a job Diana accepted as ideally suited to her. But as one friend said unconvincingly 'She is always quoting the example of Audrey Hepburn as the kind of helpful person she doesn't want to become. She admired Miss Hepburn, of course, but she represented the film-star photo-opportunity role that the Princess wants to get away from.'

A year that had started so brightly for Diana was now ending once more in confusion. Her Christmas with the rest of the royals at Sandringham was kept to the barest minimum – arrival on Christmas Eve followed by a tense Christmas Day then an immediate exit. Diana longed to be alone with her boys. Charles resented her very presence and even wanted a statement issued clarifying that there was no reconciliation on the cards.

On Boxing Day Diana flew to Washington. At least here she would be sure of a welcome. Her host was Lucia, consistently the most important person in her life, and a friend whom she had begun to miss terribly. She had been devastated when a few weeks previously it was announced that Lucia's husband had been appointed Brazilian ambassador to the US. But she quickly decided to take advantage of the situation. Her escape from the cauldron of intrigue in London to the transatlantic haven of the Flecha de Limas filled Diana with relief. She needed shelter from the storm.

With her public retreat now complete, what did the future hold for Charles? In one sense, the way was clear for him to take the initiative, put his troubles behind him and prove to the public that he was a man fit to be King. And yet ... In many ways the removal of Diana would turn the spotlight back to the unsavoury side of his own personal life. The affair with Camilla. The cuckolding of her husband, his obedient friend Andrew Parker Bowles. The prospect of him treating the royal divorce in the same cavalier fashion as he had the marriage. The year 1994 would see the relaunching of Charles. Would it also be the year to make or break him as future King?

16

Through the Minefield

The countdown to divorce had begun. Yet as 1994 dawned, little was clear. Diana was staying true to her instinct that she should not be seen to initiate a dissolution. However, neither would she stand in Charles's way if he wished to make the running. Charles, on the other hand, wanted the marriage ended as soon as possible. After all that had happened, he told friends, where was the sense in prolonging the agony?

The Prince had a point, although even politicians and courtiers close to him were worried about his judgement. 'What of the Camilla Factor?' they asked. It was spelt out to Charles that he should cut himself off from his mistress, at least until the dust from divorce settled. If he could not bring himself to take this step, then he should make certain he was not seen with her in public. If even this was unacceptable, then he should mentally prepare himself for the realisation that he could never be crowned King. 'I'm afraid, sir,' one senior politician told him, 'the country simply would not accept her, either as your Queen or consort.'

In reality, the Camilla Factor was a constant headache at the Palace. It had been intended to use 1994 – Charles's twenty-fifth anniversary as Prince of Wales – as the vehicle to relaunch him as King-in-waiting. The investiture anniversary itself, and a June fly-on-the-wall TV documentary and biography by Jonathan Dimbleby, were integral parts of this strategy. The run-up to divorce, and the way it was presented publicly, were clearly crucial.

Yet although Diana was safely out of the way, Camilla's influence was now taking hold. It was she who had stamped out the Project Zenda initiative by telling Charles she would not countenance it. How would she react if it appeared the Palace was now trying to push her sideways?

The Prince himself was making one thing crystal-clear. If circumstances were right (in other words, if two marriages were dissolved) he would marry Camilla against the advice of his most trusted aides. In any case he would continue to see her. He knew full well that in stating this he had raised the stakes. The Archbishop of Canterbury, Dr George Carey, had confirmed that Charles could be crowned King if he was separated or even divorced. But if he remarried, then Camilla would, by definition, become his Queen. Privately, Dr Carey was insisting that he would never crown her.

As the constitutional arguments raged, the image-makers continued to look for practical ways of rehabilitating Charles. The divorce of his sister Anne was cited as a successful public-relations exercise. She had remained extremely low-key, kept her second marriage clear of anything remotely newsworthy and got on with what she perceived as her duties. Andy and Fergie had taken a similar line. The only time they made news was when they were pictured together laughing and joking, as if for all the world they had not separated. If they decided to get divorced, it would at least be seen as amicable.

Charles, unfortunately, could not follow their lead. He could not carry on without his beloved Camilla. And in courting her, he also courted burgeoning controversy.

Despite this, some of those involved in the relaunch of the heir's image remained up-beat. The Food Minister Nicholas 'Bunter' Soames, grandson of Sir Winston Churchill and Charles's lifelong friend, continued to proclaim that the Prince would be King. 'He is not understood,' Soames would say, 'because he won't conform to what the press want him to do. He won't create a photo opportunity. He regards that as a sort of absurd trivia. He is too intellectually honourable and he won't be a fraud.'

Ironically, barely a month into 1994, Charles became locked into the kind of photo opportunity his advisers both dreaded and dreamed of. During his seventeen-day tour of Australia and New Zealand, the Prince was due to present prizes to schoolchildren in Tumbalong Park, Sydney. Up until then, his presence had been a flop among Australians, many of whom were considering the merits of their country's future as a possible republic. As one radio presenter had remarked: 'Indifference [to Charles] is rising to fever pitch.'

But events at Tumbalong Park changed the atmosphere completely. A twenty-three-year-old student brandishing what looked like a hand-gun ran towards the stage firing shots. They were blanks, but neither the Prince nor anyone else knew that. As the student leaped on to the stage and confronted the royal guest, Charles merely stared at him and fiddled with his cufflinks.

Seconds later screams rang out as security men jumped on the student. Dozens of people sprang from their seats. Photographers and reporters ran haphazardly about trying to work out what was happening. A woman's voice appealed for calm over the intercom, assuring everyone that the situation was under control. To the side of the stage, the struggling intruder was being carted away.

Amid this sea of turmoil, Prince Charles walked slowly up to the microphone as though the whole drama had been a scheduled part of the proceedings. 'It is, if I may say so,' he began, 'an enormous pleasure to be here . . .'

Next day the papers were full of it. 'Plucky Prince

Makes Poms Proud' bellowed the *Sydney Morning Herald*. It seemed the macho, all-action Charles of the late eighties was back – and in style.

Later the Prince gave his version of events to Australian TV chat-show host Ray Martin. He joked that 'a thousand years of breeding' had gone into his personality. His account which followed could have been a caricature of the British aristocracy in a crisis: 'I was standing up there on my own wondering what on earth was going to happen next. I was told I had to give prizes to two young achievers.

'I could not understand why nobody was appearing to collect their prizes – I thought perhaps they were coming up the centre aisle like all the others did. The next minute this chap leaps out of the crowd and starts running. I thought, "He must be hellish keen on receiving his prize." I had never seen anyone run so fast. I heard something go bang, bang, and thought: "This is very peculiar."

'The trouble is, these things happen so fast. I remember just watching in amazement. Should I give him the prize as he ran past? Was he going to stop by the time he reached me? The next thing I knew I was barged out of the way by my policeman and this chap collapsed in a heap on the platform.'

He added: 'I can't worry about whether somebody is going to come out of the crowd and bonk me on the head. If you think of these things all the time you can't get on with life.'

At home the incident gave Charles a massive leg-up in the battle to re-establish his reputation. 'Two Shots that Triggered a Royal Rebirth', enthused the *Sunday Telegraph*. Perhaps the paper was right. But Charles knew, and everyone around him knew, that he stood no chance of being truly reborn until he publicly confronted the issue that dogged his every step: his adultery with Camilla Parker Bowles. Soon he would be obliged to meet his confessor, TV presenter Jonathan Dimbleby.

The concept of the Dimbleby documentary and subsequent book had been carefully assessed by Charles's advisers. At last he was surrounded by people who knew the media inside out; spotting pitfalls was their business. As well as his astute private secretary, Commander Richard Aylard, his worldly-wise press secretary Allan Percival and his vivacious public-relations guru Belinda Harley, he could now call on the likes of Colin Byrne, a former Labour Party press officer, Grand Metropolitan chairman Sir Allen Sheppard and Julia Cleverdon, chief executive of Business in the Community.

The whole team knew how much was riding on Dimbleby's work. The 'big question' – about the Prince's affair with Camilla – would have to be asked and answered if the programme were not to be labelled a pitiful whitewash. If handled correctly, a smooth progression towards early divorce could continue. If botched, Charles would be once more out on a limb.

His confession, when it came, lasted only a few seconds. Yet it was perhaps the most compelling piece of true-life theatre ever broadcast on British television.

The ITV documentary, entitled 'Charles: The Private Man, the Public Role', had begun with the predictable footage of hand-pumping, foreign tours and family get-togethers. It was not until ninety minutes into the documentary that Dimbleby asked the question the world was waiting to hear. Had the Prince tried to be faithful and honourable to his wife?

'Yes, absolutely,' replied Charles.

'And you were?' Dimbleby ventured.

'Yes,' said Charles. There was a short pause. 'Until it became irretrievably broken down, us both having tried.'

That was enough. With divorce a possibility just six months hence, the heir to the throne, future head of the Church of England and Defender of the Faith, had just admitted to his prospective subjects that he was guilty of adultery. In the annals of British history there had been nothing quite like it.

But Charles went further. He made it clear that despite Diana's pleas, despite the counsel of his advisers, despite the subtle pressure from the Queen and the Prime Minister, he was not going to give Camilla up. Dimbleby put it to him that his relationship with her from the very start of his marriage had been responsible for its breakdown.

'What is your response to that persistent criticism?' he asked.

Charles hit back with a weak joke: 'That's the persistent criticism is it?' he smiled. Then he launched into a rambling explanation of his affair.

'Well I, the trouble is you see, that these things again, as I was saying earlier, are so personal that it's difficult to know quite how to, you know, to talk about these things in front of everybody, and obviously I don't think many people would want to. But, I mean, all I can say is there's been so much speculation and feeding on every other kind of speculation so it all becomes bigger and bigger. But all I can say is, um, that, I mean, there is no truth in, in so much of this speculation, and Mrs Parker Bowles is a great friend of mine and I have a large number of friends.

'I am terribly lucky to have so many friends who I think are wonderful and make the whole difference to my life, which would become intolerable otherwise. And she has been a friend for a very long time and, along with other friends, and will continue to be a friend for a very long time and I think also most people, probably, would, would realise that when their marriages break down, awful and miserable as that is, that so often, you know, it is your friends who are the most important and helpful and understanding, encouraging, otherwise you would go stark raving mad and that's what friends are for.'

Dimbleby asked whether the split with Diana had damaged his own reputation and that of the monarchy.

Charles replied: 'Well, obviously, I don't recommend it to anybody. Any breakdown of a marriage is obviously a dreadful thing and unfortunately causes great unhappiness and consternation and everything else, inevitably. So I suppose at the same time it's inevitable that in the wake of something like that you get all sorts of turbulence. Obviously, I'd much rather it hadn't happened and I'm sure my wife felt the same. It wasn't through lack of trying, you know, on both parts, trying to ensure these things work. No, I accept that I'm sure there's a certain amount of damage. I mean, you can't avoid it with something of this unfortunate nature.'

Then Dimbleby turned to the key point . . . Divorce. Was it a possibility? Charles played a straight bat to that. He could hardly, in any case, set out details of the deal being done. Wouldn't his most interested viewers be Diana's lawyers?

'That sort of question is very much in the future and if it happens then it will happen,' he said. 'At the moment it is not a consideration in my mind and anyway I think it is very personal and private between my wife and myself and that's how it will remain.' The Prince then went on to emphasise that divorce would not be an impediment to him being crowned King. Finally, as if to ram home the point that he was not an uncaring husband, Charles said of his failed marriage: 'It's the last possible thing that I ever wanted to happen. It's not something that I went into marriage, you know, with the intention of this happening, or in a way, in a cynical frame of mind. I mean, I'm on the whole not a cynical person and, you know, it sounds self-righteous to say so but I have on the whole tried to get it right.'

And what was Diana doing as Charles bared his soul to the nation? Certainly not at home watching TV. She was attending a gala dinner at the Serpentine Gallery in Kensington Gardens where her close friend, the gallery trustees' chairman, Lord Palumbo, was waiting to meet her. The Princess looked stunning in an off-the-shoulder, above-the-knee, black chiffon dress, set off by a ruby-and-pearl choker. She knew this was one occasion guaranteed to get photographers jostling around her. As she flashed her radiant smile, it was as though she was telling the nation: 'Look folks, this is what he's missing!'

Charles had played a high-risk gamble but he seemed to have pulled it off. On 1 July, just four days after the documentary was screened, *The Sun* published the results of an opinion poll which showed 54 per cent of the population now believed he was fit to be King. Hours before his adultery confession, 63 per cent had been against him. 'Charles Rules OK', said the newspaper, 'Nation's Sympathy Swings to Him'. Even Camilla's close family was impressed. Her father, Major Bruce Shand, said: 'I was fascinated by what the Prince had to say about all sorts of issues, including the failure of his marriage. I believe he came across as very fair-minded and sincere. I am in no doubt he will make a perfect King.' His son-in-law was similarly unfazed by the royal confession. 'Nothing has changed,' Andrew Parker Bowles told friends.

The only setback for Charles was in the reaction of the Church. In his interview he had spoken of his preference for the monarch to be called Defender of Faith, rather than Defender of *the* Faith. That one, small word made a world of difference to Anglican churchmen. Without it, their future leader would be regarding them no differently from any other religion in Britain. The arrangement would, naturally, suit Charles's personal life admirably. In taking his Coronation oath he would no longer have to swear to maintain the 'Protestant reformed religion' nor would he have to 'preserve inviolably' the Church of England as set out under the 1701 Act of Settlement.

It would certainly smooth the way for Britain's first divorced monarch for centuries. And from there, who could say? A future marriage to Camilla perhaps?

17

Believe Nothing. Trust No One

With daggers drawn, and the divorce courts looming, Charles and Diana's most valued personal aides became their lawyers. It was no longer enough to concentrate on winning the public-relations war, important though that remained. Like any couple engaged in an acrimonious dissolution of marriage, the Windsors needed to 'dish the dirt' on each other. Anything to swing a judge on their side.

Charles's divorce tactics were driven by complex forces. He wanted Diana out of his life, of that he was sure. He knew he could otherwise never truly settle down with the woman he loved. But there was an even greater desire in his heart, the desire to fulfil a destiny for which he had already trained twenty-five years. The desire to be crowned King.

Author Richard Tomlinson, writing in the *Daily Mail*, drew a neat comparison with the plight of Charles's great-uncle, the Duke of Windsor. The Duke, he pointed out, had also been bedevilled by a scandal of forbidden love (namely that of American divorcee Wallis Simpson). Like Charles, the Duke had been a reluctant public performer, a man who had seen no point in compromise for the sake of political appeasement. 'But,' Tomlinson wrote, 'there the similarities end. For in one critical respect Charles is quite different from the Duke of Windsor. While the Duke was prepared to forfeit the throne to marry the woman he loved, Charles has made the opposite calculation. In such an indecisive man, his determination to be King is striking. It is enough to ensure the succession.'

This then was the foundation of Charles's strategy. His priority would not be the freedom to love Camilla, though he regarded that as a huge bonus. But he needed a marriage settlement which eased his path to the throne, and that surely meant pushing for an early dissolution.

The way he saw it, the longer the period of time between the legal end of his marriage (the decree absolute) and his succession the better. Time would heal the emotional scars of 'Camillagate' and perhaps fog the memories of his subjects. Time would allow senior Church and state figures to prepare the wider public for the notion of an adulterer as Defender of the Faith and head of the Church of England. Time would also permit discussion of, and changes to, religious doctrine that had always been considered sacrosanct. Indeed, as we have seen, Charles had set the ball rolling by admitting his liking for the title 'Defender of Faith'.

Rarely in history can the omission of the word 'the' have taken on such huge significance. It implied that Anglicans would no longer regard their monarch as their religious figurehead. They would have to fall in line with the multitude of other faiths, large and small, which had taken root in Britain and the Commonwealth. It would mean that, as far as the King was concerned, the Archbishop of Canterbury was to be regarded as on a par with the Chief Druid. Logically, even Satanists could claim Charles as their figurehead, since devil worship is unarguably a question of faith.

Before floating his proposal to millions of TV viewers during the Dimbleby documentary, Charles sought the counsel of the Archbishop of Canterbury, George Carey. Perhaps he hoped the 'progressive' Archbishop, who had manfully led the Church through the schism caused by the ordination of women, would be a powerful ally. In fact the Archbishop could not give the Prince unequivocal backing, or anything like it. To thousands of Anglicans it would seem as though centuries of tradition were being wiped out for the convenience of one man and his mistress.

There was also the Queen's view to consider. She had always believed that her anointment in Westminster Abbey was the moment when, spiritually, she was ordained by God to fulfil her role as Queen. She held this part of the Coronation so sacred that she had always refused to let it be seen on television. Her heir, the nation now discovered, took a more flexible view.

In an interview with the Labour politician Roy Hattersley for *Night & Day* magazine in April 1994, Charles asserted: 'Naturally I look at life differently from the Queen. The Coronation was a long time ago and a different climate exists today.' Intellectual opinion, he predicted, will 'have changed even more in another forty years'. Later Hattersley recounted how a tongue-in-cheek Charles had advised him to read the speech by King Magnus in George Bernard Shaw's *The Apple Cart*. It includes the lines: 'I should never have dreamed of entering on a campaign of recrimination ... my character is far too vulnerable. A king is not allowed the luxury of a good character. Our country has produced millions of blameless greengrocers but not one blameless monarch.'

The Prince's grandiose plan for reforming Anglican law may have been intellectually and spiritually stimulating. But it mattered not a jot to his lawyers. Having been given instructions to work towards an early divorce, they needed as much clear, no-nonsense direction from Charles as possible. They found it in short supply.

One of the Prince's greatest failings, acknowledged even by his friends, is his poor capacity for man management and decision-making. During the late seventies and early eighties, a string of private secretaries discovered this character flaw the hard way. Sir David

Checketts, who held the post for thirteen years up until 1979, was edged out because his avuncular manner was considered irritating. His successor, Edward Adeane, was picked from a family of courtiers and might have expected to enjoy a long run. Adeane's father had, after all, been private secretary to the Queen for nineteen years and his grandfather, Lord Stamfordham, had the same job for most of George V's reign. In fact Adeane's working relationship with his boss ended in acrimony after just six years. They had a furious row about the Prince's constant forays into politics and, as usual, Charles got his way. He appointed a well-known City figure, Sir John Riddell, as a replacement but again the chemistry didn't work. As for Riddell's successor, Major General Sir Christopher Airy, he lasted barely a year.

Charles is one of life's natural prevaricators. His contribution to any debate tends to be long-winded and his decisions are based on instinct rather than on laborious analysis of fact. Unlike his mother, he cannot absorb information easily and prefers what politicians like to call 'the broad-brush approach' to a problem. On many official occasions this side of his character has delighted amateur impressionists within the tabloid newspaper royal pack. Screwing their faces into tortuous expressions, they ask each other in agonised tones: 'But what does it all actually mean?'

The Prince's legal team, schooled in the precise language of the law, must have found their client hopelessly indecisive. Confronted with a particular aspect of the divorce on which his opinion was required, Charles would waffle around the subject. The words 'yes' and 'no' seemed anathema to him — unless they were quickly followed by some qualifying phrase.

This personality trait has dogged Charles for years. His former speech writer, Byron Rogers, once pointed out his infuriating habit of distancing himself from whatever he was saying, no matter how thoroughly his aides had checked it in advance. The examples are legion.

'Of course, urban renewal is a vast subject,' he would say, 'and far too big for me.' When Jonathan Dimbleby asked him if he would one day be King, the obvious answer to give was 'yes'. He actually replied: 'Well, in the ordinary course of events, one imagines so.' Even before his marriage, when he was asked about falling in love with Diana, he managed to alienate romantics everywhere by remarking: 'whatever love is'.

Charles's instructions to his lawyers were inevitably bound to be contradictory. On the one hand, he wanted a quick, clean divorce. On the other, he didn't want Diana pushed too hard. Throughout 1994 he had become increasingly concerned about her mental state and the risk that she could suffer a complete breakdown. If that happened, he reasoned, the public would quickly decide who was to blame . . . him.

The Princess, of course, had been through the mill

before. The anguish of her own parents' marriage break-up had never left her and she knew that to get her way against one of the world's most powerful families she would need both ruthlessness and cunning. The woman Charles had once scathingly dubbed 'Diana the Martyr' now needed to be 'Diana the Devious'. As one close friend advised her at the time: 'Believe nothing. Trust no one.'

The Princess made her position clear. Her priority was to retain a close relationship with Wills and Harry and, while she would eventually wish to be free to pursue other relationships, divorce itself was a secondary consideration. Let Charles push for it as hard as he liked; it merely helped establish her negotiating position.

Tactically, her reasoning made sense. In her new role as a private person, it was theoretically far easier to slope off on a discreet dinner date with one of her men friends than it was for Charles to risk being seen in Camilla's company. If an early divorce went through, the Prince would be free to indulge his affair much more openly. Why make it easy for him? If he would not give his mistress up, at least he would be denied the satisfaction of acknowledging her publicly. The affair, still regarded by the public as a sordid, tacky business, would continue to be cloaked in secrecy and shame.

There was another advantage to this approach. Diana knew that her rival had been putting pressure on Charles to make decisions on their future together. The longer he could be made to prevaricate, the greater the stress on his relationship with Camilla. Diana did not want her husband back. But she was damned if she would concede victory to Camilla without a bruising tussle.

By the late summer of 1994, Diana was telling friends that she would resist a divorce until after the Duke and Duchess of York had legally ended their marriage. This would have the dual purpose of allowing her to gauge public reaction while establishing a base line for financial settlement. It would also emphasise to Charles that she would not be bounced into any quick-fix deal on the grounds that it suited him. If he wanted to be free from her quickly, she told her advisers, then the price would have to be right. Once her marriage was dissolved, her negotiating strength would dissolve with it.

The lawyers were beginning to understand just how astute Diana could be. After years of dealing with the intricacies and scheming that characterised Palace politics, directing her own divorce settlement was hardly an overwhelming prospect. Even solicitors experienced in the affairs of society figures recognised that here was a particularly sharp client. Usually their clients had to be led and guided every step of the way. Diana seemed to have versed herself in the legal processes involved and, moreover, she believed she held a strong hand. There was another intriguing, though perhaps not surprising, aspect to her strategy. Diana was overtly suspicious. Suspicious of Charles, of the Palace, of the Church, of the police and secret services – all of whom, she reasoned, might have good cause to undermine her in the service of the Establishment. Hadn't she already fallen victim to this through the making of the 'Dianagate' tape? Hadn't there been a whispering campaign about her relationships with the likes of James Hewitt, David Waterhouse and James Gilbey? She believed she was being watched, quite possibly bugged and occasionally followed.

Three incidents, quite separate in themselves, illustrate her feelings well. The first has already been mentioned: the abrupt departure of the Princess's once-favoured personal detective, Ken Wharfe, at the end of October 1993. The official version of events (that he was unhappy and wanted a new job) stretches credulity. It is hard to believe that he would have chosen to quit in defiance of Diana's wishes, especially as she was then facing the emotional trauma of planning her withdrawal from public duties. For months observers had noticed a detachment and coolness between them.

Did she believe he had been turned against her? Did she demand his resignation? Or had Ken Wharfe's bosses at Scotland Yard told him bluntly that he was getting too close? Had they been jolted into action by Charles's supporters, anxious to isolate Diana as far as possible from any potential police allies? Whatever the truth, the Princess seems to have believed Wharfe had been 'got at' and was no longer firmly on her side. She felt no personal animosity towards him. The tears she shed when he left stemmed from a growing conviction that her enemies were bent on lousing up her life.

The second incident was symptomatic of her fear that she was being bugged and watched. In early May 1994 she arranged a hush-hush meeting with the tabloid *Daily Mail*'s royal reporter Richard Kay. The purpose, she said, was to give her side of the story following claims that she had been photographed topless while sunbathing in Spain. The pictures, chivalrously bought and 'buried' by the owner of *Hello!* magazine, Eduardo Sanchez, were according to Diana 'like a rape'.

Had she felt free of prying eyes and straining ears, Diana could have met Kay at any number of discreet restaurants, maybe even the address of a trusted friend. Subterfuge was hardly virgin territory to her. She had, after all, done a thorough job of secretly arranging author Andrew Morton's briefings for the book which exposed her sham of a marriage. The fact that she chose to meet Richard Kay in her green Audi convertible parked in a quiet Knightsbridge street near Harrods suggests she believed nowhere was safe. The car, at least, could be regularly swept for bugging devices.

Diana and Kay had established a rapport early in the journalist's eight-year stint as a royal rat-packer. He was charming, intelligent and a sympathetic listener, and they had enjoyed several off-the-record conversations at private receptions during foreign tours. It helped that Kay's editor-in-chief was none other than newspaper doyen Sir David English, a man who acted as her unofficial press adviser during the early years of her marriage.

Unfortunately for the Princess, the hour-long Knightsbridge car rendezvous turned out to be a public-relations disaster. A freelance photographer followed her and captured pictures of Kay getting into her car. He sold the prints to *The Sun* and, under the headline 'Two-faced Diana', the story read: 'Princess Diana kept a secret rendezvous with a top royal reporter – just hours after complaining about intrusions into her life.' The impression given was that Diana was up to her old tricks again.

The Princess, however, suspected that the real skulduggery was being masterminded by her ex-husband's clique of Establishment loyalists. She feared there was a plot to break her down and discredit her through stealth and guile, letting her know her every move was being watched. She suspected traps were being laid, rumours circulated, fabrications engineered. And all with the declared aim of easing Charles's journey through the divorce maze.

Final proof of this, to Diana's eyes, came in the third incident: the publication of a sensational newspaper story alleging that the Princess had pestered a married male friend with silent and 'nuisance' telephone calls after becoming infatuated with him. The astonishing claims embroiled Diana in a fresh scandal which went far beyond the implications of the 'Dianagate' affair and threatened to blow apart all of her carefully-laid plans for the future . . .

18

The 'Phone Pest'

At 5.30 p.m. on 18 August 1994, the Princess of Wales stepped off her British Airways flight from Boston to Heathrow with a spring in her step. Sporting a navy blazer and Bermuda shorts, she looked relaxed and suntanned. She had just enjoyed a glorious two-week break in Martha's Vineyard, the eastern seaboard playground for America's glitterati, with Lucia Flecha de Lima and some other close friends. Apart from the weather and the company, the trip had been memorable for one other reason. Not a single paparazzo had managed to squeeze off a shot of her.

It was a feeling of contentedness that would not last. While she had been away, her private life had once again been the subject of frantic press activity. Post-holiday storm clouds were gathering ominously around her.

Rumours had been flying for months about Princess

Diana's devotion to married millionaire Oliver Hoare. A handsome Old Etonian art dealer, Hoare, aged forty-eight, was three years older than Prince Charles — but looked and acted ten years younger. Diana seemed besotted with him.

His increasingly close friendship with the Princess of Wales meant shared boxes at the ballet and discreet dinners together or with friends. Although he had always seemed a gallant ladies' man, Hoare was married to the aristocratic and beautiful oil heiress, Diane de Waldner, a devout Roman Catholic. She knew of the gossip about her husband and the Princess but laughed it off. Oliver was, after all, a long-time friend of Prince Charles; and Diane's mother, Baroness Louise de Waldner de Freundstein, was one of the oldest friends of the Queen Mother.

Diane and Hoare had met in France while he was still a student and she was on the Paris staff of Christies auction house. They married at Kensington Register Office on 27 May 1976 when he was thirty and she twenty-eight. Their first home was his bachelor flat in Kynance Mews, Kensington, but they moved soon after starting their family the following year.

Hoare first met the Princess of Wales in the early eighties through his long-standing friendship with Charles. Diana would pop in to see the dapper Old Etonian at his Ahuan art gallery in London's plush Belgravia district. He would unveil a little of his life story: how he studied art in France and later joined auctioneers Christies as a dealer. How he honed his knowledge by befriending Islamic *tarikats*, mystics who unlocked doors to a huge circle of wealthy and influential clients. And how in the cultural cauldron of Istanbul he became regarded as one of the world's leading authorities on Islamic art.

Diana was fascinated. She felt she shared much in common with Hoare: an interest in mysticism, personal fitness (he is an enthusiastic jogger), art and good conversation. She was also captivated by his impeccable manners and charm. As the celebrated gossip columnist Taki put it: 'What he has is bedroom eyes, an almost effete manner, and an old-fashioned politesse. It can lead to the wrong conclusion.'

A woman art curator was even more succinct. 'He's good-looking and full of humour,' she said. 'Easy to fall in love with.'

Throughout the late eighties, Diana remained close to Hoare, regarding him as dependable, easy-going and trustworthy. Her one regret was that she had to 'share' him with Charles. Indeed, the Hoares were among the very few royal confidants permitted to entertain Charles and Camilla at the same table.

Sometime in 1991, however, the friendship between Hoare and Diana dramatically deepened. As self-appointed marriage mediator, he was probing her most hidden thoughts, hopes and fears for the future. On occasions their meetings would dissolve into shouting matches – she accusing him of seeing only Charles's point of view; he intoning that she should grow up and stop playing silly mind games. In a curious way, the frankness of these rows may have set up an emotional bond between them. Was it Diana or Oliver who misread the signals? Certainly, it was a bond they both later found hard to break.

The bombshell for the Hoare family – and total humiliation for the Princess of Wales – came on 20 August 1994, just forty-eight hours after her home-coming from her holiday on Martha's Vineyard. On that day, Diana strode confidently out of her Chelsea health club and was confronted by a *News of the World* reporter. He asked her about a series of nuisance phone calls – up to twenty a week, he understood – which she had allegedly made to the Hoares' £2 million Kensington home.

Confused and panicky, she raced for the safety of her car without comment. She needed time to think and a shoulder to cry on. Her eventual response to the threatened publication of the report was almost as extraordinary as the news story itself.

Back at Kensington Palace, Diana pondered over whom she should turn to. Her trusted private secretary Patrick Jephson was spending the weekend at his Devon country home. Lord Mishcon, her lawyer, could not be contacted. Press secretary Geoff Crawford was away on holiday. There was only one other within her circle who could advise her. Reaching for her personal telephone book, she dialled the most unlikely helpmate, a man upon whose advice she had come to rely in the past – the royal reporter of the *Daily Mail*, Richard Kay.

An hour or so later Kay was driving her around west London as she poured out her troubles – again followed and photographed by undercover journalists. The pair cobbled together a 'damage-limitation' story which was to be presented in the *Mail*. But before it could be published, the *News of the World* hit the streets. The front-page headline blared: 'Di's Cranky Phone Calls to Married Oliver'.

The story alleged that Diana had plagued Hoare with calls just to hear his voice. Hoare and particulary his wife had regularly picked up the phone at their Chelsea mansion to be greeted by silence. It seemed to Diane that someone was gunning for them.

The calls had started in September 1992, a period when the Waleses were at each other's throats and still three months away from the separation announcement in the House of Commons. The calls, mostly silent, puzzled Diane Hoare, and at first she tried to ignore them. But, according to detectives, the final straw came when Diane took a call in which an unidentified female screamed a tirade of abuse – laced with some rich Anglo-Saxon swear words. Diane told her husband: 'This has got to stop.' She demanded that he report the matter to the police.

Hoare agreed. 'Whoever it is just wants to hear the sound of my voice,' he explained to investigating officers. 'They just keep hanging on as long as I talk. If I put the phone down they just come back. I would be polite and say, "Hello, who's calling? Who's there?" It's frightening for me and my family.'

Detectives approached British Telecom's Nuisance Calls Bureau, which uses revolutionary new technology to track down the originating numbers of incoming malicious calls. Hoare was instructed to punch code numbers into his telephone whenever the silent caller struck. This would alert a computer at BT's exchange in Vauxhall, south London, which within seconds would automatically scan hundreds of thousands of connections. The offending number would be displayed on screen for investigators and logged in databases.

On 13 January 1994 Oliver Hoare used the system for the first time. His phone rang at 8.45 a.m. but there was only silence at the other end. Spurred into action, the Vauxhall computer alerted BT operators and identified a line in Kensington Palace, normally used by Prince Charles. Four minutes later came another call, this time from one of Diana's lines. A third was made at 8.54 a.m., a fourth at 2.12 p.m. and a fifth at 7.55 p.m. – all from Charles's phone. There were no more that day.

Over the next five days, BT logged the following nuisance calls to the Hoares' house – 15 January: 4.55 p.m., call from Diana's private line. 17 January: 5.53 p.m., Diana's private line. 18th January: 10.41 a.m., Diana's mobile phone. 11.36 a.m., private line within

Kensington Palace. 5.52 p.m., same private line. 11.35 p.m., Diana's private line in Kensington Palace.

The next day Kensington detectives called on Oliver Hoare and showed him the list of originating numbers. He immediately recognised one of them as a direct line to Diana. The policemen asked whom he knew at Kensington Palace. Hoare went white as he admitted: 'Well, there's Prince Charles, there's the Princess of Wales . . . and that's about it. That's the private line of the Princess of Wales.'

Hoare told the officers he would not dream of pressing charges. Instead he would handle the situation by shouting warnings down the phone the next time a nuisance call came in. He would threaten to summon the authorities to trace the line.

The tactic worked, but only for a few days. Calls began arriving from public telephone boxes in Notting Hill and Kensington. One came from the home of Diana's sister, Sarah McCorquodale. Exasperated, the local police decided to hand the case over to Commander Robert Marsh, head of the Royal Protection Squad and, coincidentally, husband of one of Prince Charles's press officers Sandy Henney. Marsh consulted a senior member of the royal household and the calls stopped abruptly. The officer spelled out the risk that if they continued, prosecution would become an option.

In March, Hoare decided it was safe to have the tracing device removed. Three days later he was photographed being driven back to Kensington Palace by Diana late at night after a Chinese meal with Lucia Flecha de Lima and another girl friend. The diners had decided to finish the evening with coffee back at Diana's place. The meal had been arranged by Lucia as a kiss-and-make-up event at which the Princess and Hoare would restore their friendship.

Hoare must have understood that, at the time the calls were made in January, Diana had been going through one of her most depressive periods. She had been forced to leave Wills and Harry with Charles and the rest of the Royal Family at Balmoral while she spent the New Year in America with Lucia. She had missed the boys terribly and had only the briefest of reunions with them before they were packed off to boarding school on 11 January. According to royal-watchers, it was no coincidence that within two days of waving them off, the calls to the Hoare residence had resumed in earnest.

So much for the background. As the *News of the World* prepared to run its 'phone pest' story, the Princess concluded she had to respond to protect her reputation. At the back of her mind must have been the implications for custody of her children. If the divorce got bloody, Charles's lawyers could paint a grim picture of her as a mother. Would she be portrayed as the ex-bulimic (who believed she was a nun in a previous life) now in the habit of making funny phone calls to a married man? It wouldn't look good to a judge charged with ensuring the welfare of a future King.

On Saturday 20 August she parked her Audi convertible in leafy Talbot Square, Bayswater, the agreed rendezvous point for her meeting with Richard Kay. It was 4 p.m. and Kay was already waiting for her in his grey Volvo. She jumped in beside him and they pulled out into the steady traffic. As they headed for the anonymity of west London's streets she told tearfully of a desire to give her side of the story. Quotes would, as usual, be attributable to a close friend.

The drive lasted two and a half hours and when they returned to Talbot Square the Princess and the journalist sat together for a while to agree what would and would not be quoted once the *News of the World* hit the streets in a few hours. They seemed relaxed and unconcerned about the risk of being recognised. Diana even left the driver's door open as they talked, convinced that her scruffy jeans, casual navy top and baseball cap were sufficient disguise. At one point she seemed to rest her head on Kay's shoulder as though seeking some physical comfort.

At 7 p.m. Kay was standing on the pavement apparently saying goodbye and offering a few last words of reassurance. He had his head through the car window, when he was interrupted by a male passerby. The man thought they'd like to know that they were being photographed from a distance. Wordlessly, Kay strode back to his car while Diana started her engine and headed the wrong way round the square. She looked worried and upset and seemed to be looking for the photographer so that she could challenge him. When she failed to spot him she drove off.

Later that evening, and the following day, they discussed how pictures of the meeting would affect the *Daily Mail* report. Kay informed her that he had given a full account of events to his senior editors. It had been decided the *Mail* could not pretend his source was a close friend of the Princess if a rival publication had demonstrable proof that the source was Diana herself. The Princess was unhappy at the decision. It breached all the rules about contact between the royals and the press. However, she had to admit that there seemed little choice.

On Monday 22 August, British newspaper readers woke up to yet another bizarre twist in the Charles and Di saga. It was the *Mail* which carried Diana's 'unprecedented' interview but *The Sun* which had pictures of her and Kay together in Talbot Square. To get the full story, it was necessary to buy both papers.

The *Mail* headline was predictably sympathetic: 'What Have I Done to Deserve This?' above a story in which Diana pleaded her innocence of the nuisance calls. 'I feel I am being destroyed,' she said. 'There is absolutely no truth in it.' Then she set out a detailed rebuttal of why she could not have been responsible for the calls.

In particular she highlighted two calls made on

13 January. She could not have made the 2.12 p.m. call because at the time she was lunching with Lady Stevens, wife of Express Newspapers chairman Lord Stevens. And that evening the 8.19 p.m. call was dialled four minutes after she left for dinner with a friend in Eaton Square.

The 4.55 p.m. call on 15 January came at a time when she and her friend Catherine Soames were watching the Clint Eastwood film *A Perfect World* at the MGM cinema complex in the Fulham Road. One recorded at 5.53 p.m. on the seventeenth came as she was having a massage at Kensington Palace with her aromatherapist Sue Beechey. As to the flurry of calls made on 18 January, she insisted that the one timed at 10.41 a.m. from her mobile phone coincided with her having her hair done at a nearby salon. She had not had her mobile phone with her at the time. A call from Kensington Palace later that day was made while she was with her lawyer, Lord Mishcon. Finally, she pointed out that her sister Sarah was certain that no calls had been made from her home.

The Princess was quoted by the *Mail* as follows: 'Somewhere, someone is going to make out that I am mad, that I am guilty by association, that the mud will stick,' she said. 'I am bemused by this constant attention, a level of intrusion that I had reasonably thought would diminish. Photographers follow me constantly. It is said that people want me to return to the public stage – well this is hardly going about it the right way.'

She acknowledged that Hoare was a friend and that she had phoned him during the call-tracing period. She even tacitly admitted that if Hoare's wife had answered the phone she might have hung up, unwittingly creating fears of a phone-pest problem. But she emphatically denied that she had made calls of a persistent and malicious nature.

'Do you realise that whoever is trying to destroy me is inevitably damaging the institution of monarchy as well? I know there are those whose wish is apparently to grind my face in it. I knew I could not rely on anyone sticking up for me, but nor could I allow such hurtful things to be said about me in silence any longer. What should I do? Close my ears and eyes to it all.

'I know everyone wants me to be having affairs, and this man fits, but it's not true. Besides, if I was as obsessed as these calls would suggest, why would I have had supper with him a few weeks afterwards?'

Diana's words were, frankly, unconvincing. She made matters worse by dismissing Kay's inquiry as to whether she had wandered around west London calling Hoare from phone boxes. 'You can't be serious,' she replied. 'I don't even know how to use a parking meter, let alone a phone box.' Perhaps it was a flippant response. It was certainly not one that answered all the questions surrounding the escalating scandal.

Nor, it could be claimed, was Kay's own explanation, given to the *News of the World* in a series of telephone calls made on the eve of publication of their original 'Cranky Calls' story. Kay's friends insist that he merely responded to the paper's persistent attempts to call him. Whatever the truth, the resulting taped conversation, in which Kay refers to Hoare as 'Mr H' and the Prince and Princess of Wales as 'Mr and Mrs W', made fascinating reading when published by the *News of the World*. According to that newspaper, Kay said: 'I want to offer you an explanation of how it could have happened. First let me say Mr H is, as you know, a very long-standing friend of Mr W. When the marriage started to come apart, he set himself up as a middle-man, self-appointed, trying to get Mr and Mrs W back together again. He thought it was a waste and he wanted to do something about it. Mrs W didn't want anything to do with it. It was unlooked-for and unwelcome. You know he reduced her to tears.

'Now I'm offering you this explanation and see how you feel about it. Mrs W has some very loyal people working for her and they took the matter into their own hands for her. She didn't give them permission to do it, but when the police became involved she took it on the chin and took responsibility for what was done in her name. They were misguided and wrong, but they could see she was upset and tried to defend her.'

The *News of the World* claimed Kay called them again later in the day. He rejected the suggestion that he was acting as the Princess's mouthpiece but conceded that a 'damage-limitation' exercise was underway. The conversation went thus . . .

News of the World: *Why would he [Oliver] think he should get them back together? You might as well put a couple of pit bulls in a room and . . .*

Kay: *Exactly. Totally unwelcome by both sides. They don't want to know.*

NoW: *But she was very upset?*

Kay: *Well I'm told he has on occasions reduced her to tears.*

NoW: *What, just with the persistence of it?*

Kay: *Yeah. You've got to remember a lot of what I hear is second-hand conversations reported by people who heard through closed doors. I'm talking about through-the-library-door rows. And from punters I have to pay money to, who want to give me stories and sometimes they may be over-egging it. All right?*

NoW: *Possible isn't it?*

Kay: *I have to say it's a possible explanation. That's all I can tell you.*

NoW: *I think it's possible but . . .*

Kay: *Look, we all desperately want to believe that she's having an affair with someone and Oliver Hoare would be good material wouldn't he?*

A woman shouts from the background at Kay's end of the line: *She's not!*

Kay: *That's right, she's not. So I'm told. All right?*

NoW: *Yeah.*

Kay (to woman): *Get off my cock. Sorry.*

NoW: *What? Who?*

Kay: *Never mind who.*

278

NoW: She's not there with you?
Kay: *You can say hello if you like.*
Woman: *Hello.*
NoW: Who's that?
Kay: *Never you mind. All right?*

The newspaper claims there was another call that same Saturday in which Kay told a journalist: 'If you're talking about damage limitation on the explanation, well, in a way I guess it is. You either take it or leave it but I'm not doing it on anyone's behalf.'

The implication of the story was that Diana was present with Kay during at least one of the calls. But according to sources at Kay's paper, the *Mail*, this is simply not true. One said: 'Richard has a girlfriend and if anyone was with him it would have been her. That reference to a woman being present is totally mischievous. It embarrassed Richard dreadfully but he's a pro and he just carried on at work as though nothing had happened.'

In its sensational story, the *News of the World* attempted to explain the unlikely relationship between the Princess and the handsome journalist. The paper claimed that Diana was sometimes 'the first voice he [Kay] hears in the morning and the last at night'. The friendship had grown so close, it added, that the journalist had begun to fear he was being kept under surveillance by MI5. He had suffered two break-ins at his home, in which nothing had been stolen, and had resorted to a private detective to check out the driver of a car which followed him. The driver was 'almost certainly' an MI5 agent.

Again the bogeymen of MI5 were being introduced into the scenario. The rest of the British press began to speculate about these and other culprits who might have been behind the scandal. The question they all posed was: If Diana didn't make the calls, then who did? Could it really be true that a loyal member of her staff peppered Oliver Hoare with up to 300 calls on the grounds that he or she didn't like him arguing with the Princess? Again, a quite incredible explanation.

Prince Charles, for his part, was livid at this fresh scandal, fearing the effects it might have on his children. According to some reports, Charles had not ruled out the involvement in the story of some maverick MI5 squad. The spooks, he theorised, may have leaked the phone-pest story to the press even if they didn't actually arrange any frame-up. Yet at the back of his mind must have been the realisation that the events of late August could only strengthen his hand during divorce negotiations.

And strengthened it most certainly was when the true depths of the relationship between his wife and Oliver Hoare was finally revealed. It took several months before the story of their 'friendship' became clearer — and showed that the Princess and the antique dealer had been engaged in a fully fledged romance . . .

In fact, Hoare and his wife actually split up for a

two-month 'cooling-off' period after rows over his friendship with the Princess. Hoare moved out of the family home and into a friend's one-bedroom rented apartment in a backstreet near Victoria Station. In an interview with the *News Of The World*, not published until February 1995, Hoare's ex-chauffeur Barry Hodge claimed that his employer had planned to buy a Chelsea studio flat which he hoped would become a secret lovenest for himself and the Princess.

According to Hodge, the art dealer began planning his new life at the end of 1993 during a temporary respite in the telephonic plague of 'silent calls' to his home. At this time, the Princess and Hoare were already in constant contact by mobile phone and would also meet at the homes of mutual friends. 'Sometimes Princess Diana would phone him more than 20 times a day while we were in the car driving around London', said the chauffeur. 'She was driving him from pillar to post. She would even track him down to restaurants during business lunches. Like the Mounties, she always got her man.'

Oliver Hoare, allegedly pursued remorselessly until he reached the end of his tether, found himself unable to maintain his marriage and accede instantly to every whim of the Princess. His wealthy wife was also beginning to lay down the law. As the secret relationship foundered, so the 'silent calls' resumed. Largely at the insistence of his wife, Hoare was forced to call the police.

But according to Hodge, it was not only phone calls that menaced Hoare's marriage ... on one occasion Diana actually called at his home. In July 1994 she turned up on his doorstep in tracksuit and floods of tears, said the chauffeur. He went on: 'Mrs Hoare was away in France at the time but Mr Hoare still wasn't particularly pleased to see her there. He took her into the drawing room, still crying, but she seemed much more cheerful when she left 90 minutes later.

'She's a lovely lady,' Hodge added, 'but you can't help getting the impression that her idea of a crisis and most other people's idea of a crisis are very different things!'

Princess Diana's reaction to these claims, when they were eventually published, was typically curt and dismissive of a boyfriend who had played such an important role in her recent romantic life. She was 'reduced to peels of laughter' by the story. Through a friend, she let it be known that she found the idea that she might consider swopping Kensington Palace for a minute apartment 'a complete hoot'.

'The truth is she views Hoare as a pretty spineless creature. Ever since his failure to help her over the nuisance phone calls business, the friendship has been one-way. He is very much more besotted with her than she is with him. She is not interested in married men.'

Those comments were allegedly made by the Princess of Wales to her friend on 19 February 1995. Yet only the previous month, someone had still been talking to her on an intimate basis. This evidence for this was a series of messages left on her pager. They went like this:

11 January: My number is –, room – (a Cleveland, Ohio, hotel). Longing to hear and love you.

11 January: Please call. Can't reach you and have to get out soon. All my love.

12 January: Think of you every minute. Feel very bad about being so far away. Love you.

12 January: Love you very much.

12 January: Hope all is well. Thinking of you all the time. Will call you around 6pm your time.

13 January: My number is –, room – (A Cincinnati hotel). Longing to hear you and love you madly.

13 January: Tried and tried to call but never possible. So concerned and wish I could help.

13 January: A lonely travelling salesman is trying to find his mate.

It could only be assumed that the 'travelling salesman' was no other than Oliver Hoare. The ardour of the messages is clear. Perhaps Diana was right in terming Hoare 'besotted' when only a month later she cynically dismissed his entreaties as being 'a complete hoot'.

So much for poor Oliver! Courted, caught – and cast out, like others before him.

The pattern horrified Diana's friends who could only ponder why the Princess would risk all over her obsession for a married man. Scotland Yard's evidence that the calls had been traced back to her astonished her close friends. It confirmed, however, what some of them had feared: Diana had cracked under the strain of her marriage break-up and her new role as a royal outcast. It was indeed a 'Fatal Attraction' – yet one fuelled more by loneliness than lust. Like actress Glenn Close in the movie about a woman who torments the subject of her obsession, the Princess could not help running the enormous risk of pursuing Hoare.

The scores of frightening silent phone calls made over a period of sixteen months had been a sign of her desperation that she had so few firm shoulders to lean on and to cry on. The calls were effectively a reproach to Hoare after he had befriended her, consoled her, shared private moments alone with her, listened to her constant, petulant, self-pitying – and then, in her view, abandoned her. Diana behaved like a spoilt, spurned schoolgirl.

A friend said at the time: 'She feels desperately isolated and clings to certain friends for constant emotional support. This they cannot always give in endless measure. They have their own commitments but Diana just does not recognise that. To be blunt, what she needs is a man in her life – and one she can call on twenty-four hours a day. It would have to be a total commitment.'

Another friend said: 'For months Diana had been on the brink of a nervous breakdown. It wasn't just the phone calls; her staff had been finding that some of her behaviour was extraordinary, to say the least. There were tears and tantrums one minute, and she'd be nice as pie the next. Her staff never knew what to expect and were deeply concerned. Yet there was no one they could turn to in confidence for advice.'

A leading psychologist described the Princess as a lonely figure desperate for love and companionship. Jack Lamport-Mitchell said: 'The phone calls were an appeal for help rather than threatening in any way. She obviously wanted to hear his voice at the other end of the line but did not have the courage to speak herself. She just wanted to make contact – it's like calling the Samaritans. Princess Diana was so driven by her obsessive emotions and her emotional needs that she was prepared to risk everything. It was a very irrational thing to do but common sense goes out of the window in a case like this. The callers are usually insecure people and often do not know themselves why they are doing it.'

Throughout the furore over the phone calls, there was one man who could have come to the Princess's aid. But although Oliver Hoare called Diana after the story broke, offering sympathy and support, he would not agree to release a public statement clarifying his position. Perhaps he realised that unless such a statement were specific, it would only complicate matters further. The danger of being specific was that he might appear to question Diana's version of events.

From his Tregunter Road mansion, the sound of silence was deafening.

Diana could be forgiven for drawing some unpalatable conclusions. A friendship she had valued had become tainted. Another of her ever-diminishing circle of confidants, a man who could have been a key negotiator during the looming divorce tussle, had distanced himself. It seemed to her that she was again in danger of being left out in the cold. Had Diana's boyfriend decided that his future lay with his old friend, the future King?

In the past, the Princess of Wales might well have crawled back into her lonely shell to bemoan her sorry lot. She had been humiliated, not for the first time. She was the laughing stock of Buckingham Palace, not for the first time. She had been deserted by her friends, not for the first time. But for the first time, she was fighting back.

The Princess of Wales had maintained dignity (or at least a dignified silence) throughout the whole 'phone pest' débâcle. The photographers were still snapping her, the columnists still writing about her, the public still fascinated by her. Diana was discovering that she did not have to humble herself to get her way. She could stand tall and win – and so she set about winning back the man for whom her obsession had wreaked marital havoc.

On Sunday 18 December 1994, Oliver Hoare arrived at Kensington Palace under cover of darkness.

He drove through the gates at speed, wearing a buttoned-up overcoat, the collar turned up, and with a scarf wrapped around the lower part of his face. There were few staff on duty and Hoare made his way to a second-floor sitting room of the royal apartments. They sat down for supper, prepared by Diana's chef, and washed down with wine and champagne. The clandestine rendezvous lasted five hours – until the early hours of the morning.

Diana had won back her 'shoulder to cry on'. Only this time she wasn't crying. She was winning . . .

19

The Tigress Turns

The phone-pest scandal was the nadir of Diana's own *annus horribilis*. A year which should have marked her withdrawal from public life had instead turned into an unremitting torrent of media speculation about her future within the monarchy. Rarely a week went by without one paper or another snatching a photograph, and columnists clamoured to outsmart each other with so-called 'think pieces' on her predicament.

The reasons for yet another media feeding frenzy were obvious to everyone. Disclosures surrounding Diana's relationship with Oliver Hoare had been sensational enough in themselves, but in the context of recent royal scandals such as 'Camillagate' and 'Dianagate' the Hoare business was certain to be quickly overtaken. Editors around the world were eagerly awaiting publication of Jonathan Dimbleby's biography on Prince Charles and Andrew Morton's follow-up to the best-seller *Diana, Her True Story*. There were also excited whispers that former Life Guards officer James Hewitt was about to publish his own account of an affair with the Princess.

All three books were to be launched within five weeks of each other during the autumn of 1994. Diana was clearly beset from all sides. She knew she could expect nothing but a tawdry betrayal from Hewitt, who had long been expelled from her social circle. Dimbleby, though a respected journalist, could hardly be expected to do her any favours, as he would inevitably present events from the Prince's point of view. As for Morton – he was no longer considered 'on side'. As long ago as 20 August 1994 Diana had issued a statement through her favourite journalist Richard Kay making clear she had had nothing to do with Morton's new tome.

The Princess's fear was that she was being outmanoeuvred, her affairs tossed between three authors with little motivation to present her case. Once, she might have accepted her lot and slunk off to heap her troubles on to the shoulders of a few remaining confidantes. Now things were different. The Hoare affair had again focused her mind on how her enemies would try to destabilise and corner her, just as they wanted to remould and promote her husband. She identified the strategy as an attempt to loosen her influence on the young Princes – the boys she once said she 'would kill for' – during the delicate divorce negotiations. This she would not tolerate. Like a tigress

Crisis at Christmas: The Princess with Wills at the Sandringham Christmas service. Immediately afterwards, Diana drove back to London for a lonely dinner at Kensington Palace.

Slick! Triumphant Diana, the international style-setter, wows New York in 1995.

And Michael Colvin MP observed tartly: 'When she married the Prince of Wales she knew jolly well what she was letting herself in for. It is perfectly possible to marry into the Royal Family and lead a sensible life. It almost looks as though this is a preconceived plot to make her more attractive to the media. Both the Princess of Wales and the Duchess of York let themselves in for these things by being seen to be competing with each other for more publicity.'

The political backlash reached Cabinet level on Tuesday 7 December, three days after the Princess had spoken out. During an informal meeting among senior ministers at Westminster – a meeting not attended by the Prime Minister – opinion was sharply divided over what was to be done. Some argued that the Prince had to give the country a clear signal that he was giving up Camilla for good. They made clear they had no confidence in Palace advisers to chart an acceptable course through the minefield which lay ahead. But others warned against taking sides and called for the couple to be given more time to rearrange their lives. Mr Major, who that very evening was discussing the same subject at his weekly audience with the Queen, favoured the latter course. He was also keen to nip in the bud any talk about Charles not becoming King.

One politician pointed out that a public rejection of Camilla might be seen as humbug by the people: 'How can he give her up when it has been going on for the best part of twenty years?'

In addition to the suggestions that media pressure and Establishment thuggery were behind Diana's resignation, there was a third idea posed. It was simply that a deal had been reached with Diana.

In exchange for quitting the royal stage, she would be assured far more time with nine-year-old Harry and eleven-year-old William, playing a pivotal role in guiding the future heir through early adolescence. She would be able to find a new home somewhere in Berkshire – sited between the boys' prep school at Wokingham, and Eton College where they would be sent later. Diana instinctively liked this arrangement. For one thing, she regarded Kensington Palace as a 'gilded cage'. For another, both she and Charles had been worried about a minor disruptive element which had crept into William's behaviour at Ludgrove. They had both agonised over whether their public war was to blame.

One friend of the Princess said: 'You can only fight a machine for so long and that's what her in-laws are – a machine. She was tired out, worn out and wanted out. But she wasn't going to show them that until they offered something in return. As far as she is concerned she got her own way, even though she was pushed into it.'

This third explanation is closest to the truth, and indeed encompasses something of the previous two. Although some newspapers persisted in floating the idea that Diana had quit because she had formed a protecting her cubs, Diana steeled herself to fight back.

But like the rest of the nation, she was first curious to know what Hewitt, Dimbleby and Morton would say about her. If the rumours were true, Hewitt's claims were potentially the most damaging. He was planning to tell how she first seduced him at Kensington Palace and how they later slept together in her bedroom at Highgrove. For so long Diana had sustained her role as the wronged party in the Waleses' split. How would she now fare if the public believed she too had enjoyed a steamy affair?

On Sunday 2 October 1994 her worst fears seemed to be confirmed. The *News of the World* carried a front-page story revealing that Hewitt was negotiating 'one of the biggest book deals in British publishing history' and that he had previously tried to tout serialisation rights to the newspaper. Under the headline 'My Three-year Affair with Di', the report hinted that Hewitt's book might be published the following day.

The paper went on to quote Hewitt's words at a meeting with *News of the World* editors earlier that year. He had told them:

We were deeply in love. In fact, Diana was so in love with me that she even contemplated leaving Charles for me. She would often come secretly to stay with me at my home in Devon and I would see her at Kensington Palace while Charles was away. I even visited her at Highgrove and would play with Princes William and Harry. I was madly in love with her and helped her in so many ways. I advised her on what clothes she should wear, how to deal with the press and even helped her practise public speaking. For three years I was the man in her life. It got so serious that I was warned to stay away from her.

The article told how Hewitt met four journalists in a suite at London's Sheraton Hotel and tried to establish how much his story could fetch. At first he was careful not to claim he had made love with Diana, but asked coyly: 'If I had slept with the Princess of Wales and was prepared to tell all, what would it be worth? It's big stuff. The biggest ever, really.' At yet another meeting, in the Basil Street hotel, Knightsbridge, Hewitt was asked directly if he had ever made love to the Princess. He replied: 'Yes.'

The newspaper's series of clandestine interviews with Hewitt during the summer of 1994 reveal that despite Diana's coolness towards him, she had not broken off all contact. Hewitt claimed he had consulted the Princess over a sanitised, and widely-ridiculed, account of his friendship with her — written for the *Daily Express* by his friend, the twenty-seven-year-old journalist Anna Pasternak. Pasternak, in fact, was the writer he had already chosen to produce his book.

In a phone call to the *News of the World* following

the *Express* piece, Hewitt insisted: 'I did it with Diana's permission. She thought it would help to, well, help prevent some of the stories going around about me and us. We heard a journalist was going to write a book that we'd had an affair. He didn't know that but he could speculate, which is equally as dangerous. That was what Diana was afraid of. So we decided to pre-empt it, to set the situation correctly. It was a pre-emptive strike if you like. But it didn't actually achieve that. The rumours grew stronger than they were before.

'The piece wasn't that bad. What did go wrong was the hype that surrounded it. Diana was happy for it to go out. But once it backfired the support I got from her was non-existent, which is her fault. The other papers were fairly derogatory about me, and I suppose it made me out to look stupid – to take the heat off her to a degree. I tell you it's most destructive. Bits were fair but most was complete crap. It's the same for those who are in the Royal Family who are constantly bombarded by it – but they have a certain amount of breathing space and they can pull through. But if I do something I don't have any help other than myself and my wits to live on and it's not easy.

'Diana told me that she was sorry that it turned out that way. But when it got too hot and too much hype [*sic*] she decided to drop it. I think she should have been a little more supportive than she has been. I spoke to her on the phone a month ago. But I don't regard myself as a friend any more because I haven't bothered myself in trying to do so – because I feel cut off. One doesn't have any support any more. Now I don't trust anybody, I have been completely duped.'

Hewitt spoke of his admiration for Prince Charles's public confession of adultery. Charles, he said, was 'jolly brave' and deserved sympathy for the way he had confronted his critics without the support of his wife. Then, in the clearest possible demonstration of his bitterness towards Diana, he dared to question the generally accepted belief that it was Charles who first broke the Waleses' marriage vows. 'People must ask themselves the question: who cast the first stone?' he said. 'Because I think we have all got things that we wish to keep private, or things which we may be ashamed of which we don't want to admit.'

One of the most intriguing aspects of the relationship between Hewitt and Diana was the *News of the World* claim that he had been secretly betraying her for at least two years. For much of that time he was a serving Life Guards officer, yet he would arrange to meet reporters in motorway service stations and underground car parks to try and sell gossip he'd picked up about the Princess. On one occasion he turned up in full battle dress in a chauffeur-driven Army Land-Rover. On another he allowed a reporter to glimpse intimate, affectionate letters which the Princess had sent to him.

'I haven't shown them to anyone,' he said. 'I have

just got to weigh up the consequences. I could be done for high treason and sent straight to the Tower.'

As she read Hewitt's claim that Sunday morning, Diana could have been forgiven for fearing the worst. She knew the book by Hewitt and Pasternak, *Princess in Love*, was already going out to dealers in a nation-wide cloak-and-dagger operation designed to by-pass the risk of a High Court injunction. Friends in the publishing business warned her that the major chains had been put on alert to take copies of a book so secret that not even its author or title could be revealed. The publishers, Bloomsbury, had asked stores to order large quantities 'on good faith' which would be supplied on a sale-or-return basis. The book contained material 'of immense public interest'.

Sure enough, *Princess in Love* hit the streets the following day. Diana need not have worried about the effect on her public image. By Tuesday it was apparent that here was a storm fit only for the smallest of teacups.

One tabloid newspaper, the *Daily Star*, carried the headline: 'A Load of Old B*!!*(#s', and urged readers contemplating buying the book to instead send the £14.99 cover price to one of Diana's favourite children's charities: Barnardos. Even the more reserved *Daily Telegraph* described it as a 'kiss-and-tell tale deep in the realms of fantasy'. It was, said the paper, a 'strange alliance between an officer who was no gentleman and a journalist who was no author'.

The problem for Hewitt and Pasternak was that nobody took them seriously. He was already discredited as a cad, a man no longer welcome at his old regiment's Combermere Barracks at Windsor or the officers' Knightsbridge house. She, at twenty-seven, was too inexperienced to carry off her 'scoop'. Worst of all was her gushing, over-egged writing style, which was mercilessly and unanimously savaged by the critics.

Pasternak described the book as an account of the love affair between Hewitt and Diana — 'their story' was the way she put it. Yet it was demonstrably not 'their' story, as Diana had played no part in any research. Pasternak conveniently ignored this fact with some detailed and intimate descriptions of the Princess's emotions during her friendship with Hewitt. One passage reads: 'For the first time in her adult life, as she lay protected and comforted by this man, she felt at peace, as if she had come home after years stranded in an empty, windswept plain.'

The description of their first night of lovemaking, allegedly after a romantic meal at Kensington Palace, reads in similar style:

All Di knew was that she ached to be in his arms, to feel secure, protected by his strength. Suddenly she could not bear it any longer. Her need was too much ... With the ease of a dancer performing a well-worn routine, she stood up, walked across to him and slipped sideways on to his lap. As she landed on him, cupping her hands behind his neck, James was both raging with desire and taken by surprise.

That she should come to him so directly, without any further flirtatious ambiguity, seemed unbelievable. Yet with his antennae on full alert, he was aware of Diana's yearning, of her deep need to be held. He took her in his arms and held her body. He kissed her tenderly, romantically.

The account ends: 'Di stood up and without saying a word stretched out her hand and slowly led James to the bedroom.'

Critics pointed out that the book contained precious few hard facts. No one was quoted, no key dates were recorded and no claims were independently substantiated. The insistence by Pasternak that Hewitt was not cut in on the deal was greeted with incredulity, especially in the light of his upwardly mobile financial fortunes. From scraping by on a paltry £7,000 Army pension, plus whatever work he could get as a riding tutor, he was suddenly the proud owner of a magnificent Georgian country mansion at Bratton Clovelly, Devon.

Within days, Diana had ridden out the brief furore caused by what Buckingham Palace called 'this grubby, worthless little book'. So much so that by the Thursday of that same week, 6 October, the *Daily Mail* was proclaiming: 'Diana Wins The Sympathy Vote'. The newspaper had commissioned an opinion poll carried out in the forty-eight hours after *Princess in Love* was published. The poll found that more than half the public still thought Charles was to blame for the marriage break-up. Only one in ten blamed Diana while 27 per cent said both parties should take their share of the blame.

With the Hewitt time bomb defused, Diana now prepared for Dimbleby's offering. His official biography, she knew, would bear no resemblance to the half-baked format of Pasternak's book. Dimbleby had already shown, in his TV documentary, that he was prepared to tackle sensitive issues such as Charles's adultery. The question now was: How far would the Prince go in defending his conduct?

On 16 October the *Sunday Times* began serialising *The Prince of Wales — A Biography* under the bold red headline: 'The Prince's Agony'. Beneath it a sub-deck read: 'How Could I Have Got It All So Wrong?'. The clear inference was that Charles was admitting the blame for the failure of his marriage. In fact, much of the book pointed up Diana's failings and the burden her very presence had come to be on an emotionally sensitive future King.

Charles made clear to Dimbleby that the marriage was rooted in confusion and agonising self-doubt. From the moment he first met Diana in 1977, at her family's Althorp Park estate in Northamptonshire, he had felt a progressive attraction to her. She was, he told friends, a woman he could easily fall in love with. Yet by the time their courtship culminated in an invitation for Diana to stay with Charles at Balmoral, he was already under pressure to make a long-term decision about their future together.

That autumn of 1980 the Duke of Edinburgh engaged the Prince in a traditional father-and-son backs-to-the-fireplace chat in which he asserted that Charles had to make up his mind about Diana's potential as a bride. Further delays, argued the Duke, would compromise her position and possibly damage her reputation. Charles should either offer her his hand in marriage – delighting both his family and the entire country – or quietly end the affair. Either way he should act soon.

Charles saw this as an ultimatum and believed his father was suggesting he had 'callously exploited' the young Lady Diana Spencer. Confused and anxious, he admitted to one close friend: 'It is just a matter of taking an unusual plunge into some rather unknown circumstances that inevitably disturbs me, but I expect it will be the right thing in the end.' He went on: 'It all seems so ridiculous because I do very much want to do the right thing for this country and for my family – but I'm terrified sometimes of making a promise and then perhaps living to regret it.'

Dimbleby observed:

It was hardly the most auspicious frame of mind in which to offer his hand in marriage. But if his betrothal to Diana was hardly the love match for which his friends had hoped, and which the nation certainly assumed, he was determined their marriage should succeed. Now that he had made what he referred to as *la grande plonge*, any unease was kept to himself. His loyalty to his fiancée was to be absolute.

Within days of the engagement announcement, Dimbleby notes, Charles was seeing a new side to Diana. She was bemused by the stuffy formalities that marked her new life within Palace circles, and felt trapped and lonely. Among those she turned to for companionship were Michael Colborne, the secretary of the Prince's office, and Francis Cornish, Charles's assistant private secretary. They soon saw how interested she was in her fiancé's previous amours, particularly Camilla Parker Bowles. At one point she confided: 'I asked Charles if he was still in love with Camilla and he didn't give me a clear answer. What am I to do?' Neither man could offer her much guidance.

According to Dimbleby, Charles was plunged into a series of Diana-inspired crises from the first days of their married life together. She displayed bizarre mood changes and felt he showed no intimacy towards her. She was already 'obsessed' with his relationship with Camilla and dismissive of his assurances. She would explode in spasmodic bouts of anger, leaving him in bewilderment and despondency.

Throughout the following year, she would berate his friends about her lack of freedom, her boredom, an absence of any clear role for her and her husband's 'heartlessness'. Confrontations developed with his senior staff over her volatile behaviour. She would sit hunched in a corner, desperate to avoid some public engagement, yet still ready to scour tabloid newspapers for a photograph of herself.

'More disconcerting,' wrote Dimbleby,

. . . was her way of so mesmerising individuals that they would find themselves drawn into her confidence and subjugated to the force of her personality, only to be expelled for no apparent reason. The first of several such victims was Everett [Oliver Everett, her private secretary], mild-mannered, courteous to a fault, yet suddenly a 'non-person' – not called to meetings, his memos and phone calls unanswered, his very presence ignored. The Princess was never seen to be offensive to him but neither did she explain what had caused her displeasure. The isolation lasted for months, a festering wound about which he maintained a loyal silence.

The book painted Diana as a woman almost constantly in the throes of severe mental trauma. It told how, shortly after the move into Highgrove, she drove off without telling anybody where she was going, 'if indeed she knew'. Despair 'lurked' about her,

her miserable moods lasted longer and her outlook was bleaker than ever. While the Prince blamed himself for landing her the role of future Queen, his friends were concerned that she wanted too much of his time, that 'in some obscure way she sought to possess him, but only in order to be able to reject him'.

Dimbleby also damningly noted that she was so self-absorbed that she had no interest in events outside her own life. Even the Falklands War could not arouse her curiosity. She 'seemed to resent the interest being shown in the Falklands rather than in her'.

In the Dimbleby book, Charles seemed determined to put right some of the imbalances he believed Diana had planted in the minds of the public through her associations with Andrew Morton. Her suicide attempts were described as 'always less serious than they at first appeared', the cuts on her arms drew blood but 'a sticking plaster invariably sufficed to stem the bleeding'. Charles also told how many of his close friends were banished from his company by Diana, who saw them as 'oilers' (sycophants).

Charles, meanwhile, emerged as a husband desperately trying to do what was right. He pleaded with his friends to remain silent about her irrational behaviour. He loyally made excuses for her, blaming the pressures of the monarchy. He was drained by the 'persistence of his wife's reproaches', yet when she was dejected or crying he tried to console her. When he realised the extent of her mood swings he arranged for her to see a psychiatrist.

And throughout it all he continued to feel 'tenderness and pity' for her, even though he admitted resentment at the way she had diverted the media spotlight from him to her. Friends of the Prince, Dimbleby wrote,

> . . . listened, cajoled and encouraged, and they rarely remonstrated with him for his outbursts of anger and petulance. They knew his weaknesses — his sudden tempers and his tendency to self-pity, self-righteousness and self-centredness — but they loved his strengths the more. If they appeased him more than was his due, it was in the knowledge that his wounds were too raw to endure further aggravation from them.

Reading all this, an independent observer would surely have concluded that Charles was a paragon of patience while Diana was always close to the edge of sanity. But the implication that it was solely her behaviour which pushed him into renewing a sexual relationship with Camilla Parker Bowles in 1986 is dubious. The logic could just as easily be reversed. Could not his ever-present devotion to Camilla during his marriage be what fuelled her manic behaviour?

How then did Charles portray his relationship with Camilla under the forthright questioning of Dimbleby? He admitted three separate affairs over a twenty-year period, the first of which started when he was a twenty-three-year-old naval officer. The Prince immediately 'lost his heart' to her and was devastated to learn during his eight months at sea that she had accepted a proposal from Andrew Parker Bowles.

For ten years their relationship was said to be no more than platonic. They would meet occasionally at parties and both Camilla and her husband received regular invitations to Windsor, Sandringham and Balmoral. Charles began to see her as his best friend and 'sounding board', someone with whom he could share his innermost hopes and fears. During the few occasions they were alone together the friendship took on a new intensity to the point where, said Dimbleby, 'it could properly be described as love'.

The Prince was warned by 'one or two' members of his family that any clandestine affair would inevitably turn to scandal if details leaked out. Tabloid treatment of a story in which the heir to the throne was caught wooing a married woman hardly bore thinking about. But Charles – who prided loyalty above all other qualities of friendship – regarded Camilla as his haven in a stormy sea. He was unwilling to drift away from her yet he saw the futility of their situation. Increasingly, he recognised that time was ticking away; that he had a duty to select a bride and produce heirs for the House of Windsor. His dilemma was an unlikely catalyst for love. Yet in Diana Spencer, according to Dimbleby, he genuinely believed he had found someone he could fall in love with.

The Prince told Diana bluntly that Camilla had been one of his dearest friends but that now he was engaged there neither was, nor would be, another woman in his life. He didn't go into detail, assuming this was enough to convince his bride that he was sincere. In fact he acknowledged to himself that his feelings for Camilla had not changed; he had merely accepted that the 'intimacy' could not go on.

At this point in his biography, Dimbleby confronted what many observers believe was the defining moment setting the marriage on course for destruction. It was the occasion in July 1981 when, a few days before her marriage, Diana discovered a bracelet amid the pile of wedding presents and cards heaped in the office of Charles's aide, Michael Colborne. Charles's version of events was that he asked Colborne to buy it for Camilla as a symbol of gratitude for her understanding and support. It had been stamped with the initials GF (Girl Friday), Charles's pet name for his lover.

Diana confronted her husband-to-be and was told he had ordered the bracelet because he did not wish to appear dismissive towards Camilla. In the heated discussion which followed he insisted that 'as an act of courtesy' he felt he should give it to her in person. According to Dimbleby: 'A few days later, true to that word, he gave her the present and said goodbye for what both of them intended to be the last time.' Charles emphatically denied Diana's later claim that he'd spent the eve of his wedding in Camilla's company.

The Prince's third affair with Camilla began 'in late 1986 or early 1987', by which time he believed his marriage had irretrievably broken down. Up until then he claimed he had made 'virtually no contact' with her and telephoned her only once to say that Diana was expecting their first baby. From 1987 onwards she was a regular guest at Highgrove, brought back into his circle along with numerous other close friends who had gained Diana's disapproval.

If the discovery of the GF bracelet stoked Diana's suspicions, the publication of Morton's book *Her True Story* in 1992 finally persuaded Charles that the marriage was doomed. Up until then he had hoped they could live separate lives while learning to be friends, the kind of marriage of convenience long enjoyed by British monarchs and their families. Now that hope was shattered. When Diana refused to put her name to a Buckingham Palace statement which said that the book was inaccurate and distorted to the point of fabrication, Charles's attitude hardened towards her. Yet he still believed it was Diana's friends, rather than she herself, who were behind the Morton episode. Only when the Queen's private secretary, Sir Robert Fellowes, confirmed that the Princess had been instrumental in assisting Morton's researches did Charles decide he would have to seek advice from the Queen. Mother and son now openly discussed the prospects for a separation.

Dimbleby made clear that it was Charles who took

the initiative. The Prince met the distinguished lawyer Lord Goodman to establish the legal implications of a split. Then, in November 1992, after Diana had refused to allow the boys to stay with him at one of his Sandringham weekend parties, he made up his mind. He could no longer conduct his life in this way. On 25 November, he met Diana privately at Kensington Palace and asked her to agree to a legal separation. She consented, and both sides instructed their lawyers to prepare the paperwork.

The Church was consulted and the Archbishop of Canterbury, George Carey, was supportive. He advised that a formal separation would send the right signals to the country as it would emphasise the solemn institution of marriage and the seriousness of vows made before God. The Archbishop's only caveats were that both sides would have to be seen maintaining close contact with their children, and that there should be no extra-marital affairs.

Within hours of the book reaching the public, Charles's motives for assisting Dimbleby were under a media microscope. Most of the reaction was critical. Newspapers felt he had been poorly advised by his staff and that the book would do nothing to restore his battered image. Buckingham Palace was particularly disillusioned because publication had upstaged the Queen and Prince Philip's historic state visit to Russia. Sir Robert Fellowes could not understand why the Prince's private secretary, Richard Aylard, had not put more pressure over the book's timing on Dimbleby's publishers Little, Brown.

Prince Philip, while careful to avoid open criticism, let slip some dark hints about his own attitude to the book. In an interview ostensibly to mark the Moscow visit, he said: 'I've never discussed private matters and I don't think the Queen has either. Very few members of the family have. I don't know why it has happened or how it has happened or what the constraints are. I'd rather not get involved in it. I've never made any comment about any member of the family in forty years and I'm not going to start now.'

Some commentators asked why Charles's close friends had not intervened to talk him out of a project which had come across as a massive exercise in self-justification. As one put it: 'The book and the television film will be remembered in history for one thing and one thing only. The point at which the heir to the throne publicly admitted adultery.'

One friend of the Prince observed: 'I thought Dimbleby would do a better job of protecting the Prince. You see, I think he [Charles] was persuaded by all this stuff that Laurens van der Post started years ago about getting in touch with his soul and all that. He started the process which has led to this embarrassing, not to say, catastrophic book.'

Despite these negative reactions, Charles's camp was at first unbowed. St James's Palace said he had 'no regrets' about the book, which it described as 'a balanced and thoroughly researched appraisal of the Prince of Wales's development as an individual and the way he has developed his role'.

The Prince's side was anxious for the book to be judged in its entirety – from Charles's views on his upbringing to his attempts to define his purpose in a future monarchy. It was a noble goal. But it was rather like suggesting that Henry VIII's marital problems should be of no greater interest to history students than his hunting trips.

As an editorial in the august *Sunday Telegraph* so succinctly put it:

> The Prince's advisers keep pointing out that a mere forty or so of 640 pages of the book deal with personal matters and that the important thing is to read the whole book. They should have thought of that before. Millions will read the serialisation, while only thousands will read the book, and the serialisation, needless to say, is carrying very little about worthy initiatives in inner cities and a great deal about love and hate. Now the boys can read that their father never loved their mother and the Queen and the Duke of Edinburgh can read that they were bad parents, and no amount of saying that these are opinions of others in the book rather than those of Prince Charles himself will draw the sting.

Dimbleby mounted a vigorous response to criticism

of the project. Speaking at a press conference (supposedly to launch his new TV political chat show but quickly hijacked by reporters), he said he had enjoyed 'great co-operation' from Charles and that his work had been seen by the Prince before publication.

'The comment and interpretation are mine and mine alone, and I stress that because some of the interpretation that I have included in the book has been relayed as if it was the Prince of Wales's views. I would also stress that, although I had a lot of time with the Prince of Wales, I also spoke to a great many other people as, doubtless, some of you know. This is a biography in that traditional sense, based on documents, letters, correspondence and interviews with a very wide range of people.'

There were other allies. Royal analyst and author Philip Ziegler said the 'remarkable biography' was a far more important study of Charles than the titillating serialised sections suggested. 'No doubt he did espouse some rather outré causes and gave hostages to fortune by the more gnomic of his pronouncements,' Ziegler observed. 'But it is notable how often the world has moved towards his point of view. The portrait which emerges from this book is overwhelmingly one of a hard-working, conscientious and thoughtful man, energetic and resourceful, painfully honest and sincere, concerned above all about the state of the nation.'

Despite these entreaties, Charles's attempts to justify his actions had clearly backfired with the public. One readers' survey by a national newspaper showed that more than 60 per cent still sided with Diana against her husband while 65 per cent felt he was no longer fit to become King.

Within a week of the first serialisation appearing, even Charles was reported to have had second thoughts and now regretted co-operating with Dimbleby. His main concerns were that the public were interpreting the views of his friends, and the author, as his own. He also felt they had confused an authorised biography with an approved one.

On 31 October, Dimbleby himself returned to the fray with an outspoken attack on the media:

Specifically, the headlines which said 'Charles: I Didn't Love My Wife' were picked up, reported and tossed around the world as if they were true. On the contrary, the book makes very clear that given the extremely difficult decisions about the whole process of marriage – inevitable if you are heir to the throne – the marriage was extremely difficult and collapsed in misery, but involved tenderness, compassion and concern on both sides.

What is so hideous is the extent to which this misery which they have both endured has been treated as a spectacle, as a feast on which piranhas can indulge themselves to the apparent benefit of a public which I believe is far more sensitive, compassionate and sympathetic and, when they understand the truth, understanding of both individuals.

Dimbleby admitted the Prince had taken a gamble. 'For many years his life was covered particularly by tabloid newspapers on the basis of innuendo, concoction, distortion and frequently downright lies week after week after week,' he said. 'But if he had stayed silent for ever he was not just being assassinated slowly by character description, he was actually being killed off by the tabloid papers. To that degree I think it was not a foolish decision.'

For Diana, the year's second big hurdle was over. Now for the third ... What did Andrew Morton have in store?

On Sunday 6 November, the Princess sat down to read his account of her affairs following the separation. News of a second Morton book had haunted her for months because she feared her enemies would again trot out complaints that she was trying to upstage Charles. Publishing it so close to Dimbleby's official biography was provocative to say the least and she had already made her feelings clear. 'I have had nothing to do with this,' she assured friends.

In fact the book *Diana, Her New Life*, again serialised by the *Sunday Times*, was a damp squib compared with the author's original blockbuster. Its revelations were largely a matter of gossip and detail, although it did set out Diana's growing dread that her children would be used as bargaining tools once lawyers began hammering out a divorce settlement.

Morton suggested the fate of the Princes was rapidly becoming an obsession for the Princess. She had always regarded William and Harry as the most precious people in her life and the thought that they could be gradually removed from her, and schooled under Charles's influence, was anathema. She began to dwell on all kinds of Machiavellian plots which she feared were being prepared against her.

These took a physical form in the shape of the boys' unofficial nanny, twenty-nine-year-old Tiggy Legge-Bourke. Diana would seethe as she studied newspaper pictures of Harry sitting on Tiggy's knee, or read that she was in the habit of calling the boys 'my babies'. It seemed obvious to the Princess that her husband's camp was trying to provide a surrogate mother and, eventually, a flavour of 'family' atmosphere. Her friends were sympathetic. 'Absolutely outrageous', one told Morton, hinting that if Diana hired a male nanny to look after the children the Palace would be in uproar.

Tiggy had been taken on by the Prince of Wales in September 1993 to help his private secretary, Commander Richard Aylard. Her official role was to arrange Charles's diary so that he could be free of engagements when it was his turn to look after the boys. In fact she became almost an instant mother-figure, arranging outings, playing hide and seek in the woods of Balmoral and generally using her effervescent personality to keep them entertained.

Her background was impeccable for a woman in

service with the Royal Family. Her father, William Legge-Bourke, was an ex-soldier who carved out a high-flying career in the City with stockbrokers Kleinwort Benson Securities. Her mother, only daughter of the third Baron Glanusk, inherited the 6,000-acre Glanusk Park estate at Crickhowell, Powys, on the Welsh borders. Tiggy herself had gone into business with her own nursery school – Mrs Tiggywinkles in Battersea, south London – until Charles came up with his job offer.

By the end of 1994, Diana's nagging unease at the role this young woman was playing in her sons' lives had extended far beyond crude jealousy. The collapse of her marriage, and her vastly-reduced public workload, had left her little to cling to but her motherhood. Now it seemed even this could not be held sacred.

Diana wrote to Charles asking him whether he believed Tiggy's relationship with the Princes was really appropriate. She got her answer when he made clear there was no question of switching her to other duties. Diana then hit back by confronting Tiggy herself. Discovering that Charles had left the boys in the nanny's care at Highgrove while he attended to urgent business, she rang up in a blind fury and demanded to speak to Tiggy.

'I am the boys' mother thank you very much,' she told her. More proof that the tigress was spoiling for a fight!

In appointing Tiggy, Charles should have guessed

that he was touching his wife's most sensitive nerve. They had had a furious row soon after the separation when she effectively told him he could stew in his own juice while she brought up the boys in Australia. Such a stinging comment roused Charles's own fatherly fears and he decided he could not dismiss her words as some idle heat-of-the-moment threat. When he consulted his advisers on how to respond they suggested that every effort should be made to encourage Diana to live abroad, because this would dilute the threat she represented to the monarchy. But she had to understand who called the shots over the children.

Palace legal advisers had anticipated the Princess making threats over custody and they had been busy combing the statute book. Sure enough, they came up with the little-known Halsbury's Statutes, which were last activated in 1717 for the convenience of George I (George had wanted to know more about the upbringing of his grandson Frederick). The statutes laid down the right of a sovereign to control the care and education of his or her immediate family, including any grandchildren. This seemed to spike Diana's guns, though in practice it would be hard to imagine the Queen wrecking her own national popularity by invoking it. Certainly Diana's lawyer, Lord Mishcon, could have been expected to contest laws written more than 270 years ago which had never once been tested in the courts.

The new, more aggressive Diana recognised she

still suffered from enormous emotional and physical problems. The disease bulimia nervosa continued to torment her and, as Morton pointed out, she railed against what she perceived as a lack of support from the 'leper colony' – her new name for the Royal Family.

However, she also recognised that Charles no longer held all the trump cards. For one thing, he seemed anxious that *she* initiate divorce proceedings since this approach would be likely to cause less hurt to his grandmother. She told friends that Charles 'seemed very jittery' when she informed him that she was in no rush to set the legal wheels in motion. And she happily accepted Mishcon's advice: 'Sit tight, they will come to us.'

Diana's suspicion that Charles wanted a speedy divorce was born out of two further convictions. The first was the common-sense view that the country would accept him more easily as a monarch if he was already divorced when he ascended the throne. A divorcing King could cause huge problems for the Church of England, of which he would be the constitutional head. It would also mean that, for a time at least, she would become Queen of the United Kingdom, whether crowned or not.

The second conviction stemmed from an approach made to her in April 1994 by Jonathan Dimbleby. He wondered whether she would like to be involved in his TV documentary. More specifically, one of the points he wanted to cover was her reason for not initiating a divorce. Rightly or wrongly, Diana believed Dimbleby was an emissary from Charles. She told the journalist that it would not be in her interests to rush things through. She felt that Charles should be made to acknowledge that it was his adulterous behaviour that directly contributed to the breakdown of the marriage.

When Dimbleby's film then carried the Prince's confession of an extra-marital affair, Diana's friends believed he had complied with her demand and 'loaded the gun' for her to fire. Some pleaded with her to take the opportunity while she could still get out with dignity. Diana took no notice. She still feared that if she began the divorce, she would carry the blame for it.

By the end of 1994, she felt she had crossed a watershed in her life. The combined dangers of Hewitt, Dimbleby and Morton had had little impact on her public image and the perceived threat to her custody of the children had turned her into a far more danger-ous foe than the Diana of late 1993, when she bowed out of public life in tears.

Crucially, she saw how William – the future King – was rallying round and protecting her. He would refuse to help photographers if he believed they had treated his mother badly.

'Why doesn't Daddy protect her,' he once asked. On another occasion he confided: 'I want to be a policeman so that I can look after you, Mummy.'

Once, showing his growing maturity, he advised her against taking a position with the RSPCA on the grounds that she would be compromised by his love of shooting. 'Every time I kill anything they will blame you,' he said.

As Camilla was Charles's rock, so Harry, and especially William, had now become Diana's. She made a point of taking them on regular visits to the Queen, as if emphasising her own position as King Mother. She fought tooth and nail to ensure she got her full share of custody. And she even began her own programme of 'training' to prepare William for his future role. This included a secret visit to meet London's homeless, accompanied by the Catholic Primate of the UK, Cardinal Basil Hume.

As Diana's stargazers and soothsayers looked into her future they could be sure of at least one certain truth. In the divorce ahead, she would be no pushover.

20

The Other Divorce

The new, more assertive Princess of Wales was now openly testing herself against the Royal Family. The Queen had hoped that Diana and Charles could call a 1994 Christmas truce, despite the obvious depth of bitterness between them. This would have enabled the young Princes to be with both their parents for the traditional holiday at Sandringham. Diana, however, would have none of it. She saw such an exercise as hypocritical and self-defeating. Besides, she was not prepared to mooch around the Norfolk estate while Wills and Harry were outside blasting wildlife with their father.

On Christmas Eve Diana grudgingly drove the boys to Sandringham, stopped the obligatory one night, and made a brief appearance at church the following day, when she and Charles made sure they walked several yards apart. She then returned to Kensington Palace and a solitary Christmas dinner prepared in advance by her chef, Mervyn Wycherley. It was a faithful repeat of her Sandringham exit the previous year.

The next two weeks were difficult for Diana. Charles was in charge of the boys for the rest of the Christmas holidays – much of which they would spend skiing at Klosters – and she had little other than her keep-fit regime to occupy her time. Yet she was emotionally much stronger than she had been twelve months before. Besides, there was little time to brood. Unknown to her, the phone lines between Charles and Camilla were hotting up as yet another twist emerged in the divorce plot. This time it was the 'other divorce', the divorce nobody was really expecting.

Shortly after 9 a.m. on Tuesday, 10 January 1995, Andrew and Camilla Parker Bowles issued a joint statement through their solicitors announcing that they intended to seek a divorce. The decision had been reached amicably on the grounds that they had lived apart for more than two years.

The statement added: 'Throughout our marriage we have always tended to follow rather different interests, but in recent years we have led completely separate lives. We have grown apart to such an extent that, with the exception of our children and a lasting friendship, there is little of common interest between us and we have therefore decided to seek divorce.'

Although Camilla was the petitioner (i.e. the partner defined legally as the one asking for a divorce decree), this was merely a convention of the English upper classes and a sop to Andrew's staunch Roman Catholic beliefs. It was considered gentlemanly for a man to allow his wife to make the petition, irrespective of her own behaviour. In fact, pressure to end the marriage had come from Andrew.

For years, following subtle entreaties from Buckingham Palace, he had loyally maintained the veneer of his marriage. As late as 1992, when the newspapers were awash with reports of his wife's affair with Charles, he had doggedly stuck to his brief, with the now-famous quote: 'No, it's not true. How many times do I have to spell it out? It's pure fiction.'

It seems that Andrew and Camilla Parker Bowles jointly reached their decision to live apart in the months after the 'Camillagate' tapes became public, and shortly before the official announcement that Charles and Diana were to separate. Yet the decision to proceed with divorce did not come until the Prince's confession of adultery to Dimbleby. Only then did Andrew Parker Bowles decide he could not be publicly cuckolded by his future King.

'I cannot go on living someone else's life,' he reportedly told friends. Reluctantly, Camilla agreed to their instructing lawyers.

Charles's TV admission was in fact a half-truth. He had indicated only vaguely that adultery had taken place after the 'irretrievable breakdown' of his marriage. Afterwards the Prince had expressed himself well satisfied with his astonishing piece of public relations, seemingly oblivious to the controversy it was bound to cause. Not only had he admitted infidelity to the adored Princess Diana, but he had admitted a sexual liaison with another man's wife.

Even with this provocation, Andrew Parker Bowles managed to keep his cool. 'Our marital situation is unchanged,' he said in a carefully-worded statement about his future with Camilla. Then, unconvincingly, he added: 'There are no plans for any separation or divorce . . .'

A few months later (as we saw in the previous chapter) his wife's role as royal mistress was publicised even more colourfully by the hapless Charles. In his autobiography, it was stated that Charles had had 'three affairs' with Camilla. The first was as a shy, twenty-three-year-old naval officer in 1972 when she was still Camilla Shand. The second was after Camilla was married, and continued from the late 1970s through to the run-up to his wedding. The final infidelity began, according to Charles, in 1986, the year that he judged his marriage to have 'irretrievably broken down'.

Andrew himself had not been entirely devoid of lady friends throughout this latter part of his marriage. He was a visitor to the Kensington apartment of divorcee Rosemary Pitman. In 1993 he was photographed leaving the south London home of Carolyn Benson, a Camilla lookalike with whom he denied anything but a platonic friendship. And when in 1994 he retired from the Army, after ending his career as a Brigadier in charge of the Veterinary and Remount Services, based at Aldershot, he was consoled by an old flame, Lady Annabel Lindsay, at her Holland Park home.

The Parker Bowleses' divorce papers revealed that in the previous two years they had spent only ninety days together under the same roof, namely their mansion at Corsham in Wiltshire. Under the intricacies of English law, they could still argue that they were 'separated', provided they had not shared household tasks such as cooking, washing and paying bills and that they had refrained from having sex or eating together. The petitioner (in this case Camilla) would have been required to swear an affidavit to this effect.

The timing of the divorce announcement was the subject of intense discussion between all parties in the weeks before Christmas 1994. Charles was given the news personally by Camilla during a meeting at Corsham. He tried to talk her out of ending the marriage, arguing that he and she could never expect to remarry in any case. His words were to no avail and the Prince left, according to one photographer, in tears.

Charles later returned for a second meeting, at which Andrew Parker Bowles was also present, and again pleaded with the couple to reconsider. They told him the situation had become untenable and that the façade would have to end. Seeing little point in further argument, the Prince persuaded them to agree delaying the announcement until January so as not to ruin everybody's Christmas.

Unlike Charles, poor Diana had been given no warning of what was to come. The first she heard of the divorce was on a news bulletin at Kensington Palace as she and her boys prepared to enjoy the last day of the school holidays together. She was not unduly surprised, although she had not expected such a move quite so soon. She also noted the view of some Buckingham Palace aides that developments over her own failed marriage were likely to move 'very quickly' from now on.

The Princess had every reason to feel satisfied with the way things had turned out. Although she had had to endure the recent Oliver Hoare and Hewitt revelations, it seemed that the spotlight was now turning inexorably back on to Charles and Camilla. Within a week they would again be the villains of the piece.

Five days after the divorce announcement, the *News of the World* carried a front-page story headlined: 'Charles Bedded Camilla As Diana Slept Upstairs'. The article, based on claims by the Prince's long-time valet Ken Stronach, revealed that Charles had made love to his mistress in the bushes at Highgrove while his unsuspecting wife was asleep inside. Stronach told how he had once had to scrub grass stains from the knees of the Prince's pyjamas. 'There was mud and muck everywhere,' he said. 'They'd obviously been doing it in the open air.'

There then followed an account of the elaborate precautions Charles would take to keep his nights of passion secret from staff. His green-stained pyjamas, for instance, were separated from the rest of his laundry and washed personally by Stronach. Camilla would always be allocated her own guest bedroom when she came to stay but as soon as all was quiet she would sneak down the corridor to snuggle up with Charles. She knew her Prince would have neutralised the personal security system which fired a network of invisible infra-red beams around his bedroom.

After their nights of passion, Stronach would meticulously remove the 'evidence'. New sheets would be placed on the bed, rumpled and creased up on Charles's side to give the impression that only one person had slept in it. Down in Camilla's bedroom, the dirty linen from Charles's room would replace the unused linen on her bed. The intention was to defuse gossip among 'downstairs' staff. 'It was very elaborate,' said Stronach, 'but it didn't fool anyone for a minute.'

Of Camilla's visits to Highgrove, he observed: 'We were told to treat her as if she was the mistress of the house. It was as if the Princess never existed.'

The following day *The Sun* newspaper joined the open season on Camilla and Charles with a serialisation of a hastily updated book, *The King's Mistress*, by journalist Caroline Graham. The book carried precise detail of the royal affair, revealing how Charles and Camilla would meet secretly at her Corsham home and enjoy cosy suppers of cold chicken and strawberries and cream at the kitchen table. They would then climb upstairs to her bedroom, glasses of red wine in hand, to make love bathed in candlelight. Charles's detective, Colin Trimming, would have to wait patiently downstairs in what used to be the Parker Bowles children's nursery.

Charles visited Corsham virtually every Sunday evening between 1989 and 1994 for these eagerly-awaited trysts. Camilla would signal his imminent arrival by shutting off all the lights and drawing the downstairs curtains, effectively imposing a blackout. Her staff were both baffled and amused by the charade. Soon Charles was nicknamed 'The Prince of Darkness' because he appeared at nightfall and always left for Highgrove before daybreak.

It was also revealed how Camilla would cancel any engagement, at whatever notice, if it meant she could be with her lover. One source said:

I remember in the summer of 1989 Camilla was meant to join Andrew for a London dinner, the retirement party for his senior officer. It was a privilege to be invited and Andrew was very excited. But just a few hours before the dinner Camilla phoned Andrew to say she had been struck down by flu and was too ill to attend. Andrew was livid.

He told me he ordered her to ring the officer's wife herself to make her own bloody excuses.

Camilla told her staff of her 'illness' and took to her bed. A few hours later Charles's car was seen rolling up the drive.

A few months earlier, in May 1989, Andrew Parker Bowles at last accepted the truth he had so long denied: that his wife was indeed the future King's mistress. According to Caroline Graham's research, the moment of realisation came during a holiday in Turkey arranged by Charles's close friend Nicholas Soames. Camilla and Andrew were among the party.

'Emotions always run high on holidays, with the sun shining and booze flowing,' said Caroline Graham's source. 'Camilla and Charles were obviously very relaxed together. It is fair to say that, even to an untrained eye, their behaviour was more flirtatious than is the way between ordinary friends. There was a kind of feverishness about them when they were together, the kind that lovers often exude.'

Andrew became more and more morose and, during one restaurant outing, began mouthing comments about the Prince's behaviour towards his wife — an action that was out of keeping with his usual demeanour.

Although Andrew was by now furious at the turn of events, he normally managed to stay true to his breeding as an officer and a gentleman. Even at the height of the 'Camillagate' tape furore, it had been Andrew, rather than Charles, who had come to Camilla's aid. It had been he who arranged a hideaway where she could weather the storm, and he who later offered a public show of unity by strolling in the grounds of Middlewick House with her at his side. He even told friends: 'Really, Charles is a very nice chap, you know.'

Camilla's reaction to publicity surrounding her affair had been to maintain a dignified public silence. But in private, her bitter rivalry with Diana would occasionally surface. When in November 1992 a newspaper had revealed that Diana referred to her as 'the Rottweiler', she was livid. She dashed into the kitchen of her home yelling: 'Get me a copy of *The Sun*. I hear that woman has called me a Rottweiler.' She then snatched the newspaper from the hands of her cook and began mumbling angrily as she saw a picture of herself alongside the breed in question.

Camilla's dislike of Diana was obvious in other ways. One friend of the Parker Bowles family said: 'Camilla read every word ever written about Diana. Every single magazine and newspaper which carried Diana's picture or even two lines about her movements was bought by Camilla. She would scour the news-stand at Sainsbury's, flicking through the papers for any mention of Diana. When one newspaper compared Camilla unfavourably with Diana, Camilla got upset.

'She cancelled one newspaper after one of Prince

Charles's visits. His detective Colin Trimming had been sitting in the playroom as usual, waiting for Charles to leave. He flicked through one of the papers and left it open at an article that was horrible about Camilla. She found it when she had popped into the playroom to get a video. Camilla was livid and said she wouldn't have the paper in the house again. But apart from the Rottweiler story, Camilla always managed to keep her cool.'

The last rites for the Parker Bowles marriage were enacted during a seventy-five-second hearing on 19 January 1995 in the Family Division of the High Court. Their names were listed alongside those of thirty-one other couples on a tatty piece of paper fixed with a drawing pin to the door of Court Number Two. Inside, Judge Gerald Angel asked the handful of curious spectators: 'Does any party or person wish to show cause against the decrees being pronounced?' There was silence.

Nodding, the judge gathered his papers and strode away. The decree nisi, costing £40, was granted. A decree absolute, costing £15, would be approved six weeks and a day later.

In this clinical, methodical manner, the marriage of Andrew and Camilla Parker Bowles was dissolved. Only the British courts could produce such a neat understatement for such a climactic moment in the history of the British monarchy. Now Camilla was a free woman. Would Charles soon be a free man?

21

Scales of Justice

For the lawyers engaged on the case of Windsor versus Windsor, professional life can never be the same again. Representing one of the Waleses in the divorce courts amounts to stumbling across an unworked diamond mine in your own backyard. In business terms, handling such a high-profile case turns the lawyers into magnets for mega-rich clients. There is also the delicious social kudos. Lawyers are no different from the rest of the chattering classes and the mere fact that they have moved in such hallowed circles marks them out as members of their profession's elite.

There is a third consideration, however, far more weighty than money or social standing. The records will document the most sensational royal divorce case since Henry VIII sidestepped the more awkward aspects of canonical law. Windsor versus Windsor is not just a ticket to legal fame and fortune. It is the stuff of history.

In Britain, people tend to think of divorce as the invention of Henry VIII. In fact it was widely accepted long before his time. It formed a recognised part of Babylonian, Hebrew, Greek and Roman law, and only with the rise of Christianity was there established the idea that marriage should be indissoluble.

Unfortunately for Henry, the Catholic Church of the early sixteenth century was not known for its progressiveness. Faced with the intransigence of the Pope, who refused to annul his marriage to Catherine of Aragon, the King did what has always come naturally to the British Establishment: he changed the rules! Even so, it was four years before legislation was passed to make him supreme governor of the English Church and Defender of the Faith (the title, ironically, first bestowed upon him by the Pope). Only then was Henry at last free to marry his lover Anne Boleyn.

In those days it was relatively simple for a monarch to bend the law to suit his needs. Not so today. As we will see in the next chapter, Charles and Diana had to complete precisely the same forms in precisely the same way as any other estranged couple. The Queen's view has no relevance legally, and is not sought by the courts. Neither can the judge, nor the registrar, attach any weight to the constitutional implications of their decision, other than the way it might affect the children.

In picking her way through the minefield of divorce, Diana needed quality advice. Her lawyer, Lord Mishcon, had been introduced to her by one of her most

trusted friends, Lord Palumbo. With a client list
which included the Duchess of York, Lord Archer,
Robert Maxwell and millionaire Gerald Ronson, Victor
Mishcon was already well versed in the personal
problems of the wealthy and famous. Though not a
divorce specialist, his fast grasp of even the most
complicated civil tort was legendary. As one observer
put it: 'Despite his seventy-nine years, his mind is still
as sharp as ever. He has great originality of thought
and also kindness and stability. Though he will fight
for his clients, it is always done with good manners
and an old-fashioned avoidance of personal acrimony.
But never think he is a soft touch.'

Mishcon was perfect for Diana's needs. His practice,
Mishcon De Reya, was the embodiment of a high-
class law firm yet it eschewed the snobbery associated
with the Queen's solicitors, Farrer and Co. Despite his
contacts with the rich and famous and his weighty
scale of fees (around £300 an hour), Mishcon has
never courted the Establishment or the media. On the
contrary, his politics are left-wing and much of his
spare time is devoted to helping the under-privileged.

His role in advising the Princess was not so much
to take her through the nitty-gritty of a divorce case.
Rather, he provided a sympathetic ear, advice on
which legal experts to engage, reliable counsel and,
always, a good idea of the implications for her future.

Under the Matrimonial Causes Act of 1973, a divorcing couple have to show that their marriage has

irretrievably broken down. There are only five reasons which will be accepted: adultery or intolerability, unacceptable behaviour, desertion for two years, five years' continuous separation (with or without both parties' consent) or two years' continuous separation (with both parties' consent).

Certainly Diana could have cited three of these reasons if she were so minded: adultery (her husband has already admitted it before some eighteen million television witnesses), unacceptable behaviour, and two years' separation with consent. Charles, for his part, could have opted for either his wife's unacceptable behaviour or the two-year rule. If he thought his hand was strong enough, he could also have filed on the grounds of adultery. Desertion would have been ruled out of the reckoning because both the Waleses had agreed to the separation. And the five-year rule was irrelevant.

So what of the choices available to Charles and Diana?

In lawyer-speak, adultery means voluntarily having sex with someone of the opposite gender, while one or other of the parties is married. It doesn't matter how long ago the act took place. However, the partner who wants divorce on grounds of adultery must show that it would be intolerable to take the cheating spouse back.

Unacceptable behaviour is loosely defined as that in which one of the parties cannot reasonably be expected to continue living with the other. Examples include physical violence, alcohol or drug misuse, psychological distress, growing apart, arguments, and even insufficient (or too much) sexual intercourse. As the pages of this book have already shown, either of the Waleses could probably have mounted a case under this category.

Unfortunately, citing unacceptable behaviour or adultery benefits only the lawyers. For that reason alone, both Charles and Diana had always understood that the sanest course was to go for a 'no fault' divorce on the grounds of two years' separation. This option required only that the Waleses had lived apart and that both consented to the end of the marriage. It is even acceptable for them to have continued living under the same roof, provided they were not living 'as man and wife'. In fact, Charles effectively moved out of Kensington Palace soon after the separation announcement in the House of Commons on 9 December 1992.

Having chosen separation as the best method of divorce, the next step was to try to agree which of the couple would be the Petitioner (i.e. the spouse who first deposits papers with the court) and who would be the Respondent. Under British law, it is not possible to file a joint petition, even though both parties might want to do so.

Soon after the separation announcement, Diana was telling friends privately that she would not agree to act as Petitioner. She felt her image in the country would take a further knock if she were seen to be taking the lead in proceedings. Charles had other worries. He agonised over the hurt a divorce would cause his grandmother. Neither did he want history to record him as the driving force behind the split. Despite these obstacles, the Waleses did agree on one thing. They both had to begin new lives. The sooner a fresh start was made the better.

To begin divorce proceedings in Britain, a Petitioner must send two copies of his or her application to any one of the 170-plus county courts with a divorce jurisdiction, or, alternatively, apply directly to the Divorce Registry at Somerset House, in London. In either case, standard forms have to be used under the terms of the Matrimonial Causes Rules of 1977.

As we have already seen, the Petitioner must also submit a marriage certificate, a 'Prayer' for the divorce to be granted, a 'Statement of Arrangements for Children' and a 'Certificate of Conciliation' confirming that both parties have been offered the services of a conciliator whose job it is to sort out arrangements for support of and access to the children.

These and other documents are deposited with the court and sent to the Respondent, who replies with his or her 'Answer' – an opportunity for the Respondent to counter any allegations made by the Petitioner.

The court then looks at both sets of documents and makes a judgment on three key matters: residency of

the children, the splitting of assets, and future maintenance of the spouse. A decree nisi is then normally
granted, followed six weeks later by the decree
absolute.

All of this presupposes, of course, that the court is
satisfied that the marriage has 'irretrievably broken
down'. No doubt about that in the case of Windsor
versus Windsor. What was in conflict, however, was
the fundamental issue of which party actually made
the first move to launch a Petition.

Prince Charles made it clear that he wished his wife
to do so, and that the grounds should be two years'
separation. But as the price of falling in with these
plans, Princess Diana drew up a list of demands that
her husband would not accept. The divorce became
bogged down at this primary stage.

Ironically, Diana, realising that she for once had the
whip hand, was happy to see things slide. She had
time to hone her demands for a share of Charles's
wealth and for sweeping rights over her children. She
also had a chance to consider less 'amicable' grounds
upon which to launch a Petition than those of 'two
years' separation'. It was at this stage that she played
her trump card – the threat to turn Charles's dreams of
a 'quickie' divorce into the nightmare scenario of a
scandal-ridden divorce action on the grounds of her
husband's adultery with her hated rival, Camilla Parker
Bowles.

Under these circumstances, Charles's lawyers would

have been forced to retaliate with the threat of a petition by Prince Charles on the same grounds, adultery, with the possibility of an additional allegation, of unreasonable conduct.

While the adultery allegation would require specific proof that Diana had enjoyed an affair or affairs during the course of the marriage, the allegation of unreasonable conduct would be less inflammatory. In legal jargon, it requires the court to be satisfied that the Respondent has behaved in such a way that the Petitioner 'cannot reasonably be expected to live with the Respondent'.

All this was no more than clever swordsmanship, however. Bringing the divorce to a quiet, unsensational conclusion had always been the lawyers' ultimate aim. A petition on the simple grounds of two years' separation requires only the following, unsensational affirmation to the court: 'That the parties to the marriage have lived apart for a continuous period of at least two years immediately preceding the presentation of this Petition and the Respondent consents to a decree being granted.'

This simple device for a 'painless' divorce was the only sensible solution for both of the royal protagonists. And despite their conflicting claims, both knew it.

It was at this stage that the respective lawyers for the Waleses came into their own. For months they had been the go-betweens in some good old-fashioned horse trading. Now each side began sharpening its bargaining tools. And, as in the case of so many destructive divorce contests, it was the children who would become unwitting ammunition in the parents' war.

The Princess of Wales would already have answered *pro forma* questions in her so-called 'Statement of Arrangements for Children'. They included such extraordinary items as . . .

Addresses at which the children now live: Principally at Kensington Palace, London, and at Highgrove House, near Tetbury, Gloucestershire, but also intermittently at Buckingham Palace, Windsor Castle, Balmoral, Sandringham and other homes of the Crown.

Number of living rooms, bedrooms etc at the address above: Several hundred.

All other persons living with the children: The Petitioner's household includes a private secretary, three detectives, a press secretary and occasionally five ladies-in-waiting. There are also valets, butlers, dressers, gardeners, telephone operators, housekeepers, and other kitchen and domestic staff. The apartments of Kensington Palace are also the home to various relatives of the children: Princess Margaret, Prince and Princess Michael of Kent and the Duke and Duchess of Gloucester. The respondent's household includes a private secretary, a deputy secretary, three assistants, a public-relations executive, a press secretary and several assistants, along with diverse advisers. Buckingham Palace also houses the children's grandparents: Her Majesty the Queen and His Royal Highness the Duke of Edinburgh.

Will there be any changes in these arrangements? Yes. As the children grow older, more time will be spent under Buckingham Palace tutelage to prepare them for their adult royal duties, in particular the duties of William as heir to the throne.

Such responses would have made unique reading for the court clerks. But Princess Diana knew that full and honest answers to the questioning about her children would help her cause. She had been told that the court would almost certainly side with her on arrangements for the boys; judges and registrars tend to take the time-honoured view that young children need regular access to their mother more than their father. In any event, Charles's hectic schedule would give him little chance for 'quality time' with his children, other than holidays and weekends. However, Diana's side also recognised that the boys, particularly William, would need to spend more and more time under the wings of Buckingham Palace aides and mentors.

Grooming an heir to the throne involves much more than ethereal discussions on court etiquette and protocol. If William was to be an effective ruler he would need a good grasp of the constitution, of national politics, of foreign affairs and of the key domestic issues of the day. These were not matters that could wait until he came of age. Indeed, the tutelage had already begun.

But while Diana accepted the need for her sons to grow up with a sense of duty, she was concerned about the prospect of some courtiers attempting to turn them against her. In briefing sessions with her lawyers, she made it clear that she should have unrestricted access and regular breaks alone with them. On this, above all else, she was not prepared to compromise.

Charles's advisers knew this would be her negotiating stance. They also knew they could mount a fair case for frustrating her demands by pointing out her unpredictable behaviour and medical history. The strange phone calls to Oliver Hoare, and her problems with bulimia, were among the most obvious examples. It could be argued on these grounds alone that she was not sufficiently stable to exercise care and control over her children.

Of course, the Prince's lawyers realised that such damaging allegations against one of the world's best-loved mothers could be levelled only behind closed doors. Were it to go public, it would subject Charles to opprobrium – as a cold, heartless figure intent on depriving his defenceless wife of her beloved sons. Such publicity would be another PR disaster.

The feeling in Charles's camp was that playing the 'unstable mother' card should be used only as a last resort in the event that negotiations turned nasty. Lawyers believed Diana could be brought to heel simply with the carrot of reasonable access to her two boys and sufficient funds to enjoy a respectable lifestyle.

Yet it would be wrong to assume Charles retained the trump cards. Diana held one that was capable of blowing away all the neat, clever strategies dreamed up by her opponents. At any time, she could decide to revert to a suit for divorce on grounds of her husband's adultery and, if necessary, she could name Camilla Parker Bowles as Co-Respondent. Such a move would engulf the monarchy in a tidal wave of embarrassment. No longer would Charles be able to brush aside his extra-marital affair with vague responses to a television interviewer. His adultery would be firmly on the record. If it didn't actually cost him the throne, it would nevertheless be another damning blow to his ambitions.

With all this in mind, the two sets of lawyers set about explaining the niceties of child contact and residency to their respective clients. Again, the royal couple were advised that they could expect no special treatment from the courts.

If the Waleses had failed to agree arrangements for their children, they would have been assigned a court welfare officer. He or she would have prepared a report for the judge pending a full trial (in private) at which both partners would put their case. In this messy scenario, one or other parent might have found themselves with greatly reduced responsibilities for the children. In such a conflict, the judge's principal duty would have been to decide residency (i.e. where the children would live) and contact (how often the parent who failed to get residency could see them). In theory, neither parent would be preferred over the other but if a father had left the family home – as Charles did – he would stand less chance of obtaining residency. It is accepted that the parent remaining in the family home is the one most likely to offer security and some continuity.

However, such guidelines flew out of the window very early in the case of Windsor versus Windsor. For a start, Wills and Harry could be said to have numerous homes: principally Highgrove, Kensington Palace, Balmoral, Windsor, Sandringham, and Buckingham Palace. They had never known much continuity of residence while their parents were married. Why should it matter after divorce?

No wonder the lawyers exhorted their Royal Highnesses never to let matters reach this point. The last thing either needed was to fill out form CHA10 (Application for a Contact Order, Prohibited Steps Order, Residence Order or Specific Issue Order) and wrangle over who was the better parent.

There had been many disagreements between the Prince and Princess over contact with the children, usually centring on holidays, especially the Christmas break, but these had always been resolved. Longer-term custody and access were matters that involved the go-betweens in months of negotiations. The next stage of the divorce settlement, the division of assets, was no less complicated.

Where do you begin to add up the assets of the Prince of Wales? In theory, Diana can claim half of everything he owns. If he inherits the throne, and gains further assets, she is even entitled to return to court to ask for a bigger share. Yet Charles could argue that much of his wealth is not within his personal gift. Many of his estates and properties are owned by the Crown and outside his control. From the court's point of view, if he can't sell an asset, then he doesn't own it.

The procedures for redistributing a couple's wealth are complex. As Petitioner, Charles would have had to furnish the court with an 'affidavit of means' stating his financial position simply and succinctly. It would have detailed the financial background and history of the marriage and included items such as the number of cars owned, savings, stocks and shares, art treasures, other valuables, land and property. He would also have had to reveal his outgoings, such as payment of secretaries, butlers and other aides, and include such fine detail as the size of his monthly telephone, gas and water bills. These might seem trivial matters, yet they again emphasise the point that the rules can not be rewritten for the convenience of royalty.

At this stage documentation is crucial. Charles would have been forced to produce bank statements, share certificates, pension policies and valuations of his private estate. Property valuations are one of the most notorious bones of contention in divorces. Often a husband and wife will cast around for the opinions of numerous surveyors until they find one that best suits their cause. In an unpredictable housing market it is difficult enough pricing an ordinary semi-detached home in suburbia, never mind Highgrove with all its royal connotations.

Charles also risked suffering the humiliation of having his personal bank accounts and credit-card statements scrutinised by Diana. She would be entitled to check on all transactions to see if there had been any surprising movement of large cash sums. But she would also have been within her rights to query smaller purchases. Just what did that £500 buy at Harvey Nichols? A new dress perhaps? Which lucky lady received that?

Charles would have had to send two copies of his 'financial application' to the courts and pay a small fee (£20 in 1994) to have them stamped. One would have been filed with the court; the other sent to Diana together with his affidavit of means. She would then have had fourteen days to respond, setting out in full her own statement of financial affairs.

By now Charles would have learned the salutary lesson applicable to all divorcing men who have been a family's main provider. It matters not whether he earned every penny ever spent. In law, none of the family assets is his or hers. He has no automatic right to a single personal possession. Everything is considered to be the couple's joint property. In an estate as large as that of the Prince of Wales, it would clearly be impossible for Diana to know every financial detail. However, if a particular bank statement which interested her was not forthcoming, the Princess could serve a Rule 2.63 Questionnaire on her husband requiring him to disclose it. He would then have no choice but to comply.

Charles's integrity in revealing his affairs is not in question. Apart from any other considerations, it would be madness for him to attempt to conceal assets in the hope of reducing his wife's cut. If she were ever to find out and haul him back to court, a judge would certainly take a dim view and impose the harshest redivision possible. The Waleses have always had a strong incentive to agree a division of assets. Failure to do so would have meant a full court hearing taking the form of a trial. Diana would have been able to call witnesses and constitutional authorities to support her claims about Charles's wealth. He in turn would have responded with his own expert witnesses. It could all have got very bloody.

A further, vital argument in any divorce is over the question of maintenance. Diana's ambition for her own court, centred on some impressive estate, infuriated Charles. Yet he has had to recognise her right to enjoy the same lifestyle in divorce as she did in marriage. The Princess, on the other hand, has had to tread carefully on three counts . . .

Firstly, she could not demand a large country mansion (something she yearned for) if it meant rejecting out of hand an offer to remain at Kensington Palace. Diana is known to find the Palace oppressive and unwelcoming, yet the courts would probably regard such objections as unacceptable. The judge was concerned with her housing and lifestyle, not her personal taste and aesthetic preferences.

Secondly, there was the question of a 'Calderbank Offer'. Either the Petitioner or Respondent to a divorce has the right to make an offer of maintenance which is not disclosed to the court during a hearing. If this offer turns out to be greater than that awarded by the judge, the party which rejected the Calderbank Offer is liable for legal costs ffrom the date of rejecting it.

Thirdly, Diana could not expect the courts to hand her a meal ticket for life. If a divorced woman no longer has pre-school-age children on her hands, a judge will normally expect her to find work which might reduce her husband's maintenance. Clearly this is somewhat difficult when the divorcing woman is the Princess of Wales. Nevertheless, it is a factor in the overall maintenance equation.

The court can grant a decree nisi — accepting that the divorce satisfies one of the five legal requirements for irretrievable breakdown — before child custody and the financial split have been agreed. But the divorce cannot be made absolute until there is the agreement of both sides. It is only when an agreement fails to materialise that husband and wife attend a trial to put their arguments to the judge.

In all the speculation about the Prince and Princess's divorce, politicians and commentators have sometimes tried to pretend that timing is irrelevant. That there would be no problem if the couple were never to divorce. That they could lead separate lives, act as dutiful parents and perform their respective duties without ever going near a courtroom. In theory this is all fine. But in practice timing is of crucial importance.

If the Queen were to die or abdicate, and Charles ascended the throne, Diana would immediately become Queen Consort – the legal wife of a reigning sovereign. She would not need a crowning ceremony in Westminster Abbey to achieve this. A Coronation would merely solemnise a title which is hers by right. However, if divorce came before Charles ascended the throne, Diana would be constitutionally no more than a private person.

This is why the Prince railed against a long delay before divorce. The prospect of Diana becoming Queen Consort filled him with dread. He would never have been able to put their marriage behind him and he could never depose her, unless Parliament agreed to pass a special Act. The nightmarish prospect of two rival courts vying for the people's affections would have become grim reality. The court battle of Windsor versus Windsor might have ended. The war of the Windsors would have stretched endlessly on.

22

Petitions in the Divorce Registry

(This is how the Princess of Wales could have prepared her Petition for the Divorce Registry. Being a member of the Royal Family offers no special privileges in a divorce action, and makes no difference to the way in which Princess Diana has to complete such forms. She is under an obligation to answer all questions put to her and to back them up with written evidence.

This applies equally to the Prince of Wales. The fact that he is the son of the Queen makes no difference in most areas of the law. Neither does a grandparent have any say over a divorce court's arrangements for grandchildren.

For the purpose of this exercise, we have taken the likely form of a Petition to be presented by Princess Diana. In the event of there not being agreement about a divorce settlement and access rights to the children, she could have had her lawyers draw up a Petition on the grounds of 'FACT A' (below): adultery.

Prince Charles's response would then have been to draw

up an 'Answer' and a 'Cross-Petition'. The Answer contains his replies to his wife's allegations. A Cross-Petition contains Charles's counter-allegations against his wife.

In this particular case, the Prince could have filed a Cross-Petition on the very same grounds as his wife's — adultery. Or he could have cited the less inflammatory grounds of unreasonable behaviour.

Alternatively, he could have hedged his bets and petitioned for divorce both on the grounds of adultery and ('in the alternative' is the neat legal phrase) on the grounds of unreasonable behaviour.

For the purpose of this exercise, we have assumed that Charles, wishing to temper the sensationalism surrounding the case, would have chosen to petition for divorce on the grounds of 'FACT B': unreasonable behaviour.

However, after all legal arguments between solicitors, the final Petition most likely to end up before the court would always have been one on the least controversial grounds: 'FACT D' — separation for two years.)

[The **bold type** in the forms below indicates the lawyers' insertions]

IN THE DIVORCE REGISTRY

The Petition of **Diana Frances Windsor** shows that

1. On the thirtieth day of July 1981 the Petitioner was lawfully married to: **Charles Philip Arthur George**

Windsor (hereinafter called the Respondent) at **St Paul's Cathedral** in the district of the **City of London**.

2. The Petitioner and the Respondent last lived together as husband and wife at **Kensington Palace, London, and at Highgrove House, near Tetbury, Gloucestershire**.

3. The Petitioner is domiciled in England and Wales. The Petitioner is a **Princess of the British Royal Family** and resides at **Kensington Palace, London**, and the Respondent is a **Prince of the British Royal Family** and resides at **St James's Palace, London**.

4. There are no children of the family now living except: **William Arthur Philip Louis and Henry Charles Albert David**.

5. No other child now living has been born to the Petitioner during the marriage (so far as is known to the Petitioner).

6. There are or have been no other proceedings in any Court in England and Wales or elsewhere with reference to the marriage or between the Petitioner and the Respondent with reference to any property of either or both of them.

7. There are no proceedings continuing in any country outside England and Wales which relate to the marriage or are capable of affecting its validity or substance.

8. No agreement or arrangement has been made or is proposed to be made between the parties for the support of the Petitioner and any child of the family.

9. There have been no applications under the Child Support Act 1991 for a Maintenance Assessment in respect of any child of the family.

10. The said marriage has broken down irretrievably.

11. FACT A
(i) *That the Respondent has committed adultery and the Petitioner finds it intolerable to live with the Respondent.*
(ii) Here insert grounds of adultery: *That the Respondent has committed adultery on diverse occasions and locations, including the marital home of Highgrove House, for many years throughout the period of the marriage with the Co-respondent Mrs Camilla Parker Bowles, of Middlewick House, Corsham, Wiltshire.*

11. FACT B (*Not Applicable*)
(This, however, would form the basis of Charles's Answer and Cross-Petition. See below.)
(i) That the Respondent has behaved in such a way that the Petitioner cannot reasonably be expected to live with the Respondent.
(ii) (Here insert grounds of behaviour)

11. FACT C (*Not Applicable*)

(i) That the Respondent has deserted the Petitioner for a continuous period of at least two years immediately preceding the presentation of the Petitioner.

(ii) (Here insert date and circumstances of separation)

11. FACT D (*Not Applicable*)

(This, however, would probably form the basis of a final Petition. See below.)

(i) That the parties to the marriage have lived apart for a continuous period of at least two years immediately preceding the presentation of this Petition and the Respondent consents to a decree being granted.

(ii) (Here insert the date and circumstances of separation)

11. FACT E (*Not Applicable*)

(i) That the parties to the marriage have lived apart for a continuous period of at least five years immediately preceding the presentation of the Petition.

(ii) (Here insert the date and circumstances of separation)

★★★★★★★★★★★★★★★★★★★★★★★★★★★★★★★★★★

(An Answer and Cross-Petition by Prince Charles would be presented on a different document but would probably be on the following grounds:)

11. FACT B

(i) That the Respondent has behaved in such a way

that the Petitioner cannot reasonably be expected to live with the Respondent.

(ii) (Here insert grounds of behaviour) *That the Respondent (the Princess of Wales) has throughout the period of the marriage behaved publicly in a manner likely to bring disrepute upon the Petitioner [the Prince of Wales] and embarrass his family, including Her Majesty the Queen, in the eyes of their friends, their servants and their subjects. Furthermore, the Respondent has received the attentions of male admirers in a manner likely to cause humiliation to the Petitioner. Furthermore, the Respondent has encouraged a book to be written and newspaper articles to be published maligning the Petitioner and likely to subject him to public disrepute and contempt.*

★★★★★★★★★★★★★★★★★★★★★★★★★★★★★★★★

(In all probability a final, agreed Petition by either party would be on the following grounds:)

11. FACT D

(i) That the parties to the marriage have lived apart for a continuous period of at least two years immediately preceding the presentation of this Petition and the Respondent consents to a decree being granted.

(ii) (Here insert the date and circumstances of

separation) *After irreconcilable differences arose be-*
tween them, the parties separated on the 9th of
December 1992, such separation being announced
on that date in the House of Commons by the Prime
Minister, Mr John Major, and since that date the
parties have lived separate and apart.

★★★★★★★★★★★★★★★★★★★★★★★★★★★★★★

(The Princess of Wales would have had to complete
the following quaintly worded 'Prayer' for the dissolution
of her marriage. The Prince of Wales would have had
to make similar requests in his Answer and Cross-
Petition.

The demands that are made in 4(a) are specifically for
the benefit of the wife. For instance, Diana could apply
for 'maintenance pending suit'. In a defended case, she
would probably need to do so if there was no agreement
for financial provision. She would also want from her
husband a lump sum and periodical payments. Her addi-
tional demand for a 'secured provision order' is rarely used
as it is applicable only to the very rich. This order, if
granted, forces the husband to put a further lump sum on
deposit, in order to generate interest to cover future living
expenses.

The demands in 4(b) are made specifically for the
children of the family. If granted, these payments would be
for the benefit of William and Harry only.

Finally, 4(c) is an order primarily on behalf of the wife, but possibly also extended to the children. A 'property adjustment order' is particularly relevant because jointly-owned property can be transferred to either of the parties by agreement – or by order of the court.)

PRAYER

The Petitioner therefore prays:

(1) That the said marriage be dissolved.

(2) That the Petitioner may be granted the Residence of the children of the family namely **William Arthur Philip Louis** born on the **28th of June 1982** and **Henry Charles Albert David** born on the **15th of September 1984.**

(3) That the Respondent may be ordered to pay the costs of this suit.

(4) That the Petitioner may be granted the following ancillary relief:

(a) *An order for maintenance pending suit*
A lump sum order
A periodical payments order
A secured provision order

(b) *A periodical payments order*
A secured provision order
A secured sum order for the children of the family

(c) *A property adjustment order*

Signed...............*(Diana Frances Windsor or her lawyer)*

Dated this day ....*(Leave blank for present)*

The names and addresses of the person to be served with this petition are:

Respondent: *Charles Philip Arthur George Windsor of St James's Palace, London.*

Co-respondent: (adultery case only): *Camilla Parker Bowles, of Middlewick House, Corsham, Wiltshire.*

The Petitioner's address for service is: *Kensington Palace, London, or Mishcon De Reya, 21 Southampton Row, London WC1.*

Address for all communications for the court to: The Chief Clerk, Divorce Registry. The Divorce Registry is open from 10 a.m. to 4 p.m. Mondays to Fridays.

★★★★★★★★★★★★★★★★★★★★★★★★★★★★★★★

(The Prince and Princess of Wales would have had to complete every item of the following forms, even to the degree of assuring the court that suitable arrangements were in place for the children's financial wellbeing and for caring for the children while the parents are absent.)

STATEMENT OF ARRANGEMENTS FOR CHILDREN

In the Divorce Registry

Petitioner: *Diana Frances Windsor*

Respondent: *Charles Philip Arthur George Windsor*

To the Petitioner:

You must complete this form if you or the Respondent have any children under 16 or over 16 but under 18 if they are at school or college or are training for a trade, profession or vocation.
Please use black ink.
Please complete Parts I, II and III.

Before you issue a Petition for divorce try to reach agreement with your husband/wife over the proposals for the children's future. There is space for him/her to sign at the end of this form if agreement is reached. If your husband/wife does not agree with the proposals he/she will have an opportunity at a later stage to state why he/she does not agree and will be able to make his/her own proposals.

You should take or send the completed form, signed by you (and, if agreement is reached, by your husband/wife) together with a copy to the court when you issue your Petition.

Please refer to the explanatory notes issued regarding completion of the Prayer of the Petition if you are asking the court to make an order regarding children. The court will only make an order if it considers that an order will be better for the children than no order.

If you wish to apply for any of the orders which may be available to you under Part I or II of the Children Act 1989 you are advised to see a solicitor.

You should obtain legal advice from a solicitor or, alternatively, from an advice agency. Addresses of solicitors and advice agencies can be obtained from the Yellow Pages and the Solicitors Regional Directory which can be found at Citizens Advice Bureaux, Law Centres and any local library.

To the Respondent:

The Petitioner has completed Part I, II and III of this form which will be sent to the court at the same time that the divorce Petition is filed. Please read all parts of the form carefully.

If you agree with the arrangements and proposals for the children you should sign Part IV of the form. Please use black ink. You should return the form to the Petitioner or his/her solicitor.

If you do not agree with all or some of the arrangements or proposals you will be given the opportunity of saying so when the divorce Petition is served on you.

PART I – Details of the children

1. Children of both parties (please give details only of any children born to you and the Respondent or adopted by you both).

(i) Forename: **William Arthur Philip Louis**. Surname: **Windsor**. Date of birth: **28th of June 1982**.

(ii) Forename: **Henry Charles Albert David**. Surname: **Windsor**. Date of birth: **15th of September 1984.**

2. Other children of the family (give details of any other children treated by both of you as children of the family: for example your own or the Respondent's). **None.**

3. Other children who are not children of the family (give details of any children born to you or the Respondent that have not been treated as children of the family or adopted by you both). **None.**

PART II – Arrangements for the children of the family (please tick the appropriate boxes)

4. Home details.

(a) The addresses at which the children now live:

Principally at Kensington Palace, London, and at Highgrove House, near Tetbury, Gloucestershire, but also intermittently at Buckingham Palace, Windsor Castle, Balmoral, Sandringham and other homes of the Crown.

(b) Give details of the number of living rooms, bedrooms etc at the address in (a): *Several hundred, but in all cases adequate for the children's needs.*

(c) Is the house rented or owned and by whom? Is the rent or any mortgage being regularly paid?
No .... ☐ *Yes* .... ☑ *Highgrove House is jointly owned by the Petitioner and Respondent and the other homes are owned by either the Crown or by Her Majesty the Queen.*

(d) Give the names of all other persons living with the children including your husband/wife if he/she lives there. State their relationship to the children. *The Petitioner's household includes a private secretary, three detectives, a press secretary and occasionally five ladies-in-waiting. There are also valets, butlers, dressers, gardeners, telephone operators, housekeepers, and other kitchen and domestic staff. The apartments of Kensington Palace are also the home to various relatives of the children: Princess Margaret, Prince and Princess Michael of Kent and the Duke and Duchess of Gloucester. The Respondent's household includes a private secretary, a deputy secretary, three assistants, a public relations executive, a press secretary and several assistants, along with diverse advisers. Buckingham Palace also houses the children's grandparents: Her Majesty the Queen and His Royal Highness the Duke of Edinburgh.*

(e) Will there be any change in these arrangements?
No .... ☐ *Yes* .... ☑ (please give details) *Highgrove House is to become the property solely of the Respondent, while the apartments at Kensington Palace are to be used solely by the Petitioner.*

5. Education and training details (please tick the appropriate boxes).

(a) Give the names of the school, college or place of training attended by each child. *William and Henry presently attend Ludgrove School, Wokingham, Berkshire, and will continue to receive a private education according to their abilities.*

(b) Do the children have any special educational needs?
No .... ☑ Yes .... (please give details).

(c) Is the school, college or place of training fee-paying?
No .... ☐ *Yes* .... ☑ (please give details of how much the fees are per term/year). *The basic fees per term at Ludgrove School are £2,675 each. From September 1995, William will transfer to public*

*school, probably Eton College, Berkshire, where
annual fees will be approximately £12,000.*
Are fees being regularly paid?
No .... ☐ **Yes** .... ☑ (please give details). **Fees
are paid by the Respondent.**

(d) Will there be any change in these arrangements?
No .... ☑ Yes .... ☐ (please give details).

6. Childcare details (please tick the appropriate boxes).

(a) Which parent looks after the children from day to
day? If responsibility is shared, please give details.
**Responsibility shared. Both boys at boarding school;
weekends generally spent with the Petitioner; holidays shared between Petitioner's principal residence
and Respondent's principal residence and Buckingham Palace, subject to official engagements.**

(b) Does that parent go out to work?
No .... ☐ **Yes** .... ☑ (please give details of his/
her hours of work). **Both parents go out to work;
working hours variable.**

(c) Does someone look after the children when the
parent is not there?
No .... ☐ **Yes** .... ☑ (please give details). **See list
of household staff above [4 (d)]. All residences also
contain servants.**

(d) Who looks after the children during school holidays? *[As 6 (a) and 6 (c)] above.*

(e) Will there be any changes in these arrangements?
No .... **Yes** .... ☑ (please give details). *As the children grow older, more time will be spent under Buckingham Palace tutelage to prepare them for their adult royal duties, in particular the duties of William as heir to the throne.*

7. Maintenance (please tick the appropriate boxes).

(a) Does your husband/wife pay towards the upkeep of the children? If there is another source of maintenance, please specify.
No .... ☐ **Yes** .... ☑ (please give details of how much). *Impossible to estimate but running into millions of pounds long-term; in any case, adequate to their needs.*

(b) Is the payment made under a court order?
No .... ☑ *Yes* .... ☐ (please give details, including the name of the court and the case number).

(c) Is the payment following an assessment by the Child Support Agency?
No .... ☑ *Yes* .... ☐ (please give details of how much).

(d) Has maintenance for the children been agreed?
Yes .... ☑ No .... ☐

(e) If not, will you be applying for: a child maintenance order?
Yes .... ☐ **No** .... ☑

or child support maintenance through the Child Support Agency?

Yes .... ☐ *No* .... ☑

8. Details of contact with the children (please tick appropriate boxes).

(a) Do the children see your husband/wife?

No .... ☐ *Yes* .... ☑ (please give details of how often and where). *On adequate occasions during weekends and school holidays and otherwise by agreement and arrangement.*

(b) Do the children ever stay with your husband/wife?

No .... ☐ *Yes* .... ☑ (please give details of how much). *As above.*

(c) Will there be any change to these arrangements?

No .... ☐ *Yes* .... ☑ (please give details of how much). *It is accepted that the children will spend more time with the Respondent and his family as they are prepared for official royal duties.*

Please give details of the proposed arrangements for contact and residence. *The Petitioner is anxious to have guaranteed contact with her children at weekends and during school holidays without the need to return to the court for variance of any order made in this case.*

9. Details of health (please tick the appropriate boxes).

(a) Are the children generally in good health?

No .... □ **Yes** .... ☑ (please give details of any serious disability or chronic illness).

(b) Do the children have any special health needs? **No** .... ☑ Yes .... □ (please give details of the care needed and how it is to be provided).

10. Details of care and other court proceedings (please tick the appropriate boxes).

(a) Are the children in the care of a local authority, or under the supervision of a social worker or probation officer? **No** .... ☑ Yes .... □ (please give details including any court proceedings).

(b) Are any of the children on the Child Protection Register? **No** .... ☑ Yes .... □ (please give details of the local authority and the date of registration).

(c) Are there or have there been any proceedings in any court involving the children: for example adoption, custody/residence, access/contact, wardship, care, supervision or maintenance? **No** .... ☑ Yes .... □ (please give details and send a copy of an order to the court).

★★★★★★★★★★★★★★★★★★★★★★★★★★★★★★

(The Prince and Princess of Wales would each have had to sign a copy of the following form, which has nothing to do with any attempt at reconciliation. A conciliator is appointed

by the court to help the parents agree terms for contact with the children in an attempt to avoid the matter escalating into a full-blown dispute.)

PART III – To the Petitioner

Conciliation

If you and your husband/wife do not agree about the arrangements for the children, would you agree to discuss the matter with a Conciliator and your husband/wife?
No . . . . ☐ *Yes* . . . . ☑

Declaration

I declare that the information I have given is correct and complete to the best of my knowledge.

Signed...................(Petitioner) (*Diana Frances Windsor*)

Date ....(*Leave blank for present*)

PART IV – To the Respondent

I agree with the arrangements and proposals contained in Part I and II of this form.

Signed.........................(Respondent)
(*Charles Philip Arthur George Windsor*)

Date ....(*Leave blank for present*)

★★★★★★★★★★★★★★★★★★★★★★★★★★★★★★★★★

(Solicitors for the Prince and Princess of Wales would each have had to sign the following form, even though no hope of reconciliation exists.)

CERTIFICATE WITH REGARD TO RECONCILIATION

IN THE DIVORCE REGISTRY

BETWEEN: *Diana Frances Windsor*

AND: *Charles Philip Arthur George Windsor*

I the Solicitor acting for the Petitioner in the above cause do hereby certify that I *have* / have not discussed with the Petitioner the possibility of a reconciliation and that I *have* / have not given the Petitioner the names and addresses of persons qualified to help effect a reconciliation.

Dated this ....day of ....199...
(*Leave blank for present*)

Solicitors for the Petitioner...
(*Mishcon De Reya*)

23

The Dreadful Cost

In the wake of Windsor versus Windsor, how should
the Royal Family take stock? What talents can the
main players offer to steer Britain into the next millennium and continue a monarchy that has ruled unbroken
in pomp and majesty since 1660? This is an exercise
which, the Queen accepts, is crucial to the family's
future. No longer has it the luxury and security to
indulge itself simply because it has a glorious history.
In an age where accountancy is God, it must start
giving value for money.

In a sense, the monarchy is like an upmarket public
limited company which has awoken to the strictures of
market forces and realised the need to keep sharehold-
ers happy. For years it has bumbled along on goodwill,
a distinctive reputation and a carefully cultivated mys-
tique. The health of its balance sheet has been determined by its popularity, its workload and the dignity
with which it conducts its affairs. Now the denizens of

what used to be Fleet Street, and the wider public, have looked into the private activities of the board and concluded that all is not well.

To avoid a takeover (i.e. an elected head of state) the company needs what business tycoons call a 'mission statement'. It needs direction and leadership and vision. Above all, it needs to take a long, hard look at its only assets which matter – its family members.

So what of these assets? What is their current track record and what potential do they offer for the future? To any independent mind, the long-term prognosis looks grim . . .

But first the good news. The monarchy still has the Queen. She enjoys almost universal popularity among all but the most committed republicans. Her subjects remember the way she accepted the awesome responsibility of the Crown with fortitude and how she has discharged her duties pretty well faultlessly ever since. Her worldwide reputation and standing as a head of state is unequalled.

'Ah,' sigh the monarchists, 'if only the rest of them were more like her.' Sadly they are not. The rest of them collectively make up the bad news.

There is Prince Philip. He can generally be relied on to say the wrong thing at the wrong time, very often to foreigners. He comes across as stiff, stuffy, haughty and out of touch.

There are the bit-part royal siblings, the Princess Royal and Prince Edward. Both have largely avoided adverse publicity in recent years – not because of any particularly adept manoeuvring on their part but rather because the hounds have had meatier prey. Remodelling the public roles of these two would be unlikely to have much impact. The Princess Royal is a tireless worker for charity but she is perceived, like her father, as being distant and crotchety. Edward, now busy carving out a career in the media, also lacks the common touch. Bouts of petulance, such as his highly public temper tantrum at the royal 'It's a Knockout' fiasco, have not much endeared him to the masses.

Then there are the Yorks. Fergie, after a protracted honeymoon period with the media, is now a public-relations disaster. She will never shrug off the toe-sucking episode with John Bryan, and her perpetual whining about poverty is an embarrassment. Andrew has emerged from the collapse of his marriage with dignity, and his gung-ho boyishness retains a certain charm. But he is awkward in public. On the rare occasions he says anything impromptu – the Lockerbie disaster, for instance – his words tend to be ill-chosen and clumsy.

And so we come to the Waleses. The future of the monarchy.

We have a might-have-been Prince who indulges in pornographic telephone conversations with his mistress, who cuckolds her husband by publicly admitting adultery before millions of TV viewers, who abandons his marriage vows despite aspiring to be Defender of the Faith, and who is stubbornly remembered in many parts of the globe as The Man Who Talks to Plants.

Then we have the Princess of Wales. She has the sympathy vote, the looks and the air of a 'natural' in public. But she is an obsessive (witness the phone-pest scandal) and her dabblings in the supernatural hardly mark her down as a haven of stability. Her bulimia illness remains a terrible strain and she has too readily absorbed the various cults of alternative therapy.

Finally there are the boys. William and Harry, the hopes for the future. No one can know what they have gone through over the last few years but to pretend they have been emotionally untouched by such a bitter parental split is naïve. Despite this, William now looks a more likely future King than his father. And perhaps that is not such bad news after all.

Predicting the future is easy. Being right is harder. Which of the current crop of writers and newspaper columnists could have foretold a decade ago that the British Royal Family would be in its present sorry state? With that caveat, it is still possible to advance views on the prospects for the three key members, those most valuable assets – Charles, Diana and William.

Where does Charles go from here? His personal life and constitutional role are, whether he likes it or not, quite inseparable. The catastrophic failure of his dalliance with Dimbleby did little to promote his case for the Crown. Indeed, there is an argument that the TV interview was part of a secret agenda specifically designed to secure an early divorce. Certainly, Charles seems to have accepted short-term pain for what he hopes will be long-term gain.

Camilla, of course, will be gradually brought in to his life, since there is no longer any reason to keep her a closet mistress. They will 'bump into' each other at the odd reception, be photographed at Sandringham and Balmoral and, in time, even permit themselves the occasional kiss in public. But there will be no sign of Camilla with the Princes, at least not until they have come of age. Such a move would cause a national uproar and could tip Diana over an emotional precipice.

Will Charles remarry? Possibly, say the Palace moguls, although whichever path he chooses will be fraught with problems. The country expects to see a spouse at his side, but another 'unsuitable' partner would land the Prince in an impossible situation. In any case, there is only one person he loves enough to make his Queen. Both Camilla Parker Bowles and Charles fear it will never happen.

The increasingly likely scenario is that the Crown will jump a generation and William V will succeed to it. But this depends on two key factors. First, that the Queen continues to enjoy her good health and lives another ten or twenty years. Second, that if she abdicates or dies earlier, Charles agrees to allow William – a boy perhaps barely out of his teens – to shoulder a lifetime's burden as head of state.

Charles would have good reason to pass on the Crown. Many Anglican bishops would be unable to square him being both Defender of the Faith and a divorcee, and he could announce that he was stepping aside to avoid a schism within the Church. With William on the throne, Charles would at last be free to marry the great love of his life. Perhaps this would also free him of his habitual depressions, the sense that no one takes any notice of him, and the gnawing self-doubt which reminds him that he has let the side down.

Opinion polls are notoriously fickle instruments. As any pollster knows, you can obtain the answers you want by tinkering with the questions you ask. Nevertheless, an authoritative poll in 1995 made sober reading for the Prince.

Asked 'Do you think Prince Charles should or should not give up his right to the throne in favour of Prince William?', more than one in three said that he should. The figure was even higher among the younger generation, with 42 per cent opposed to the notion of a King Charles III. It got worse. More than half those questioned said Charles set a poor example of how to behave and 32 per cent said he was bad for Britain's image; 31 per cent said he had low moral standards and 29 per cent said he was a weak individual.

These figures bear witness to the dreadful cost of the Windsor versus Windsor divorce. Charles may believe that time will soothe these malcontents. Yet his would-be subjects have long memories.

What of Diana? We have already seen how her immediate future is dictated by her concern for her boys. She has found little peace since withdrawing from public life; indeed the decision has made her a more desirable target for photographers and newsmen. Faced with an unworkable, self-imposed exile on home ground, the fashionable wisdom is that Diana will seek to establish herself abroad. A flurry of five transatlantic trips in 1994 and early 1995 fuelled the speculation that she will settle in America.

The reasoning behind this is straightforward enough. Americans are fascinated, both by the royal dynasty they rejected in 1776 and the beautiful Princess who has come to symbolise its modern-day role. Thus, society hostesses dream of presenting Diana over cocktails, gossip columnists muse about possible future escorts, and everyone from cab drivers to cowboys gobbles up stories about her possible Atlantic crossing.

Diana, for her part, loves the American lifestyle particularly the New York version. She likes the fast-food culture and the glitz, the classy shops and the baseball-cap-and-jeans fashion sense. Above all, she likes Americans. 'They accept you for what you are, not for who you are,' she has told friends.

This is the crux of the matter. After a decade of feeling stifled by royal etiquette and obsequious official functionaries, Diana wants a flavour of freedom, the same freedom she had as a bachelor girl. She concedes that she is flattered by the interest people take in her, and that she loves to take centre stage at a party. But she hates all the curtseying and the ma'aming, the false smiles and the transparently rehearsed conversational gambits. She believes that in America she would have the chance to join the ranks of high-profile working women.

One of the role models who helped feed this ambition was the late Jackie Kennedy-Onassis – the closest anyone ever got to being an America surrogate Queen. Jackie O managed to knuckle down to a publishing job in New York despite her celebrity status. Diana is convinced that she too could join the ranks of New York's commuter army in a way that would be unthinkable in London. She is further heartened by the way Jackie O hit back at a particularly persistent paparazzi by successfully suing for harassment.

Diana's circle of influential American women friends could probably ease her into any job in the country. She has power-lunched with Hillary Clinton, exchanged gossip with *Washington Post* proprietor Katherine Graham and joked girlishly with Elizabeth Dole, wife of Senate Republican leader Bob. In doing the rounds, she has benefited from the highly attuned advice of the woman she trusts perhaps above all others: her friend at the Brazilian embassy, Lucia Flecha de Lima.

Some senior advisers to Diana, people she respects, have cautioned her against embracing America. They say she would be too distant from the institution that gave her her status in the first place and that, in time, she would become a celebrity also-ran on the party circuit. She has little truck with this line. For one thing, she is convinced she could find the prestigious working role she craves. For another, she sees America as a far longer-term opportunity — longer-term because she clearly realises that to move there in the immediate wake of divorce would give Charles a free hand in raising the boys, a prospect that appals her. Having battled so resolutely for her share of custody, she is hardly likely to throw it all away.

It is argued that America might give her the chance to remarry, even to have more children. Proponents of this course insist that a remarriage in Britain would be impossible because, in the received wisdom, 'no suitor would take her on'. That may have been the case while her relationship with Charles was disintegrating, but with a signed and sealed divorce, it theoretically no longer applies. And the argument that no man could handle the resulting tabloid interest is no more than an interesting speculation. It depends on the man.

It is not difficult to see how Diana could fall in love. The problem for her will be in sustaining the affair. For one thing, she will have to consider the feelings of the boys. She will be mindful that a new man in their lives might unwittingly create an emotional barrier between them and their mother. If they reacted by wishing to spend more time with Charles, rather with their aspiring stepfather, it would break her.

Secondly, there are the practicalities of a long-term affair. After her experiences of the early 1990s, Diana will be extremely cautious about whom she trusts – if indeed she can trust anybody. Meeting a boyfriend in public would be hugely risky, and her standard disguise of jeans, T-shirt and baseball boots would not always be enough to fool trailing paparazzi. London's freelance photographers are so used to stalking her that her face, figure, even the way she walks, are burned into their brains.

Then there is the inevitable question: Which man? Many old flames such as Hewitt and Gilbey are out of the running for good. Others have been dropped from her circle for reasons that mystify them. In any case, most of her favoured male friends are either married or spoken for. The last thing she needs right now is to be caught up in an adulterous affair of her own.

Of course, Diana could meet someone completely new. But she would then want time to test the relationship before committing herself. Could she retain her privacy? Would the suitor himself be patient – and trustworthy – enough to stay the course? And what of Buckingham Palace's reaction? Would there not be some embittered aides waiting to wield the knife?

The likeliest scenario is that Diana will have to serve a long exile, one in which her boys would be allowed a period of stability. But it will be an exile which will test her mental reserves to the full – and which will be a constant reminder of the lonely existence endured by her divorced mother Frances.

Money will be the least of her problems. During divorce settlement negotiations, Diana successfully established that her annual spending touched £500,000, a sum befitting her position as mother of the future King. This has helped determine her once-and-for-all settlement of, it is believed, around £15 million. To raise this, Charles has had to go to his mother's coffers. His Duchy of Cornwall assets amount to around £90 million but he is allowed to touch only the income – around £4 million a year (taxable at 40 per cent). Although his lawyers attempted to drive through a £4 million settlement, this was uncompromisingly dismissed by Diana's lead negotiator, Lord Mishcon.

The Princess knew she would also have to be provided with a suitable town house or grace and favour royal apartment. In addition, she has always wanted a country retreat, and numerous large mansions in the home counties and the Welsh borders have been discreetly assessed. Inevitably, her main base will become the unofficial court of the Princess of Wales. More appropriately, bearing in mind the lonely future ahead, it will perhaps be dubbed 'Fortress Diana'.

Her relationship with the Royal Family remains cool. She is conscious of their attempts to mend bridges with her but suspects that this is largely for the sake of the Princes and the need to keep her on-side as their best public-relations ambassador. She is fiercely defensive of her right to bring up Wills and

Harry as she sees fit. She does not see why she should bend to help a family who, she believes, have acted so shabbily towards her during her marriage break-up.

In prophesying the future, there is one shadow from the divorce which will for a long time hence affect the reputation of the participants – and have a deleterious effect on the innocent victims of this marital conflict. It is the question: Who is to blame?

Apportioning blame is one of Britain's favourite pastimes. Churchmen preach sternly against it, sociologists try to find 'real' reasons for it and politicians trade in it and on it. In the dictionary of the politically correct, it is an unfashionable word. Yet where a royal marriage break-up is concerned, everyone is busy apportioning it. And why not? History books are about interpreting 'facts', or at least what are popularly assumed to be facts. And well into the next century, historians will be analysing the Waleses' marriage and apportioning blame for its epoch-making demise.

Both partners will have their childhoods dissected. The break-up of Diana's parents' marriage will be cited as one reason for her insecurity (fully justified) about her husband's relationship with Camilla. Diana's upbringing in the backwoods of the aristocracy will be seen as having ill prepared her for the royal match to come. Her failure, it will be said, was in being dazzled by the romance and glitz of the British monarchy. She fell in love with the image easily. She had to work too hard to remain in love with the man.

And Charles? His failures as an individual will be laid at the door of his parents. Prince Philip was too ogre-like, too severe a figure for a sensitive young boy. Charles developed an overbearing sense of siege mentality, a fear heightened by his father's blundering attempts to 'toughen him up' at Gordonstoun. The Queen herself will not escape her share of blame. She was too preoccupied with her sense of duty, too unwilling to show affection in public, too immersed in affairs of state. As a result, they produced a confused, unhappy, uncertain heir with a poor sense of judgement.

These are, of course, one-sided views. There are many facets to the failure of the Waleses' marriage – the attentions of the media, the influence of the Queen Mother (who cold-shouldered the Princess), Diana's illnesses (which would have put a strain on any marriage) and the couple's huge workload (which reduced the time each of them had to discover each other).

Above all, their respective friends and interests were poles apart. He enjoyed hunting, shooting, fishing, polo, painting and walking on inhospitable Scottish mountains. She liked pop music, partying, lively restaurants and fun parks. Partners with diverse interests often make a marriage work. But, just occasionally, those interests must coincide. In the case of the Prince and Princess of Wales, they never did.

It will take time for such a legacy to be laid to rest. There is no time, however, to await events. The future is here and now. And the future is Prince William and brother Harry.

Constitutionally, William is the boy born to be King. It is he who will have to cast off the baggage of his parents' marriage and lead the monarchy forward into a brave new dawn. The portents already look forbidding . . .

It is not inconceivable that Prince William may find his future subjects (all Britons are classed in law as the monarch's subjects) becoming 'citizens' of a new Republic of Great Britain. Britain's entrenchment within the European Community is now highlighting the major differences between its constitution and those of its neighbours.

In Britain, every civil servant and MP swears an oath of allegiance to the Crown. In every other European monarchy, the Crown swears allegiance to the State. Similarly, the monarch is the one person in Britain who is above the law. The monarch has personal immunity from a huge raft of legislation, including anti-discrimination and equal-opportunities measures. This is one of the reasons why a Queen who has more non-white than white subjects in the Commonwealth has been able to employ an all-white staff at Buckingham Palace.

It is far too early properly to judge Prince William's character or how he will respond to the challenge. We simply do not know enough about him. Some senior courtiers warn that he has absorbed a huge amount of emotional flak – although, on the positive side, they point out that the Waleses' separation may be the best thing that could have happened to him. With the rows, the silences, the tensions and the competitive element removed from the young Prince's domestic surroundings, he at least has the chance to begin his teens in a stable atmosphere.

There is little doubt that William is terribly introverted. His early confidence (at the age of seven he once booked a meal for two at San Lorenzo as a surprise for his mother) has all but vanished. He cannot identify with the more carefree attitude of brother Harry. He is said to blame himself for the divorce and considers himself responsible for shielding Harry from it.

Before the separation announcement, this sorry child would lock himself into the bathroom at Kensington Palace. Yet he would refuse to use the toilet – behaviour which psychologists suggest is a form of body control adopted by those who feel unable to control events around them. After the royal separation William bravely told his parents: 'I hope you will both be happier now.'

At boarding school, William was forever finding excuses to telephone his mother. His manners, normally impeccable, would disappear on occasions and staff noticed how he sometimes seemed to be locked in a dream world. On outings with Diana, Harry would be the one running in all directions. William would be holding his mummy's hand.

Academically, William looks to be well up to scratch. He has remained in the top third of his class throughout his education and came in the top six in the vital mock exams for entrance to Eton. He is particularly strong in history, Latin and English. He has a well-developed sense of humour, inherited from his father and regarded as another indication of an intelligent mind. When a classmate once argued with him, he hit back with the threat: 'I'll have you beheaded!'

Despite his social reticence, the Prince is, unlike his brother, an excellent team player. He made the soccer First XI at Ludgrove and earned a reputation as a creative passer of the ball. As a horseman, he shows immense promise. During one Christmas holiday at Sandringham, the Queen laughingly told Diana: 'He was riding so fast I could hardly keep up.'

Prince Harry is largely the antithesis of his brother. Whereas William likes healthy eating, Harry likes fry-ups and chocolate feasts. While William is uninterested in military matters, Harry is addicted to them. And while William is usually polite in company, Harry displays a schoolboy cheek that stays only just on the endearing side of impertinence. Harry can be forgiven his boisterous manner, however; it is his elder brother on whose young shoulders the weight of responsibility must already be feeling weighty.

The obvious difficulty for Prince William as he grows up will be the uncertainty surrounding his succession . . . the same uncertainty which has plagued his father. William must assume he will one day be King, even though doubts about the monarchy's future are unlikely to go away. But he cannot have any clear idea when duty will call.

Much depends on the country's attitude to the Charles–Camilla relationship in the years ahead. The Queen may want to choose her moment to step down, and the politicians and bishops will want to have their say. William could be a twenty-year-old or a sixty-year-old King. It must be an unnerving prospect to a sensitive young boy.

But this chapter is about predictions and conclusions. The Queen, it is already clear, will try to stay on the throne as long as possible, and at least into the next millennium. She will rely on time healing Charles's shattered image and hopefully allowing the Commonwealth to accept him more readily as King. It is for this reason that, in early 1995, the Queen urged both Prince Charles and Prince Andrew to speed up their divorce proceedings to allow the younger royals a fresh dawn. A rescue of the institution had been delayed too long.

Both Queen Elizabeth and Prime Minister John Major strongly believed the uncertainty had been undermining the monarchy by fuelling debate over the constitutional link between Church and Crown. Were that link to be broken, the Windsors risked losing their very purpose – their legal claim to the throne as set out under the 1701 Act of Settlement.

Assuming the Queen's health allows her to 'buy

time', Charles can work on his rehabilitation. His confession of adultery was the start — perhaps the hardest part of all. Now the rebuilding will continue. Charles still wants the throne. He wants it badly.

But does he deserve it? Has he earned it? Is he worthy of becoming King?

Many observers, including a sizeable quota of the Cabinet, believe his case is already past saving. Until the adultery confession, they argue, Charles still had the slimmest chance of turning his fortunes around and claiming his birthright. But the moment he bared his soul to Jonathan Dimbleby, he threw it all away. To return to our opening analogy of the royals as a public limited company, Charles is out of the running for chairman. In the eyes of too many, he is a moral bankrupt.

And so William will be prepared to step forward. He remains the main casualty of Windsor versus Windsor, a boy torn between his duty to the monarchy, the expectations of his father and his love for his mother. He will shape the destiny of all of them.

APPENDIX 1

The 'Dianagate' Tape Transcript in Full

HIM: And so darling, what other lows today?

HER: So that was it, I was very bad at lunch. And I nearly started blubbing. I just felt really sad and empty, and I thought: 'Bloody hell, after all I've done for this fucking family.'

HIM: You don't need to. 'Cos there are people out there, and I've said this before, who are going to replace that emptiness. With all sorts of things.

HER: These articles and, um, horoscopes . . . It's just so desperate being in . . . in . . . innuendo, the fact that I'm going to do something dramatic because I can't stand the confines of this marriage.

HIM: I know.

HER: But I know much more than they know because . . .

HIM: Well interestingly enough, that thing in *The People* didn't imply either one of you.

HER: No.

HIM: So I wouldn't worry about that. I think it's common knowledge, darling, and amongst most people, that you obviously don't have . . .

HER: A rapport?

HIM: Yeh, I think that comes through loud and clear. Darling, just forgetting that for a moment, how is Mara?

HER: She's all right. No. She's fine. She can't wait to get back.

HIM: Can't she? When's she coming back?

HER: Saturday.

HIM: Is she?

HER: Mmmm.

HIM: I thought it was next Saturday.

HER: No, Saturday.

HIM: Not quite as soon as you thought it was.

HER: No.

HIM: Is she having a nice time?

HER: Very nice.

HIM: Is she?

HER: I think so. She's out of London. It gives her a bit of a rest.

HIM: Yeh. Can't imagine what she does the whole time.

HER: No.

HIM: The restaurant. If you have a restaurant, it's so much a part of your life, isn't it?

HER: I know, people around you all the time.

HIM: That's right. The constant bossing and constant ordering and constant sort of fussing. And she hasn't got that. She's probably been twiddling her fingers wondering what to do.

HER: Hmmmm.

HIM: Going to church every day.

HER: I know.

HIM: Did you go to church today?

HER: Yes I did.

HIM: Did you, Squidge?

HER: Yes.

HIM: Did you say lots of prayers?

HER: Of course.

HIM: Did you? Kiss me, darling. [*Sound of kisses being blown down the phone*].

HER: [*Sound of laughter and returns kiss.*]

HIM: I can't tell what a smile that has put on my face. I can't tell you. I was like a sort of caged rat and Tony said: 'You are in a terrible hurry to go.' And I said: 'Well I've got things to do when I get there.' Oh God [*sighs*], I am not going to leave the phone in the car any more, darling.

HER: No, please don't.

HIM: No, I won't. And if it rings and someone says: 'What on earth is your telephone ringing for?' I will say: 'Oh, someone's got a wrong number' or something.

HER: No, say one of your relations is not very well and your mother is just ringing in to give you progress.

HIM: All right, so I will keep it near me, quite near to me tomorrow, because Father hates phones out shooting.

HER: Oh, you are out shooting tomorrow, are you?

HIM: Yeh. And darling, I will be back in London tomorrow night.

HER: Good.

HIM: All right?

HER: Yes.

HIM: Back on home territory, so no more awful breaks.

HER: No.

HIM: I don't know what I'd do. Do you know, darling, I couldn't sort of face the thought of not speaking to you every moment. It fills me with real horror, you know.

HER: It's purely mutual.

HIM: Is it? I really hate the idea of it, you know. It makes me really sort of scared.

HER: There was something really strange. I was leaning over the fence yesterday, looking into Park House [*the house on the Sandringham estate where Diana was brought up, now a home for disabled people*] and I thought: 'Oh, what shall I do?' And I thought: 'Well, my friend would say go in and do it,' I thought: 'No, cos I am a bit shy' and there were hundreds of people in there. So I thought: 'Bugger that.' So I went round to the front door and walked straight in.

HIM: Did you?

HER: It was just so exciting.

HIM: How long were you there for?

HER: An hour and a half.

HIM: Were you?

HER: Mmm. And they were so sweet. They wanted their photographs taken with me and they kept hugging me. They were very ill, some of them. Some no legs and all sorts of things.

HIM: Amazing, Leonard Cheshire.

HER: Isn't he.

HIM: Yeh, amazing — quite extraordinary. He devoted himself to setting up those homes. To achieve everything, I think it's amazing. Sort of devotion to a cause.

HER: I know.

HIM: Darling, no sort of awful feelings of guilt or . . .

HER: None at all.

HIM: Remorse?

HER: None. None at all.

HIM: Good.

HER: No, none at all. All's well.

HIM: OK then, Squidgy. I am sorry you have had low times . . . try darling, when you get these urges you just try to replace them with anger like you did on Friday night, you know.

HER: I know. But do you know what's really quite un . . . whatever the word is? His grandmother is always looking at me with a strange look in her eyes. It's not hatred, it's sort of interest and pity mixed in one. I am not quite sure. I don't understand it. Every time I look up, she's looking at me and then looks away and smiles.

HIM: Does she?

HER: Yes. I don't know what's going on.

HIM: I should say to her one day: 'I can't help but ask you. You are always looking at me. What is it? What are you thinking?' You must, darling. And interestingly enough, one of the things said to me today is that you are going to start standing up for yourself.

HER: Yes.

HIM: Mmm. We all know that you are very capable of that, old Bossy Boots.

HER: I know, yes.

HIM: What have you had on today? What have you been wearing?

HER: A pair of black jodhpur things on at the moment and a pink polo neck.

HIM: Really. Looking good?

HER: Yes.

HIM: Are you?

HER: Yes.

HIM: Dead good?

HER: I think it's good.

HIM: You do?

HER: Yes.

HIM: And what on your feet?

HER: A pair of flat black pumps.

HIM: Very chic.

HER: Yes [*pause in tape*]. The redhead is being actually quite supportive.

HIM: Is she?

HER: Yes, she has. I don't know why.

HIM: Don't let the [?] down.

HER: No, I won't. I just talk to her about that side of things.

HIM: You do? That's all I worry about. I just worry that you know she's sort of . . . She's desperately trying to get back in.

HER: She keeps telling me.

HIM: She's trying to tag on to your [?]. She knows that your PR is so good, she's trying to tag on to that.

[*The couple go on to talk about someone they both know . . .*]

HER: Well, he is sort of heterosexual. And everything else, I think.

HIM: Heterosexual.

HER: Yes.

HIM: Is he?

HER: Yes.

HIM: What do you mean, heterosexual?

HER: Everything.

HIM: Oh he's everything?

HER: Yes.

HIM: That's not heterosexual, darling! Oh Squidge [*laughs*]. Do you know what heterosexual is?

HER: No.

HIM: You and me – that's hetero.

HER: Yes.

HIM: The other's sort of, um, alternating current. I don't know how you . . . What is it? [*pause*] 'Bi'. Is he 'bi'?

HER: [*Diana's voice is now much softer and in the background*]. Harry, it's in my bathroom. [*louder*] What's that you said about babies?

HIM: Is he 'bi'?

HER: You didn't say anything about babies, did you?

HIM: No.

HER: No.

HIM: Why darling?

HER: [*laughing*] I thought you did.

HIM: Did you?

HER: Yes.

HIM: Did you darling? You have got them on the brain.

HER: Well yeh, maybe I . . . Well, actually, I don't think I am going to be able to for ages.

HIM: I think you've got bored with the idea, actually.

HER: I'm going to . . .

HIM: You are, aren't you? It was a sort of hot flush you went through.

HER: A very hot flush.

HIM: Darling, when he says His Nibs rang him up, does he mean your other half or PA rang him up?

HER: Eh? My other half.

HIM: Your other half.

HER: Yes.

HIM: Does he get on well with him?

HER: Sort of mentor. Talk in the mouthpiece – you moved away.

HIM: Sorry, darling, I'm resting it on my chin, on my chinless. Oh [*sighs*], I get so sort of possessive when I see all those pictures of you. I get so possessive, that's the least attractive aspect of me really. I just see them and think: 'Oh God, if only . . .'

HER: There aren't that many pictures, are there? There haven't been that many.

HIM: Four or five today.

HER: Oh.

HIM: Various magazines. So darling, I . . .

HER: I'm always smiling, aren't, I . . .

HIM: Always.

HER: I thought that today.

HIM: I always told you that. It's the old, what I call the PR package, isn't it? As soon as you sense a camera . . . I think you can sense a camera at a thousand yards.

HER: Yes.

HIM: That smile comes on. And the charm comes out and it stays there all the time, and then it goes away again. But darling, tell me, how was your tea party?

HER: It was all right. Nicholas was there and his girlfriend Charlotte Hambro. Do you know Charlotte?

HIM: Yes. She was there, was she? How was that?

HER: It was all right. I went in in terrific form.

HIM: Where are they staying then? Nicholas's?

HER: They are all staying with her sister down the other side of Fakenham.

HIM: Oh, Jeremy?

HER: Yes.

HIM: Was he there?

HER: Yes. Difficult man.

HIM: Very difficult man. Saw him at the ballet the other night.

HER: Oh, he's always there.

HIM: Yes, always. So quite a long drive, then?

HER: Yes. But the great thing is, I went in and made a lot of noise and came out. And no one could have picked a thing on me.

HIM: Were they all very chatty?

HER: Yes. Very very very.

HIM: Very kowtowing?

HER: Oh yes.

HIM: Were they?

HER: Yes, all that.

HIM: Darling, you said your yesses and noes, please and thank-yous. You stared at the floor and there were moments of silence . . .

HER: No, no, no, no. I kept the conversation going.

HIM: Did you?

HER: Yes.

HIM: What about?

HER: Oh God, anything.

HIM: What's she like? His wife looks quite tough.

HER: Suzanne? I think she's quite tough. I think she's given quite a tough time.

HIM: Is she?

HER: Yes.

HIM: So there with Charlotte and Willy Peel.

HER: Yep.

HIM: I don't know him at all.

HER: She's a very sexy number.

HIM: Quite. Bit worn out I reckon.

HER: [*laughs*] Ya.

HIM: Bit worn out, I reckon, darling. I wish we were going to be together tonight.

HER: I know. I want you to think of me after midnight. Are you staying up to see the New Year in?

HIM: You don't need to encourage me to think about you. I have done nothing else for the last three months. Hello.

HER: Debbie says you are going to go through a transformation soon.

HIM: I am?

HER: Yes. She says you are going to go through bits and pieces and I've got to help you through them. All Libra men, yeh, I said: 'Great I can do something back for him because he's done so much for me.' We are quite keen to know when you were born.

HIM: Are you? Squidgy, laugh some more. I love it

when I hear you are laughing. It makes me really happy when you laugh. Do you know I am happy when you are happy.

HER: I know you are.

HIM: And I cry when you cry.

HER: I know. So sweet. The rate we are going, we won't need any dinner on Tuesday.

HIM: No. I won't need any dinner actually. Just seeing you will be all I need. I can't wait for Ken to ring. And I will be thinking of you after twelve o'clock. I don't need any reasons to even think about you. Mark Davis kept saying to me yesterday: 'Of course, you haven't had a girlfriend for ages. What's the transfer list looking like? What about that woman in Berkshire?'

HER: Oh God.

HIM: And I said: 'No Mark, I haven't been there for months.' He said: 'Have you got any other transferees in mind?' I said no. We then went off on a walk and we started talking about Guy Morrison. He was telling me how extraordinarily Guy had behaved towards me at Julia's party. And he said: 'Oh well, the only reason he probably didn't want to speak to you was because you had been speaking to you-know-who for a long time.' And so I just didn't sort of say anything. And I said: 'I suppose that is my fatal mistake.' And Mark said: 'You spend too much time with her' and that was that. Then he said: 'I wonder whom she's going to end up with?' And I said: 'What do you mean?' And he said: 'Well she must be long overdue for an affair.' And I said: 'I've no idea. I don't talk to her about it. And I have only spoken to her twice since I saw her.' And that was it – I just kill every conversation stone dead now. It's much the best way. Darling, how did I get on to that? Oh, the transfer list. So I said no, there was no list drawn up at the moment. And even less likely there was anybody on it. I tell you, darling, I couldn't. I was just thinking again about you going all jellybags and you mustn't.

HER: I haven't for a day.

HIM: You haven't?

HER: For a day.

HIM: For a day. Why? Because you have no other people in the room. There were only three of us there last night. Four, actually, Mark, Antonia, their nanny and myself, and that was it. And I definitely didn't fancy the nanny, who was a twenty-three-year-old overweight German.

HER: Did you just get my hint about Tuesday night? I think you just missed it. Think what I said.

HIM: No.

HER: I think you have missed it.

HIM: No, you said: 'At this rate, we won't want anything to eat.'

HER: Yes.

HIM: Yes, I know. I got there.

HER: Oh well, you didn't sort of put the flag out. You didn't put the flag out.

HIM: What, the flag?

HER: Oh . . .

HIM: Squidge, I was just going over it. I don't think I made too much reference to it.

HER: [*laughs*] Mmm, oh bugger.

HIM: I don't think I made too much reference to it. Because the more you think about it, the more you worry about it.

HER: All right. I haven't been thinking a lot else.

HIM: Haven't you?

HER: No.

HIM: Well I can tell you that makes two . . . I went to this agonising tea party last night. You know, all I want to do is to get in my car and drive around the country talking to you.

HER: Thanks [*laughter*].

HIM: That's all I want to do, darling, I just want to see you and be with you. That's what's going to be such bliss, being back in London.

HER: I know.

HIM: I mean it can't be a regular future, darling, I understand that. But it would be nice if you were at least next door, within knocking distance.

HER: Yes. What's that noise?

HER: The television, drowning my conversation.

HIM: Can you turn it down?

HER: No.

HIM: Why?

HER: Because . . .

HIM: The boys [*indistinct*].

HER: It's covering my conversation.

HIM: All right . . . I got there Tuesday night, don't worry, I got there. I can tell you the feeling's entirely mutual. Ummmmm, Squidgy, what else? It's just like unwinding now. I am just letting my heartbeat come down again now. I had the most amazing dream about us last night. Not physical, nothing to do with that.

HER: That makes a change.

HIM: Darling, it's just that we were together an awful lot of time and we were having dinner with some people, and it was the most extraordinary dream — very vivid — because I woke up in the morning and I remembered all aspects of it. All bits of it. I remembered sort of what you were wearing and what you had said. It was so strange; very strange, and very lovely too.

HER: I don't want to get pregnant.

HIM: Darling, it's not going to happen.

HER: [*Sigh*]

HIM: All right?

HER: Yeah.

HIM: Don't worry about that. It's not going to happen, darling. You won't get pregnant.

HER: I watched 'EastEnders' today and one of the main characters had a baby. They thought it

was by her husband but it was by another man.
Ha ha!

HIM: [*sighing*] Squidgy ... kiss me [*sounds of kisses by
him and her*]. Oh God, it's wonderful, isn't it? This
sort of feeling. Don't you like it?

HER: I love it.

HIM: Um.

HER: I love it.

HIM: Isn't it absolutely wonderful? I haven't had it for
years. I feel about twenty-one again.

HER: Well you're not. You're thirty-three.

HIM: I know.

HER: Pushing up the daisies soon, right?

HIM: No more remarks like that. It was an agonising
tea yesterday with, er, do you know Simon Prior-
Palmer?

HER: I know who you mean, yes.

HIM: And his wife Julia, Julia Lloyd-Jordan, you must
remember her.

HER: Yes, I do.

HIM: Do you?

HER: God, yes ... who was she after? Eddie?

HIM: I can't remember. She lived in that flat in Cadogan
Gardens, didn't she, with Lucy Manners.

HER: Yes, she did.

HIM: She lost weight. You lived there for a while,
didn't you?

HER: No, it's the wrong place.

HIM: Oh! But the umm ... honestly, I loved going

to [?]. I mean, they've got quite a nice house and things. And there was quite a nice Australian, er, Polish sort of friend of theirs who was staying. And God — Simon! He's thirty-eight years old, but honestly he behaves older than my father. I cannot believe it. I find it so exhausting when there's people that age. They behave as if they're fifty.

HER: I know.

HIM: Anyway, we did time there. And that was it. We got back. A very quiet dinner. Mark was sort of exhausted from last night. And that was it really. He was talking about . . . hunting gets you gripped doesn't it?

HER: It does.

HIM: I mean, he drove six hours yesterday.

HER: [*laughter*] My drive's two and a half to three.

HIM: No I'm talking about both ways. He drives three hours from Hungerford. He was hunting with . . . can't remember who he was with; oh yes . . . the Belvoir yesterday.

HER: The Belvoir, umm.

HIM: That was three hours there and three hours back.

HER: God.

HIM: And he'd done the same on Wednesday to the Quorn.

HER: How wonderful.

HIM: Darling, ummmm. Tell me some more. It's just like sort of ummm . . .

HER: Playing with yourself?

HIM: What?

HER: Nothing.

HIM: No, I'm not actually.

HER: I said it's just like, just like . . .

HIM: Playing with yourself.

HER: Yes.

HIM: Not quite as nice. Not quite as nice. No, I haven't played with myself, actually. Not for a full forty-eight hours. [*Both are now laughing.*] Not for a full forty-eight hours. Um, tell me some more.

HER: I don't know. It's all quiet.

HIM: How was your lunch?

HER: It wasn't great.

HIM: Wasn't it? When are the Waterhouses turning up?

HER: Next Thursday, I think.

HIM: Oh, I thought they were coming today.

HER: No, Thursday.

HIM: To hold on to you . . . I've gone back to another point about your mother-in-law, no, grandmother-in-law. I think next time, you just want to either outstare her and that's easy.

HER: No, no.

HIM: It's not staring . . .

HER: No, no listen — wait a minute. It's affection, affection — it's definitely affection. It's sort of . . . it's not hostile anyway.

HIM: Oh, isn't it?

HER: No. She's sort of fascinated by me, but doesn't quite know how to unravel it, no.

HIM: How interesting. I'm sorry — I thought, darling, when you told me about her, you meant hostile.

HER: No, I'm all right.

HER: So do I.

HIM: I haven't spoken to you for twenty-eight hours. I've thought of nothing else.

HER: I know, I know.

HIM: Oh, that's all right. If it's friendly, then it doesn't matter.

HER: It's all right. I can deal with that.

HIM: My stars said nothing about 1990 — it was all very sort of terribly general.

HER: Fine, but it's definitely him *within* the marriage.

HIM: Right.

HER: It's not . . .

HIM: [*interrupting*] Did you see the *News of the World*?

HER: No.

HIM: 'He's got to start loving you' . . .

HER: Yes, I saw that. Yeh. She . . .

HIM: Did you? I thought: Well there's not much chance of that.

HER: No. I know. But, um, definitely she said I am doing nothing. I am just having a wonderful, success-ful, well-awaiting year.

HIM: A sort of matriarchal figure.

HER: I know. She said anything you want, you can get next year.

HIM: You should read *The People*, darling. There's a very good picture of you.

HER: Ah.

HIM: Oh no, it's . . . where is there a good picture? In the *Express*, was there? I think there's a . . . wearing that pink, very smart pink top. That excellent pink top.

HER: Oh, I know, I know.

HIM: Do you know the one I mean?

HER: I know.

HIM: Very good. Shit hot, actually.

HER: Shit hot [*laughs*].

HIM: Shit hot.

HER: Umm. Fergie said to me today that she had lunch with Nigel Havers the other day and 'all he could talk about was you'. And I said: 'Fergie, oh how awful for you.' And she said: 'Don't worry, it's the admiration club.' A lot of people talk to her about me, which she can't help.

HIM: I tell you, darling, she is desperate to tag on to your coat-tails.

HER: Well, she can't.

HIM: No, she absolutely can't. Now you have to make that quite clear . . .

HER: If you want to be like me, you have got to suffer.

HIM: Oh, Squidgy!

HER: Yah. You have to. And then you get what you . . .

HIM: Get what you want.

HER: No. Get what you deserve, perhaps.

HIM: Yes. Such as a second-hand car dealer [*laughs*].

HER: Yes, I know [*laughs*].

HIM: [*laughing*] Do you know, as we go into 1990, honey, I can't imagine, you know, what it was that brought us two together on that night.

HER: No, I know.

HIM: And let's make full use of it.

HER: I know.

HIM: Full use of it. Funnily enough, it doesn't hold any sort of terror, any fright for me at all.

HER: [*the sound of a knock on the door*] Hang on. Come in, come in please. Yes, it's OK, come in. Hang on. What is it? Ah. I'd love some salad, just some salad with yogurt, like when I was ailing in bed. That would be wonderful. About eight o'clock. Then everybody can go, can't they.

MALE VOICE: Bring it up on a tray?

HER: That would be great. Edward will come down and get it.

MALE VOICE: 'We'll bring it up.'

HER: All right, bring it up. That'll be great, Paul. No, just salad will be great, Paul. Thanks, Paul.

HIM: How much weight have you lost?

HER: Why?

HIM: Darling, I am sure lettuce leaves aren't going to keep you strong. You'll run out of energy driving to London.

HER: I am nine and a half stone.

HIM: Are you? Are you? Nine and a half. So are you staying in tonight?

HER: I am, because I am babysitting. I don't want to go out.

HIM: Oh, I see. So is he going?

HER: Yes. He doesn't know that I'm not yet. I haven't told him that yet.

HIM: I was going to say, darling. That was shitty. You can't face another night like last Friday, absolutely right. But you are there, darling.

HER: I know.

HIM: 1990 is going to be fine.

HER: Yes, but isn't it exciting.

HIM: Really exciting.

HER: Debbie said, I'm so excited for you. It's going to be lovely to watch . . .

HIM: I don't know, I've been feeling sick all day.

HER: Why?

HIM: I don't know. I just feel sick about the whole thing. I mean wonderful. I mean straight-through real passion and love and all the good things.

HER: Becky said it would be all OK, didn't she? The most fulfilling year yet.

HIM: You don't need to worry, do you?

HER: She's never questioned someone's mental state, or anything like that.

HIM: What, his?

HER: Yes. Nobody has ever thought about his mind. They've always thought about other things.

HIM: [*unclear*] ... something very interesting which said that serious astrologers don't think that he will never make it.

HER: Yah.

HIM: And become a [?].

HER: And Becky also said this person is married to someone in great power who will never make the ultima ... make the ultimatum or whatever the word is.

HIM: Absolutely ... Oh Squidgy, I love you, love you, love you.

HER: You are the nicest person in the whole wide world.

HIM: Pardon?

HER: You're just the nicest person in the whole wide world.

HIM: Well darling, you are to me too. Sometimes.

HER: [*laughs*] What do you mean, sometimes?

HIM: Sometimes. What else ... I really haven't got much else, darling. I got up quite late, went for a walk this morning; went for a walk this afternoon. Had lunch. I only got angry because Mark gave the nanny too much wine and she was incapable of helping at lunch.

HER: I love it.

HIM: He's a rogue, Mark ... David [?].

HER: Oh, Wills is coming. Sorry.

HIM: Is he going?

HER: No, no.

HIM: He's such a rogue, darling. He's the man you met once [?].

HER: I remember. But I didn't recognise him.

HIM: He's incorrigible.

HER: Would I like him?

HIM: He's a sort of social gossiper in a way. He loves all that, Mark. He's got a very comfortable life, you know. He hunts a lot.

HER: He's got the pennies?

HIM: He's got lots of pennies. He calls all his horses 'Business' or 'The Office' because when people ring up and he's hunting midweek, his secretary says: 'I'm sorry, he's away on Business.'

HER: [*laughs*] It's great to hear it.

HIM: But, umm . . . an incredible, sort of argument last night about subservient women in marriage.

HER: Well, you're an expert.

HIM: I kept very quiet actually. I could think, darling, of nothing but you. I thought: 'Well, I should be talking to her now.' You know, it's five past eleven.

HER: I know.

HIM: You don't mind it darling, when I want to talk to you so much?

HER: [*enthusiastically*] No. I *love* it. Never had it before.

HIM: Darling, it's so nice being able to help you.

HER: You do. You'll never know how much.

HIM: Oh, I will darling. I just feel so close to you, so wrapped up in you. I'm wrapping you up, protecting.

HER: Yes, please. Yes please ... Do you know, that bloody bishop, I said to him ...

HIM: What's he called?

HER: The Bishop of Norwich. He said: 'I want you to tell me how you talk to people who are ill or dying. How do you cope?'

HIM: He wanted to learn. He was so hopeless at it himself.

HER: I began to wonder after I'd spoken to him. I said: 'I'm just myself.'

HIM: They can't get to grips that, underneath, there is such a beautiful person in you. They can't think that it isn't cluttered up by this idea of untold riches.

HER: I know. He kept wittering about one must never think how good one is at one's job. There's always something you can learn around the next corner. I said: 'Well, if people know me, they know I'm not like that.'

HIM: Yes, absolutely right. So did you give him a hard time?

HER: I did, actually. In the end I said: 'I know this sounds crazy, but I've lived before.' He said: 'How do you know?' I said: 'Because I'm a wise old thing.'

HIM: Oh, darling Squidge, did you? Very brave thing to say to him, actually. Very.

HER: It was, wasn't it.

HIM: Very full marks. Ninety-nine out of 100.

HER: I said: 'Also I'm aware that people I have loved

and have died and are in the spirit world look after me.' He looked horrified. I thought: 'If he's the bishop, *he* should say that sort of thing.'

HIM: One of those horoscopes referred to you – to Cancerians turning to less materialistic and more spiritual things. Did you see that?

HER: No I didn't. No.

HIM: That's rather sad, actually. Umm, I don't really like many of those bishops especially.

HER: Well, I felt very uncomfortable.

HIM: They are a funny old lot.

HER: Well, I wore my heart on my sleeve.

HIM: They are the ones, when they've got a five-year-old sitting between them, their hands meet. Don't you remember that wonderful story?

HER: Yes, yes.

HIM: Gosh, it made my father laugh so much. Go on, darling. When you wear your heart on your sleeve . . .

HER: No, with that bishop, I said: 'I understand people's suffering, people's pain, more than you will ever know,' and he said: 'That's obvious by what you are doing for the AIDS.' I said: 'It's not only AIDS, it's anyone who suffers. I can smell them a mile away.'

HIM: What did he say?

HER: Nothing. He just went quiet. He changed the subject to toys. And I thought: 'Ah! Defeated you.'

HIM: Did you? Marvellous, darling. Did you chalk up a little victory?

HER: Yes, I did.

HIM: Did you, darling? Waving a little flag in your head.

HER: Yes.

HIM: How marvellous. You ought to do that more often. That flag ought to get bigger.

HER: Yes, my surrender flag [*chuckling*] . . .

HIM: You haven't got one?

HER: Yes.

HIM: What a big one?

HER: Well, medium.

HIM: Is it? Well, don't wave it too much.

HER: No.

HIM: Squidge, in this layby, you know, you understand how frightened people feel when they break down in the dark.

HER: I'm sure.

HIM: I suddenly thought someone could have shot at me from the undergrowth. Or someone suddenly tried to get into the car. I always lock the door for that reason.

HER: Gosh! That's very thoughtful. That's very good of you.

HIM: I know. Darling how are the boys?

HER: Very well.

HIM: Are they having a good time?

HER: Yes, very happy. Yah. Seem to be.

413

HIM: That's nice. Have you been looking after them today?

HER: Well, I've been with them a lot, yes.

HIM: Has he been looking after them?

HER: Oh, not really. My God, you know . . .

HIM: Have you seen him at all today, apart from lunch?

HER: I have. We went out to tea. It's just so difficult, so complicated. He makes my life real, real torture, I've decided.

HIM: Tell me more.

HER: But the distancing will be because I go out and – I hate the word – conquer the world. I don't mean that. I mean I'll go out and do my bit in the way I know how and I leave him behind. That's what I see happening.

HIM: Did you talk in the car?

HER: Yes, but nothing in particular. He said he didn't want to go out tonight.

HIM: Did you have the kids with you?

HER: No.

HIM: What, you just went by yourselves?

HER: No, they were behind us.

HIM: Oh, were they? How did he enjoy it?

HER: I don't know. He didn't really comment.

HIM: No. Oh, Squidgy.

HER: Mmm.

HIM: Kiss me please [*sound of kisses*]. Do you know what I'm going to be imagining I'm doing tonight at about twelve o'clock. Just holding you so close to me. It'll have to be delayed action for forty-eight hours.

HER: [*giggles*].

HIM: Fast forward.

HER: Fast forward.

HIM: Gosh, I hope Ken doesn't say no.

HER: I doubt he will.

HIM: Do you?

HER: He's coming down on Tuesday and I'm going to tell him I've got to go back on Tuesday night. And I've got to leave and be back for lunch on Wednesday. But I can do that.

HIM: You can?

HER: And I shall tell people I'm going for acupuncture and my back being done.

HIM: [*shrill laugh*] Squidge, cover them footsteps.

HER: I jolly well do.

HIM: I think it's all right. I think those footsteps are doing all right, actually, from both points of view. I'm going to set off, actually. Hold on. It's getting hot in here. It's like an oven.

HER: Well, I've got to kiss my small ones.

HIM: Oh no, darling.

HER: I've got to.

HIM: No Squidgy, I don't want you to go. Can you bear with me five minutes?

HER: All right . . .

HIM: Just five.

HER: What have you got on?

HIM: I've got the new jeans I bought yesterday.

HER: Good.

HIM: Green socks. A white and pink striped shirt.

HER: How very nice.

HIM: A dark apple-green V-neck jersey.

HER: Yes.

HIM: I'm afraid I'm going to let you down by the shoes.

HER: Go on, then [*giggles*].

HIM: You can guess.

HER: Your brown ones [*mock shriek*]. Your brown ones. No, those black ones?

HIM: No, I haven't got the black ones, darling. The black ones I would not be wearing. I only wear the black ones with my suit.

HER: Good. Well, get rid of them.

HIM: I have got those brown suede ones on.

HER: Brown suede ones?

HIM: Those brown suede Guccis [*laughs*].

HER: Oh I know, I know.

HIM: The ones you hate.

HER: I just don't like the fact it's so obvious where they came from.

HIM: Di, nobody wears them any more [*at this point the conversation cuts off, then resumes*].

HIM: I like those ordinary Italian things that last a couple of years, then I chuck them out. It was a sort of devotion to duty. I was seeking a sort of identity when I brought my first pair of Guccis twelve years ago.

HER: Golly.

HIM: And I've still got them. Still doing me proud, like.

HER: Good.

HIM: I'm going to take you up on that, darling. I will give you some money. You can go off and spend it for me.

HER: I will.

HIM: Will you? [*laughs*].

HER: Yep, I'm a connoisseur in that department.

HIM: Are you?

HER: Yes.

HIM: Well, you think you are.

HER: Well, I've decked people out in my time.

HIM: Who did you deck out? Not too many I hope.

HER: James Hewitt. Entirely dressed him from head to foot by me. Cost me a lot that man. Cost me quite a bit.

HIM: I bet he did. At your expense?

HER: Yeh.

HIM: What, he didn't even pay you to do it?

HER: No.

HIM: God! Very extravagant, darling.

HER: Well, I am, aren't I? Anything that will make people happy.

HIM: No, you mustn't do it for that, darling, because *you* make people happy. It's what you give them . . . [*call breaks again, then resumes*].

HER: No, don't. You'll know, you'll know.

HIM: All right. But you always say that with an air of inevitability [*giggles*]. It will happen in six months' time. I'll suddenly get: 'Yes, James Who [*giggles*] I don't think we've spoken before.'

HER: No.

HIM: I hope not. Well, darling, you can't imagine what pleasures I've got in store this evening.

HER: It's a big house, is it?

HIM: It's a nice house. Thirty people for dinner or something.

HER: God.

HIM: I know. Do you want me to leave the phone on?

HER: No, no, better not.

HIM: You won't be, from 9.30? Why not?

HER: No, tomorrow morning.

HIM: I can't, I can't ... all right, tomorrow morning. Shall I give you a time to call me?

HER: Yes, I won't be around from 9.30 to 11.

HIM: Why not?

HER: I'm going swimming with Fergie.

HIM: Are you taking the kiddies?

HER: Might well do.

HIM: You should do. It's good for you. Get them out. It gives you enormous sort of strength, doesn't it. Have the lovebugs around you.

HER: I know, I know.

HIM: Beautiful things pampering their mother.

HER: Quite right.

HIM: That's what she wants. I think you should take

them darling. At least you are not battling with the rest.

HER: No, I'm not.

HIM: Are you . . . [*call breaks again, then resumes*].

HER: I'd better, I'd better. All the love in the world — I'll speak to you tomorrow.

HIM: All right. If you can't get me in the morning . . . You're impatient to go now.

HER: Well, I just feel guilty because I haven't done my other business.

HIM: Don't feel guilty. They'll be quite all . . . [*call breaks again, then resumes*].

HIM: Just that I'll have to wait till Tuesday. All right.

HER: All right.

HIM: I'll buzz off and simply behave. I'll approach the evening with such enormous confidence now.

HER: Good, good.

HIM: And you, darling. Don't let it get you down.

HER: I won't, I won't.

HIM: All right.

APPENDIX 2

The 'Camillagate' Tape Transcript in Full

HIM: He was a bit anxious actually.

HER: Was he?

HER: Ah well.

HIM: Anyway, you know, that's the sort of thing one has to beware of. And sort of feel one's way along with – if you know what I mean.

HER: You're awfully good at feeling your way along.

HIM: Oh stop! I want to feel my way along you, all over you and up and down you and in and out.

HER: Oh!

HIM: Particularly in and out.

HER: Oh, that's just what I need at the moment.

HIM: Is it?

[*At this point the person making the recording speaks over the couple to record the date as 18 December (although the tape is now believed to have been recorded in the early hours of the morning of 19 December).*]

HER: I know it would revive me. I can't bear a Sunday night without you.

HIM: Oh, God.

HER: It's like that programme 'Start the Week'. I can't start the week without you.

HIM: I fill up your tank!

HER: Yes you do.

HIM: Then you can cope.

HER: Then I'm all right.

HIM: What about me? The trouble is I need you several times a week.

HER: Mmm, so do I. I need you all the week. All the time.

HIM: Oh, God. I'll just live inside your trousers or something. It would be much easier.

HER: [*laughing*] What are you going to turn into, a pair of knickers? [*Both laugh.*] Oh, you're going to come back as a pair of knickers!

HIM: Or, God forbid, a Tampax. Just my luck! [*Laughs.*]

HER: You are a complete idiot! [*Laughs.*] Oh, what a wonderful idea.

HIM: My luck to be chucked down a lavatory and go on and on for ever, swirling round on top, never going down.

HER: [*laughing*] Oh darling.

HIM: Until the next one comes through.

HER: Oh, perhaps you could come back as a box.

HIM: What sort of box?

HER: A box of Tampax, so you could just keep going.

HIM: That's true.

HER: Repeating yourself. [*Laughing*] Oh darling, oh I just want you now.

HIM: Do you?

HER: Mmm.

HIM: So do I.

HER: Desperately, desperately, desperately. Oh, I thought of you so much at [*indistinct*] Yaraby.

HIM: Did you?

HER: Simply mean that we couldn't be there together.

HIM: Desperate. If you could be here. I long to ask Nancy sometimes.

HER: Why don't you?

HIM: I daren't.

HER: Because I think she's so in love with you.

HIM: Mmm.

HER: She'd do anything you asked.

HIM: She'd tell all sorts of people.

HER: No, she wouldn't, because she'd be much too frightened of what you might say to her. I think you've got – I'm afraid it's a terrible thing to say – but I think, you know, those sort of people do feel very strongly about you. You've so, such a great hold over her.

HIM: Really?

HER: And you're . . . I think as usual you're underestimating yourself.

HIM: But she might be terribly jealous or something.

HER: Oh! [*laughing*] Now that is a point! I wonder – she might be, I suppose.

HIM: You never know, do you?

HER: No. The little green-eyed monster might be lurking inside her. No, but I. But I don't know they'd betray you – you know, real friends.

HIM: Really?

HER: I don't. [*Pause*] Gone to sleep?

HIM: No, I'm here.

HER: Darling, listen, I talked to David last night. It might not be any good.

HIM: Oh no!

HER: I'll tell you why. He's got those children of one of those Crawley girls and their nanny staying. He's going. I'm going to ring him again tomorrow. He's going to try and put them off 'til Friday. But I thought, as an alternative, perhaps I might ring up Charlie.

HIM: Yes.

HER: And see if we could do it there. I know he is back on Thursday.

HIM: It's quite a lot further away.

HER: Oh, is it?

HIM: Well, I'm just trying to think. Coming from Newmarket . . .

HER: Coming from Newmarket to me at that time of night, you could probably do it two and three-quarters. It takes me three.

HIM: What to go to, um, Bowood?

HER: Northmore.

HIM: To go to Bowood?

HER: To go to Bowood would be the same as me really, wouldn't it?

HIM: I mean to say, you would suggest going to Bowood, uh?

HER: No, not at all.

HIM: Which Charlie then?

HER: What Charlie do you think I was talking about?

HIM: I didn't know because I thought you meant . . .

HER: I've got lots . . .

HIM: Somebody else.

HER: I've got lots of friends called Charlie.

HIM: The other one, Patty's.

HER: Oh! Oh, there! Oh, that is further away. They're not . . .

HIM: They've gone.

HER: I don't know – it's just, you know, just a thought I had. If it fell through, the other place . . .

HIM: All right. What do you do? Go on the M25 then the M4 is it?

HER: Yes, you go, um, and sort of Royston or M11 at that time of night.

HIM: Yes, well that will be just after; it will be after shooting anyway.

HER: So it would be, um, you'd miss the worst of the traffic. Because I'll, er . . . you see the problem is I've got to be in London tomorrow night.

HIM: Yes.

HER: And Tuesday night 'A' is coming home.

HIM: No.

HER: Would you believe it, because I don't know what he's doing. He's shooting here or something. But, darling, you wouldn't be able to ring me anyway, would you?

HIM: I might just. I mean, tomorrow night I could have done.

HER: Oh darling, I can't bear it. How could you have done tomorrow night?

HIM: Because I'll be [*yawning*] working on the next speech.

HER: Oh no, what's the next one.

HIM: A 'Business in the Community' one: rebuilding communities.

HER: Oh no, when's that for?

HIM: A rather important one for Wednesday.

HER: Well, at least I'll be behind you.

HIM: I know.

HER: Can I have a copy of the one you've just done?

HIM: Yes.

HER: Can I? Um, I would like it.

HIM: OK, I'll try and organise it.

HER: Darling.

HIM: But I, oh God, when am I going to speak to you?

HER: I can't bear it, um . . .

HIM: Wednesday night?

HER: Oh, certainly Wednesday night. I'll be alone Wednesday, you know, in the evening. Or Tuesday. While you're rushing around doing things, I'll be, you know, alone until it reappears. And early

Wednesday morning, I mean, he'll be leaving at half past eight ... quarter past eight. He won't be here Thursday, pray God. Um, that ambulance strike — it's a terrible thing to say this — I suppose it won't have come to an end by Thursday.

HIM: It will have done?

HER: Well, I mean, I hope for everybody's sake it will have done but I hope for our sakes it's still going on.

HIM: Why?

HER: Well, because if it stops, he'll come down here on Thursday night.

HIM: Oh no.

HER: Yes, but I don't think it will stop, do you?

HIM: No, neither do I. Just our luck.

HER: It just would be our luck, I know.

HIM: Then it's bound to!

HER: No it won't. You mustn't think like that. You must think positive.

HIM: I'm not very good at that.

HER: Well I'm going to, because if I don't I'd despair. [*Pause*] Hmm. Gone to sleep?

HIM: No. How maddening.

HER: I know. Anyway, I mean, he's doing his best to change it, David. But I just thought, you know, I might just ask Charlie.

HIM: Did he say anything?

HER: No, I haven't talked to him.

HIM: You haven't?

HER: Well I talked to him briefly but, you know, I just thought I . . . I just don't know whether he's got any children at home. That's the worry.

HIM: Right.

HER: Oh darling, I think I'll . . .

HIM: Pray, just pray.

HER: It would be so wonderful to have just one night to set us on our way, wouldn't it?

HIM: Wouldn't it! To wish you a Happy Christmas.

HER: [*Indistinct*] Happy. Oh, don't let's think about Christmas. I can't bear it. [*Pause*] Going to go to sleep? I think you'd better, don't you darling?

HIM: [*Sleepily*] Yes darling.

HER: I think you've exhausted yourself by all that hard work. You must go to sleep now . . . Darling?

HIM: Yes darling?

HER: Will you ring me when you wake up?

HIM: Yes, I will.

HER: Before I have these rampaging children around. It's Tom's birthday tomorrow. [*Pause*] You all right?

HIM: Mmm, I'm all right.

HER: Can I talk to you, I hope, before those rampaging children . . .

HIM: What time do they come in?

HER: Well, usually Tom never wakes up at all. But as it's his birthday tomorrow, he might just stagger out of bed. It won't be before half past eight. [*Pause*] Night night, my darling.

HIM: Darling . . .

HER: I do love you.

HIM: [*Sleepily*] Before . . .

HER: Before about half past eight.

HIM: Try and ring?

HER: Yeah, if you can. Love you, darling.

HIM: Night darling.

HER: I love you.

HIM: Love you, too. I don't want to say goodbye.

HER: Well done for doing that. You're a clever old thing. An awfully good brain lurking there, isn't there? Oh darling, I think you ought to give the brain a rest now. Night night.

HIM: Night darling. God bless.

HER: I do love you and I'm so proud of you.

HIM: Oh, I'm so proud of *you*.

HER: Don't be so silly. I've never achieved anything.

HIM: Yes you have.

HER: No I haven't.

HIM: Your great achievement is to love me.

HER: Oh, darling. Easier than falling off a chair.

HIM: You suffer all these indignities and tortures and calumnies.

HER: Oh darling, don't be silly. I'd suffer anything for you. That's love; it's the strength of love. Night night.

HIM: Night, darling. Sounds as though you're dragging an enormous piece of string behind you, with hundreds of tin pots and cans attached to it. I think it must be your telephone. Night night, before the battery goes. [*Blows kiss.*] Night.

HER: Love you.

HIM: Don't want to say goodbye.

HER: Neither do I, but you must get some sleep. Bye.

HIM: Bye, darling.

HER: Love you.

HIM: Bye.

HER: Hopefully talk to you in the morning.

HIM: Please.

HER: Bye. I do love you.

HIM: Night.

HER: Night.

HIM: Night.

HER: Love you for ever.

HIM: Night.

HER: G'bye. Bye, my darling.

HIM: Night.

HER: Night, night.

HIM: Night.

HER: Bye, bye.

HIM: Going.

HER: Bye.

HIM: Going.

HER: Gone.

HIM: Night.

HER: Bye. Press the button.

HIM: Going to press the tit.

HER: All right, darling. Wish you were pressing mine.

HIM: God, I wish I was, harder and harder.

HER: Oh darling.

HIM: Night.
HER: Night.
HIM: Love you.
HER: [*yawning*] Love you. Press the tit.
HIM: Adore you. Night.
HER: [*Blows a kiss.*]
HIM: Night.
HER: G'night my darling. Love you.